New Mansions for New Men

By

DANE RUDHYAR

Lucis Publishing Company
New York
1938

COPYRIGHT, 1938, BY LUCIS PUBLISHING CO.

PRINTED IN THE UNITED STATES OF AMERICA
BY THE STRATFORD PRESS, INC., NEW YORK

To Malya

whose spirit communes with the Source
whence symbols arise and dreams flow
—moulds of a reality-to-be,
this book is dedicated.

The author acknowledges gratefully his indebtedness to Paul G. Clancy for the permission to make use in this book of the material which was printed in American Astrology under the titles "New Mansions for New Men", "Cosmic Tones for Solar Men" and "Meditations at the Gates of Light" through the years 1935, 1936 and 1937.

Contents

Foreword   xi

MANSIONS OF THE SELF

Prelude	3
First Mansion — "To Breathe"	12
Second Mansion — "To Own"	19
Third Mansion — "To Know"	26
Fourth Mansion — "To Establish"	33
Fifth Mansion — "To Release"	41
Sixth Mansion — "To Improve"	48
Seventh Mansion — "To Relate"	55
Eighth Mansion — "To Renew"	62
Ninth Mansion — "To Understand"	69
Tenth Mansion — "To Achieve"	75
Eleventh Mansion — "To Transfigure"	82
Twelfth Mansion — "To Transcend"	103

MUSIC OF THE SPHERES

Prelude	99
The Song of Light	89

The Song of Life 111

Saturn —— Lord of Boundaries 119

Jupiter —— Organizer of Functions 129

Mercury —— Weaver of the Threads of Life 138

Mars —— He-Who-Goes-Forth 148

Venus —— Queen of the Celestial Bees 157

Uranus —— Master of Transformations 167

Neptune —— Master of Ecstasy 178

Pluto —— Sower of Celestial Seed 189

Asteroids and Comets —— Servants and Messengers of Universal Harmony 198

The Constellations and the Milky Way 207

MEDITATIONS AT THE GATES OF LIGHT

1. At the Southern Gate 219
2. At the Eastern Gate 232
3. At the Northern Gate 242
4. At the Western Gate 253
5. The City of Light 265

Foreword

THIS BOOK, UNDERSTOOD AS A WHOLE, IS IN TRUTH AN EPIC revealing through symbols taken from ancient astrological lore the basic cycles of the development of human consciousness.

In "Mansions of the Self" the spiral-like process of formation of the individual Soul through the twelvefold field of experience is outlined. In "Music of the Spheres" the functions, powers and faculties which this Soul must use and harmonize, if it is to reach fulfillment and operative wholeness, are evoked and linked with those "wandering stars"—sun, moon, planets, planetoids—which trace orbits of light round our planetary abode.

The "Meditations" lead us finally to the realm of light which is the substance of the Soul on its own plane. They seek to convey the significance of those cyclic modifications of the light—symbolized by the zodiacal signs—which mark not only the passage of the year but the spiritual changes of attitude of man to his divine Source. It is these changes that tell of the Soul's progress in its adventure in spiritual realization, that reveal its trials and its hopes on the path toward the inward communion with the essence of all Meaning: the goal of all consciousness.

Consciousness: how it is formed through the fields of experience—how it is activated by the life-energies which pour through the total organism of man—how it is substantiated through progressive realizations of the essence of being. Such is the real theme which is developed through the many stanzas of this poem.

The book which preceded this, *The Astrology of Personality*, was an attempt to reformulate traditional astrology in terms of the modern philosophical and psychological outlook. It was therefore in form a "treatise", and aimed at a strict, logical continuity and coherency of thought. It established new foundations for a consistent system of symbolism, using astrological factors as its symbols. Its goal was the formulation of an "algebra of life", using organic life-qualities as its primary elements, defining these qualities particularly at the psychological level in terms borrowed from C. G. Jung's analytical psychology.

This present work adds to its predecessors, as it were, a new dimension. It is addressed to the intuitional faculties, rather than to the philosophical mind. In this sense it is a more "esoteric" work, which evokes depths rather than describes surface-relationships. Thus it is essentially a poem and not a treatise. It deals with life through symbols taken from experience.

It is therefore a book for everyone who wishes to go deeper into the substratum and the meaning of human experience in terms of consciousness and understanding—though the person familiar with astrological values will obviously reap a richer harvest of significance because of associations of ideas with which he or she has dealt in a practical or even a theoretical manner. It is however a book which leaves many things unsaid. It suggests more than it states. It provides subjects for meditation and introspection. It opens new vistas or transforms old landscapes, vivifying them through the light of a more direct and less traditional—often an antiquated—meaning. But it is not a textbook for the lazy or formalistic mind hoping to find all things neatly catalogued and described.

Indeed it should be read as a poem, an epic of the human Soul. But not a poem in the modern sense of "literature"; rather a poem as poetry was understood in olden times, as an initiation into life-mysteries *sub speciem aeternitatis*—as a revelation of permanent and essential meanings through symbols that have power because great beings who lived them poured power into them.

The symbols which are derived from astrology have indeed power. Countless millions of men have believed in them, have worked with them, lived through them, experienced them and poured life, joy, fear, expectation, disappointment, tragedy into them. These symbols are great primordial Images of the universal memory of men. Their potency is as great as that locked in the countenance of gods hoary with age and laden with the devotion of multitudes.

Today is a new birthday for ancient gods. New men call for new symbols. Their cry rises, beyond their logical intellects ashamed of mystical longings, for new gods to worship and to use in order to integrate their harrowing mental confusion and to stabilize their uprooted souls: young gods, fresh and radiant with the sunshine of a new dawn, glorified with the "golden light" of a new Sun of Power, ecstatic with virgin potentialities after the banishment of ancient nightmares; gods whose urge for living springs from a deeper well of being than of old, whose compassion is vibrant and clear, whose energies burn free in skies wondrous with vistas of total and inescapable wholeness; gods whose abodes are no longer confined to heavenly realms but whose hearts beat in unison with every human heart and whose minds illumine the consciousness of all men; gods made human with the divinity of our inextinguishable quest.

A Mandala for "new men"

The use of symbolic patterns for meditation and magical work is worldwide—from Tibetan *mandalas* to Gothic rose-windows. In this, as made visual to M. R., the twelve petals of the "Lotus of the Sky" have rolled back away from the apparent center revealing another dimension of spiritual depth, the hidden core of being. The flaming 8-pointed effulgence, which is the "Heart of the Sun," discloses the 6-pointed and 5-pointed stars. These figures add to 19, the sacred Solar number. The Venusian "bees" represent the three Souls of Man, come to draw the divine ambrosia from the "Heart of the Sun."

Mansions of the Self

Prelude

THE WORLD IS BEING MADE ANEW IN THIS MYSTERIOUS, AWE-inspiring twentieth century. A new consciousness of the wholeness that is man is being developed, a consciousness almost hierarchical in its scope, inasmuch as it accepts the existence of several levels of being and reinterprets all things in terms of these levels and of the effort which mankind as a whole and in its individuals is constantly making to shift its focus of being from one level to the next higher. It is not enough for us who would plumb the depth of man to accept ancient interpretations and let our mind dwell in the old mansions built by our ancestors. It has been said that in every age the depth of a civilization could be evaluated by inquiring into the profundity of its grasp of this most essential of all concepts, the concept of the self. Today more than ever we need a revaluation of the concept of selfhood, a deepening and extension of it so that a new and ordered inclusiveness may take the place of the exclusiveness which was patent throughout the Christian era.

Thus the significance of the idea of "level". From it a new inclusiveness and a new sense of ordered development of the principle of individual selfhood may be derived. The man's ego may be seen not as a static unchangeable reality of a metaphysical character, but as a functional center of being growing through its very functioning in scope, depth and significance; growing progressively through measured and meaningful steps, which may recur in cyclic series if life be fulfilled at every step.

Such steps vary obviously with every individual, inasmuch as every man lives through phases of experience which in a sense are unique and never duplicated. Likewise the exact relationship of the stars and planets in the skies can most assuredly never be duplicated. In even such a small factor as the oscillatory motions of the poles of the earth it seems doubtful that the poles should ever return exactly to the same position, so complex is the interplay of elements involved in their movements. Nevertheless the unique individual must pass on his way to death or immortality through portals which are identical in racial significance. Men may decorate the walls of their dwellings in unique ways as they move from one mansion to another on the road to perfection; but the mansions are there to be inhabited by each and all. The fine lines which the bare feet make upon the sands of life are different with each individual, but the steps are the same—if they be taken at all. And some never progress beyond the very first steps.

It is to such collective and generic factors that symbols apply—and perhaps nothing but symbols may ever truly apply. Because where the intellect attempts to reduce these large factors to definite laws and rigid formulations, there the very essence of these factors may be lost irrevocably. Even the most collective, and thus apparently the most objective and measurable, elements in the progress of the human being are still *living* factors. They may be not at all individual, and thus not to be influenced basically by individual fluctuations; nevertheless they are factors of *experience*. Numbers and categories are not elements of experience. But the type of symbols which we encounter in astrology, or in all these ancient systems of life-interpretation not entirely dominated by the intellect, are drawn from facts of experience, from realities lived. The very fact that they are susceptible of many shades of interpretation vouches for their living quality.

Symbols however may die the death of all memories supplanted by a fresher crop of living experiences at a new level of being. New men call for new symbols. New mansions must serve the call of new human needs. Just as the introduction of modern machines and the uprooting of the physiological earth-conditioned instincts of the modern city-man are forcing us slowly to adopt new types of dwelling places conditioned for new needs, and a new concept of the woman's function, likewise—as mankind becomes re-polarized at a more mental level of being—we must find new symbols for our basic conceptions of the self. New mansions must be built for new men.

"In my Father's house are many mansions," said Jesus. But we are indeed in an age in which the very house of the Father may need to be rebuilt to fit the new generation of men fashioned by new planetary and stellar energies. It has been said that the upheaval which is making humanity reel with wars and mental conflagrations is merely the by-product, as it were, of an "initiation of the planetary Logos". This is the occultist's somewhat cumbersome way of saying that the whole earth is moving to new fields of galactic space, that mankind is being transformed from within by the onsurge of new powers, that the Father is rebuilding His mystical house, that the Self is being known in new ways through the challenge of new relationship.

It is for us, who have not forgotten that at the birth of all cycles the world belongs to poets and bards bringing new names to a race ecstatic with birthing and confused with the crashing of the old, to read the signatures which the new Ideas, that are God-born, inscribe upon the open book of the world. Thus we may be true "star-gazers", deciphering new relationships, new patterns slowly forming in that sky of all skies: the heart and mind of man.

It is as poets that we write, summoning symbols that may

be pregnant with futurity of meaning. We are taking the old forms of that most wondrous and most adaptable of all symbolisms, astrology, and blowing into their faded structures a new breath of life. We are making them more inclusive. We are balancing them on new levels of being in the perilous ascent toward unscaled heights of significance. We hope thereby that men may be refreshed in the experience of new images; that they may be led to experience more deeply, as they meet them, old concepts swinging in tune to new rhythms of thinking and feeling, illumined by a refreshed intuition of the goal that is man's.

There are many facets to the wholeness of the perfected human being. There are many portals which man must enter before a round of experience is completed and the individual has learnt the basic functions fulfilling which he proves himself truly human. These are the mansions of astrology, the twelve mansions or "houses" into which the fullness of space surrounding man at birth is divided. In order to understand with a greater touch of reality what these twelve mansions represent we must realize the meaning of the relationship between man just achieving his first declaration of independence—the first cry—and space pressing upon him from all possible directions. This new-born babe is Life *particularized*, made an individual and unique entity. Space around him is Life *universal*, total, mother and womb all-encompassing.

For this new-born infant, to live means to assimilate as much of this surrounding Life as his individual framework and character will enable him to assimilate. To assimilate; not to absorb. Mere absorption is not living experience. To experience vitally is to assimilate; to make the absorbed contents one's own, to transform and interpret them in terms of one's own individual nature and center of reference: the Self. What is absorbed but not assimilated causes physical, mental or spiritual indigestion. It poisons the consciousness. Mere awareness is not enough. Consciousness, that is, awareness referred to the individual center of synthesis (con-sciousness), is necessary.

This process of assimilation of life-contents is a generalized aspect of the body's metabolism. Everything that surrounds us is potential food to our consciousness, even though much of it is undigestible or poisonous. Individual selfhood *as an abstraction* is a primary factor of being human; but in order to become a concrete reality of the inner world of the psyche the abstract "I am" must become substantial as Soul. The psyche must be fed with life-contents; its many molecular energies must become integrated as a psycho-mental organism. Man must pass through a twelve-tone gamut of experience, learning to fulfill twelve basic functions of living as a conscious, social being.

This twelvefold process of development it is which astrology symbolizes by the twelve "houses"—twelve 30-degree sections of the total space surrounding the place of birth, above and below the soil, extending to theoretical infinity. The line of horizon is the basic line of segmentation. It defines two realms of experience, two phases of development of consciousness: the below-the-soil realm of strictly individual awareness, and the above-the-soil realm of social and outer awareness —the invisible and the visible, that which is conditioned by the self and that which is conditioned by the not-self (the world of sensations and of relationship with others).

A detailed study of these twelve mansions of the individual soul, as it slowly forms and establishes itself as a complex of memories and anticipations, has been made in our previous work, *The Astrology of Personality*. We have shown that there are two methods of approaching the cycle of these "houses": a static and timeless one according to which man's complete field of experience is analyzed into twelve separate departments or modes of activity—and one which follows up step by step the development of man's awareness of life, linking every progressive phase to the preceding and the following ones and presenting a view of the process of soul-development as it unfolds through the series of experienced moments.

This last mentioned approach is much the more fruitful and the better fitted to the type of thought which characterizes our century. It deals with the material of experience and with the actual focus of man's consciousness as it shifts from one phase of life to another. It reveals to us not an abstract realm of intellectual formulas but a living whole of experience, constantly and continuously readjusting itself to new needs and new goals, dimly perceived yet eagerly fought for. It is this approach which will yield to us new symbols for the twelve mansions of the self: symbols which are the products of actual organic and social experience, symbols which should enable us to gain a new and fresher perspective upon a cyclic process which is hoary with age yet ever as young and mysteriously virginal as those who tread with immature steps the path of living.

This path does not extend its reaches in a straight line. Every living process is essentially cyclic. Wherefore we must postulate the existence of various "levels" of being and experience. It is true that all men live upon the same earth and, whether they be young or old, foolish or wise, eat much the same food and perform much the same necessary actions for the perpetuation of their physical organisms. But to that physiological level of experience another may be added, and perhaps yet another. Man's mind and soul operate in ways which, if not independent from physical realities, at least have a definite rhythm of their own. The individual may live, as an individual, a psycho-mental life free within certain limits from the pull of the earth.

Even if constrained by physiological needs he can center his consciousness in a realm in which these needs have an utterly transformed significance and are seen in a new light. New needs arise. The same basic symbols may apply to this new level, but transfigured by the new light and the new realizations. Indeed—and this is the proof of the validity of the symbols—they do apply to all levels, for life is unalterably one. But man may face it in different ways, from different levels. The reality is the same, but the truth about the reality differs on every level. Facts are the same, yet the light of a new meaning makes them almost unrecognizable; for man's world is essentially a world of significance, and thus man creates his own world as he deliberately gives to old forms new meanings.

It has been shown elsewhere that the archetypal span of man's life *in terms of individual consciousness* is 84 years, or three cycles each of 28 years. To these three cycles correspond in a general manner three levels of man's development as a conscious self. At the beginning of each of these cycles man experiences—theoretically—a birth. To the physical birth corresponds thus, at the age of 28, a psycho-mental or "second" birth, and at the age of 56 a spiritual or "third" birth.

The first 28 years represent the physiological part of man's development. Man functions primarily as a *racial* being, in terms of heredity and geographical-social environment. His experiences are conditioned mostly by the collective norm, and if he sways away from it, it is because of the pressure of wrong and unhealthy conditioning, of psychological maladjustments and bodily illness.

On the basis of such abnormalities and of more or less conscious inner urges welling from the past, man achieves a certain amount of distinctiveness. He becomes different from the norm. He may thus emerge from the collective womb of his race as an individual. Theoretically this second birth occurs around the 28th birthday. *If it does*—and in most cases it does not and man lives his life as a collective being barely differentiated from the mass—then the individual slowly establishes himself at the psycho-mental level, operating there as an individual, learning from individual experiences, giving to all things a significance really his own; learning also to utilize his very complexes and abnormalities so as to break through the boundaries of the mass-mentality and to discover new angles of vision—finally realizing that these new angles are not to stand *against* the normal ones but should rather complement and vivify them.

On the basis of this new and mature understanding the individual may grow into the higher realm of the spirit, when he finds those "who belong to the same brotherhood", those with whom he forms a higher collectivity of the Spirit founded on individual selfhood, and no longer—as at the racial level—upon a common physiological ancestry and a tribal tradition conditioned by blood and climate. This "third birth" is only a potentiality which a very few indeed really experience. Yet the trend it represents is more or less felt by those individuals who, after the years of maturity, face life in a broader and less separative way; who serve their race or their ideals with a wisdom accumulated from the tragic struggles of the period of individualistic focalization.

These three 28-year periods and the levels of conscious focalization to which they have just been correlated are obviously rather theoretical and abstract. In the living experience of living men there are no sharp lines of demarcation, and cycles in the individual may not necessarily fit in with the above-mentioned generic ones. Nevertheless, the formulation of such cycles is as valid as the assignment of a definite age to physiological crises of growth such as puberty and the change of life. All that is necessary is to think of such cyclic figures in terms of a living process never rigidly to be measured by yardsticks and clocks, but always to be experienced through identification with the surge of the Life-force which is the reality and substance beyond or within all manifestations of consciousness and of selfhood.

As we move in thought through the twelve stations of the path which to many is known as a *via dolorosa*, yet which should be realized instead as a glorious process of life-metamorphosis leading to the birth of the Living God within our illumined Soul; as we touch upon symbol after symbol and see them unfold in significance from level to level of understanding, we must never lose touch with the reality of our living experience. We must ever let the symbols live within the actuality of our quest for richer living. They are not dead butterflies pinned upon the pages of a curiosity-seeker's album. They are live seeds. They would be futile indeed, and all this would be in vain, if men and women here and there, in all lands, were not to glow more brightly and live more understandingly with the fire and the wisdom that these symbols have stirred within their souls.

First Mansion
To Breathe

IF WE SEARCH FOR A SYMBOL FIT TO CHARACTERIZE AND FORCEfully to suggest in terms of outer activity the primordial essence of pure being, we shall find none better suited than the ancient and immemorial symbol of the breath. To breathe: such is the first action of individualized being. To breathe is to be independent and, relatively at least, self-sufficient, complete —alive. To breathe is to inhale the whole world, to open oneself to air that has coursed through myriads of lungs, that the sun has kissed, the earth has scented, the stars have blessed. To breathe is to declare, tragically yet with passionate fervor: I am. The song of the breath is the song of the "I am". Stop breathing and very soon the song is ended. For a few minutes life goes on; but, the individual—the "I am"—having withdrawn, having refused to contact the whole living world through the magical performance of breathing, the body loses its significance and disintegrates; it has been rendered useless, meaningless.

Breath is the first mansion: the mansion of the "I am". In it, human life celebrates its individual selfhood. Thus in old India, the land of pure and spiritual individual selfhood, where the Self—*Atman*, the absolute Breath—was the only true divinity, the act of breathing was regarded as most sacred. Spiritual development was there a matter of reaching the Self, of becoming identified with the Self that is changeless, formless, conditionless, absolute.

To the Self many paths were seen to lead; but somewhere on every path a moment came when the traveler had to meet the Breath; when man had to cease breathing as an animal—instinctively—and to begin breathing as a man—deliberately. From this moment, man began to act as a master of the life-force. He began to operate at a higher level of individual selfhood, establishing slowly his own rhythm of being, his own valuations, his own universe.

The first type of breathing is the instinctive, animal type. It is racial, natural, unconscious, automatic. It is safe, but superficial. It refers to the collective, to the mass, to the *earth*—to the first birth. It is controlled in the human body by the autonomous nervous system, balanced by the complementary action of the expanding, accelerating sympathetic, and of the contracting, retarding para-sympathetic groups of nerves.

The second type of breathing is deliberate, mental. It is based on the development of the individual, which it furthers *for weal or for woe*. It is conscious, deliberate, deep. It carries the seed of great danger—of illness and insanity. It is based on a law of polarization and of operative wholeness which belongs to the world of mind, the realm of formation and of mastery— for good or for ill. It is the true breath of *air*—the song of the second birth. It is controlled by the cerebro-spinal nerves, by the axis of individual selfhood: the spine—the "pillar of fire", the living symbol of the potentially immortal "I".

The third type of breathing is hard to understand, for it belongs to the realm of spirit and of *light*. It is superconscious, ecstatic, high. It is the solar breath—of which very little can be said, save that it gives light to the soul and immortality to the individual who fully partakes of it. The old Hindu books deal in veiled utterances with the mystery of it. It is the mystery of the third birth, under the many forms which it may take throughout the evolutionary cycles of collective mankind.

Following this analogy of the breath, so vital and fundamental for an understanding of essential being, one may say likewise that there are three types of "I am", three types of individual selfhood. They can be correlated, at least symbolically, to the three types of breathing and to the three births.

The first type is the instinctive, animal-like ego which is rooted in the blood. It is the integrative power of the body. It correlates through the blood-stream all organic functions, and its rhythm may be known from that of the heart-beats. It is born of the fact of organic living. It is the result of the fact that the body is an organic whole capable of maintaining itself in a condition of at least relative health; this, largely through the operation of the muscular system, to which the heart organically belongs. Being rooted in the blood, it is indissolubly bound to the tribal whole; to a family, an ancestry, a tradition, a tribal system, a tribal religion—and to a certain geographical location: "my country". It is the earth-born ego, who, childlike, proclaims "I am!"—with adequate muscular gestures, whether it be of sex or speech.

It *is*; and in order to continue to be and to grow in stature, it *owns*. My country, my family, my wife, my home, my possessions—mine! Because this earth-born ego owns and must own in order to expand; because expansion in the realm of earth-substance necessarily means *to have* more of anything which can be owned; and because as every ego naturally and instinctively desires to expand, these wills to expand must of necessity come into conflict—then, there must be craving, violence, hatred, war. Thus the possessive ego becomes the passional and imperialistic ego; the feudal lord dominating his possessions, surrounded by fear and hatred, fighting a losing fight against the inevitable death. He that is of the blood must perish by the blood. All deaths are due either to congestion or poisoning of the blood-stream, or else to the exhaustion of the muscular and glandular systems which maintain the organism as an operative whole. The ego that is born of the dust must return to the dust. Such is the old mansion for men who belong to the old—to the order that is rooted in the blood. And alas! while humanity as a whole is striving to refocus its élite at a higher level, nevertheless the man of the mass is still completely centered around this ego born of blood and muscles.

At the higher level, reached through the portals of the "second birth"—portals opened by the Buddha and the Christ for the first time in a collective and planetary way—the "I am" establishes itself upon another foundation. It is reborn of air and of tone. It becomes itself a foundation. It creates its own universe as an individual, a bestower of significance upon all physical facts of the earth. It separates itself from the earth, as the perfume separates itself from the flower to flow upon the waves of air; as the tone separates itself from the throbbing bell to wing its way through the countryside.

The individual. How much misunderstanding accompanies this potent word! The idea it represents is difficult for many persons to grasp, because it implies two different operations. The first one implies a separation from the earth, the mother, the family, the tribe—and from the sense of ownership. Through it man has to stand alone, as if without foundations, as if without friends or possessions. It is darkness—for, remark, the first astrological house is *below the horizon*. It is yet the unseen. It is that which presses upward from the depth; that which separates itself from the depth and the dark—and emerges at the line of awareness: the horizon and the "Ascendant".

Thus the individual is never a static reality. He is a surging upward from the depth—as the tone surges from the hollow of the bell. And as he surges onward, he seems to lose contact with the "mother", the earth, the home—and to become a wanderer and an exile. And it is because he is an exile that he can become the foundation of a new order of life; just as the Pilgrim Fathers became the foundation of a new social order. But in proportion as there is in the exile a sense of clinging to the old ideals and the old possessiveness that is of the blood, in this same proportion does the new order fail to be vitally significant and great.

Because the individual at first becomes an exile and a lonely wanderer, he realizes the need to make a covenant with other exiles; a covenant guaranteeing the rights of each and all on the basis of equality and of individual freedom. This covenant of free men—and no longer of blood-kinsmen bound by the traditions of their ancestral earth—is the foundation of the new order. This new order begins on a Plymouth Rock, for the same reason that Peter—which means "a stone"—was chosen by Jesus as the rock upon which His church was to be built. Such a rock, in the astrological symbolism of the second birth, corresponds to Aries 19°—the point of exaltation of the Sun, in the first zodiacal mansion of the Sun, which becomes the symbol of the wanderer: Man. The number 19 is the number of the Sun, or rather of him who becomes a manifestation, an *avatar*, of the Sun.

Then the individual, having thus become a separate entity, is ready for the second phase of the process. He joins hands and will with other separate individuals; and on that foundation of covenanted individuals is born the new order, the real democracy, which is—when it exists in reality—a spiritual idea projected into a pattern of organization. This "joining of hands" is deeply symbolical; but it means the establishing of a new order only if each participant has become previously "separate"; only if each individual has proven to himself and to God his own individualhood by the new breath—which is a symbolical way of saying that the individual has become free from bondage to the earth and to the blood, whence comes the sense of passion, of jealousy, of possessiveness and covetousness, and the craving for conquest and ruthless expansion.

Expansion on the earth-plane means violent conquest and the enslavement—physical or moral—of others. But on the plane of air, expansion means the achievement of more inclusive co-operation with others, more inclusive wholeness. No one will fence in the air and say: my air, for myself only to breathe. If one did so, one would sooner or later die suffocated. One cannot possess air and live. Air belongs to all and is breathed by all; and it unifies every living thing, as it courses through the lungs of would-be enemies as well as of entranced lovers.

Thus the individual of the second birth, living on the plane of air, which is that of vitalizing wholeness, finds himself both a unique personality without roots in a binding past, and one creative center joined through unity of purpose and of work with many similar creative centers. Similar, yet each different; graded as to activity and work in a hierarchy of creative deeds, yet all equals in a community of essential being.

On this foundation, which will become the true Aquarian order, a new consciousness develops which in time transcends itself, and reaches to the "third birth", which is of the realm of light. Of this, it is almost useless to speak; for today the great struggle is between earth-values and air-values, the cravings of the blood-self and the purposes of the breathing self. The old mansion says: "I am—and all others shall bow to this, my triumphant cry of selfhood. They shall be my slaves and my reflections." The new mansion calls for new men who know, each and all: *I am That*—I am the particular being with a particular purpose and destiny, and I will fulfill them. I recognize that each of my companions has his particular purpose and destiny, which I will not only allow him, but help him to fulfill. And this shall be the new nobility of Man, that every individual, whatever his blood, his sex, and his past, shall join hands with other individuals as free human beings, to create and to manifest upon the earth the Glory of the One Individual in whom "we live and move and have our being."

What may lie beyond such a realization can only with the most extreme difficulty be manifested through a present-day human personality. Witness the agonies and the strange aberrations of those mystics who claim to have become identified with God in a universal birth of light. That such a birth is possible, there can be little doubt. But what is being born is so incongruous with the normal basis of earth-conditioned present-day humanity, and it is so nearly impossible to find on our planet, as it is materially constituted today, substances to sustain the being of those who have reached this identification with God, that such an exalted and universal state of being can hardly be substantialized and become harmonious personality.

In the first mansion, being is only an Idea, an archetype, a mere "breath". It is, in terms of consciousness, an intuition, a flash of illumination, a pure, unsubstantiated realization. It has form, but not yet substance. It is the "Son of God" before he has met the "daughters of the earth". It is joy before the crucifixion into the flesh. But the vistas opened to that joyous, heaven-born realization of being will become the incentive beyond the ponderous, groping steps of a more substantial development of personality. Being will operate through all the vicissitudes of becoming; and the courage to go forth and to prove to the universe that quality and that tone which constitute man's innermost individuality will be found by concentrating again and again upon that "original Impulse" which is of God—even if all else be heavy with the refuse of the past and the mire of earth.

Second Mansion
To Own

IF BREATHING IS THE FIRST STEP OF INDEPENDENT AND INDIVIDual being, the second step is: *to own*. As the "I am" becomes aware of itself through the breath a new intuition or awareness necessarily follows: this sound, this breathing, these lungs —are my own. *I own!* . . . Which means: I am not merely an abstract airy spirit wafted upon the winds. There is something in which I am. I have a basis, a substance in which to be concrete. There are flesh, bones, blood, tissues which belong to me. I am real—because I own. I have power—because I own some portion of the earth. I need not be afraid of non-existence—because these possessions which are mine are guarantees of continued existence. I am strong—potent.

All existence is based on ownership. Being, as pure spirit, begins to "exist" the moment there is something it can call "mine". "I am!"—this very cry of individual being involves possessions. The "I" may be considered as a pure abstraction; but the "am" necessitates *something* to be in. A body, of course. And the body is our first possession—even though we do not realize at first the meaning of it in its totality. Yet we recognize one by one all the instrumentalities through the use of which being proves itself to itself. And we say proudly: these hands, this flesh are mine. In and through them I am.

As we grow, as our life-path leads us through many mansions, we ceaselessly extend our sense of ownership. Our possessions increase; also the burden and responsibility thereof. We begin to differentiate between this and that type of possession. We put different valuations upon our several possessions. We come to realize that what we own as an individual being has been in other hands before. And we begin to classify possessions into *inherited* and *acquired* possessions.

Inherited are all the things or elements which have come to us without any deliberate individual effort. The first of those is the aggregate of organs and cells which we learn to consider as our body. Our parents—especially our mother—gave it to us. Our food and clothing, the thoughts and traditional valuations which our immediate surroundings impressed upon us for many years of childhood, caused relatively little individual effort for us to appropriate. They were all *foodstuffs:* physical or psychological. And we ate them, digesting them in a very automatic, unconscious manner. We could not struggle for different ones. We could only refuse to absorb that which, in a dull unconscious way, we did not like. Through refusal, rebellion, disobedience, suffering, deprivation, craving, ambition, envy, we learned to give to possessions our own individual valuations. A tragic path, which all must tread. The path of illness, of frustration and of woe. What we own is bound to make us suffer; for it is only as we suffer from the things we own—or fail to own—that we begin to function as a real individual, consciously; that is, as one who is able to put upon everything owned or susceptible of being owned the stamp of his own creative significance. Without some extent of deprivation and suffering there can be no individual selfhood as such. Consciousness is born of relative want; it may die, however, from too much deprivation.

Possessions, at the level of the physiological birth and the physiological organism, are matters of more or less vital necessity—or at least they seem so, to us. Without them the ego cannot be what he is. The ego is bound to his traditional possessions, as he is bound to his own body. He demands them as the very means for his existence; and therefore he is not able to evaluate them objectively, because he cannot separate himself from them. To let go of them would be inconceivable. What could an ego do without his body? To lose it means extinction—death or profound sleep. What could a normal person, rooted in blood-traditions and racial-physiological habits, do without his traditional concepts and feelings? To lose them would mean psychological death.

Thus the terrific implications of "exile". An exile is an uprooted tree. He must live psychologically on his treasure of accumulated remembrances; otherwise he is as one dead. Every contact inflicts on his ego a wound. He is an "I" without the "am". He lives psychologically in a world of fantasies, shrinking from any new confrontation, trying to compensate for this ceaseless frustration by many and varied means of spiritual escape, unless he accepts his new situation, and faces his new world as one born out of the mother womb—although, it may seem, without a mother to feed him.

When a man is thus deprived of his root-possessions, there are two ways open for him: he may go on dreaming of the past, in constant agony of deprivation—however cleverly he may hide the fact from his consciousness!—or else he may accept the separation as a matter of fact and begin at once to find new possessions. In so doing a new situation faces him, and the possibility of using a more deliberate choice in the re-gathering of possessions. He has separated himself from that which was his own by physical birthright: his ancestral life and his very substance. He can now select, consciously, freely, as an individual, what he will call his own.

But very often he does not. He merely accepts his new surroundings and absorbs what they radiate, just as unconsciously as he drank his mother's milk—only the mother's milk was vital, whereas the new psychological foodstuffs he ingests are not synchronous with his own rhythm. He and they are not born of the same earth and the same tradition. Thus the new life is one lived on the surface of being; intellectually and socially satisfying perhaps, but vitally and spiritually inoperative. And this is the tragedy of so many modern city-lives!

On the contrary, the man who has passed deliberately through the second birth goes to search for what is his own, by individual choice. Slowly, painfully, through many false enthusiasms and crucifying repudiations, he gathers his own earth, the substance of his truly individual body. Only thereafter can he say vitally and creatively: "I am". And he will say it really for the first time. For what he owns now, he has valued objectively. He is no longer identified with his possessions as a matter of fact. He uses them deliberately, by choice. And this is the new meaning of possessions. To own is now only to use. Creative and significant use must be the foundation and only justification of ownership.

It is this distinction between possessions with which the ego identifies himself subjectively and possessions which the ego uses objectively which constitutes the fact of the "new birth" in this second realm of life—the realm of ownership. The difference is that which lies at the root of the conflict between a capitalism rooted in the right to inherit social possessions without individual effort or valuation, and socialism, collectivism, or technocracy. "No ownership without individual use and significant use" might be the motto of the new age. From this follows in logical social sequence the right for each individual to own what he can use significantly and creatively; which means that individual frustration can then become a thing of the past. With it would disappear the psychological complexes which confuse or torture modern mankind, even though these can become the foundation upon which a new step of spiritual development and the birth of great individuals are made possible.

Frustration is due to the impossibility that exists for the ego to find the proper substance in which to become actual and concrete. In a spiritual sense it is the only real crucifixion. Great spiritual beings at certain times of the earth's history—

and ours is one!—cannot find adequate parents to provide them with fit bodies and fit psychological environment. Yet the cyclic tide calls for their birth. A new era must be ushered in, and they are the heralds and the seed. Will they, can they refuse the call to service and to earthly embodiment? Tragically, yet out of boundless compassion for this poor troubled earth, the great Avatars and Heroes are thus born in races which provide no adequate soil or "food" for their egos fully to manifest.

Therefore they must become rebels and exiles. Painfully, step by step, they must build their own bodies of manifestation—mental-spiritual ones, as long as there are no physiological ones available. This means working in a state of constant tension, of "dissonant harmony"; ceaselessly integrating the farther opposites, ceaselessly moving on and on over the crushed memories of what are bound to appear as failures and emotional ruins, yet which are the nearly unavoidable result of an "equation of destiny" to which the Soul assented—a compact with God. Of such a tragic march over graves, mind is the result. From frustrated ownership life moves on to knowledge—the third mansion.

The degree of frustration permitted, justifiable or useful to man, not only as an individual but also as a collectivity, constitutes a major problem, the solution of which is most important in determining the existing type of culture or civilization. What is at stake here is the relation between the first and the second mansions; between the new impulses to be and the load of past unfulfillments which these impulses—or monads—have to meet as they attempt to exteriorize themselves as individual selves. The first mansion establishes the goal of the individual; the second, what society (as the sum-total of the race's past) provides him with at the start of his journey toward this goal.

The problem is thus involved in, or is the consequence of, the racial *karma*. It is the nature of this *karma*, the nature of the race's antecedent failures and "sins", which determines the relationship between individuals and society. It does that by regulating the degree of frustration or deprivation to be endured by the new-born individual selves. The poverty or wealth of individuals and of the average man and woman in any particular society, the opportunities for development offered to the children—psychological and spiritual as well as physical and mental—the type of ideology dominating this society and its educational institutions, and in a larger planetary sense the fertility of the soil and the nature of its various resources:—all these factors and a few others determine the proportion of relatively individual thinkers and creators to the collective mass.

In ages of deprivation or psychological perversion a few geniuses stand far above the depressed masses of the people. Great thinkers face enslaved or dulled populations. Only the very great individual Self can hope to overcome the handicaps of birth in such a society. The very suppressed energy of the masses' unfulfillment goads him to victory in order to establish a balance of spiritual realization in the race as a whole— for the same reason that a mother frustrated in her passionate yearning to be a singer may give birth to a great musician, and that the child with an inferiority complex forces himself up to success.

In ages of plenty and of harmonious opportunities for mental and spiritual development the average man and woman can blossom forth. The race level is high, but no great individuals shine forth to compensate for the racial low. Mankind's achievements are collective rather than individual. Thought is collectively absorbed like good and healthy food, but not being wrenched from a hostile environment, it lacks a certain character of dynamic intensity and spiritual fire. It is the flowering of the earth, rather than a glorious downpour of the Spirit making deity manifest through an individual.

It is written in the *Bhagavat Gita* that Krishna, the divine Incarnation, takes birth on earth in periods of darkness and perversion in order to re-establish the reign of the Spirit. This is the universal law. Deity manifests only through an individual personality who, spurred on by the dismal materiality of his race, consciously or super-consciously overcomes the spiritual or mental or physical frustrations caused by his heredity and immediate environment, and *in spite of them* becomes a grail for divinity. Great Spirits become godlike Personages or geniuses not because of conditions in which they were born, but in spite of them. "Notwithstanding" is the key-word of spiritual realization, of any truly individual realization. Only the lowest depths are a fit match to the activity of the highest "Flames", who, overcoming the most crushing burdens, prove themselves "Sons of God".

Third Mansion
To Know

THE THIRD MANSION THROUGH WHICH THE INDIVIDUAL MUST pass on his quest for wholeness and operative mastery is that of knowledge. *I know* is the natural sequence to "I am" and "I own"; for it is only out of the conflict between these last two elements of being that the third arises: knowledge. It is only as the ego senses the inadequacy of that which he owns —his body and his inherited mechanisms of action—in his efforts to express what he inherently is, that the need to know the whence, how, and whither of these possessions is made imperative.

Knowledge is ever born out of fundamental and irreducible oppositions. It is because spirit (the Self) is never adequately expressed by matter (the body and all the ancestral past of any newborn entity) that man, individually or collectively, becomes the thinker, the knower. And the search for knowledge is endless, for there never will be any material aggregation which will satisfy the needs of the spirit. There can be no material organism—be it the most cosmic or divine—that ever will be an absolutely adequate vehicle for the "I am" who is to dwell therein. Therefore there will always be "divine discontent" and the need for knowing what may be done about it. There will ever be restlessness and motion and search; and ever new ways will have to be devised for the "I am" to operate adequately through what he owns by birthright. And the worlds will keep on whirling; and the demon of speed will dizzy universes and men; and intellects will search feverishly for the eternally elusive secret of perfect adequacy of matter to spirit. Such is the mystery of the third mansion—the eternal Gemini.

The twain will never meet. They will stand for all eternities like Greek columns, Doric and Ionic, in the frigid ecstasy of knowing that they are ever inseparable and ever unsatisfied. It is this dualism and this subconscious despair that make minds reel in the search for God—the Integrator, the Harmonizer, the Perfect Solution of the irreducible dilemma. But perhaps there is no Integrator to be called upon or searched for in empyrean loneliness—save it be that one perpetual effort which links the twain, in conflict, in love, in sorrow and compassion. That effort is *intelligence*. It is the power to see a situation whole, and thus to make it whole. It is the power to refuse ever to stand still, ever to admit incapacity—yes, it is even the power to laugh at the two stupidly eternal columns facing each other in mysterious inadequacy. For even laughter can be a solution—perhaps an escape, perhaps also a chant of triumph, as O'Neill has shown in his sublime epic, *Lazarus Laughed*, the drama of the confrontation between eternal renewal (spirit) and eternal decay (matter); between the future and the past.

Between these two columns, past and future, something may happen: the present. And the present is "intelligence". Intelligence is the power to bring the past performance up to the new demands of the future—the ideal. Intelligence is the Initiate of old, standing between the two columns and by his power bringing to the candidate integration, operative wholeness. And how wonderful are these old myths! The Initiate who has failed and turned destructive is Samson, who, betrayed by matter (Delilah), stands between the two columns of the Temple and pushes them apart, hurling death at himself and at the betrayers.

In these symbols rests, for those who know how to read symbols, the secret of the intellect: divine, yet devilish where the would-be god is betrayed; integrating knowledge which projects into all organic behavior the power to improve itself and to cope with new situations—or the disintegrating worship of formalism which turns every creative performance into dead routine and clever automatism.

In the man of the first birth the third mansion means nerve-coordination and instinctual intelligence. It refers to essentially self-protective and self-reproductive mechanisms. Man is the creature of his heredity; he lives, a racial being, surrounded by brothers, sisters, and all his blood-relatives. His life-performance is easily integrated and wholesome, for it is relatively adequate to the as yet feeble demands of the individual self. The latter is barely able to assert itself through taking advantage of the situation provided by communal and tribal living. By playing brother against brother, this against that, he acquires power. At any cost the individual must find ways of asserting himself against the collective, against the parents. The present moment for him is centered round the urge to free the future from the inertial domination of the past. Cunning, restlessness, lies, bribery are the first stages. By constant repetition, habits are formed; the performance is improved. Competition, self-interest, cleverness, superficial brilliancy, sophistry are developed. Formalism is the ideal, for the self being more collective as yet than individual, the forms needed are stable and communal, generic and not individual. Individuals perfect the technique; but the creative power resides in the tribe, in the blood.

When mankind as a whole has reached a relatively high stage of civilization; that is, when the earth-substance itself—the raw materials of human endeavor, physiological and psychological—has become refined and thoroughly leavened by the mental operations of many generations, then the forms of knowledge may be very high. Yet, for the man of the first birth, this knowledge remains collective. It is merely assimilated intellectual foodstuff; not the result of creative thinking, of the fecundation of ideas. Thus today a child is born with the inherited power to deal at ease with cars, radios and machines in general, this power implying no creative thought or originality on his part.

When man has passed the threshold of the second birth, when he has become ever so dimly aware of his true "I am" and has either revaluated what was his own or acquired new possessions, then there is no longer need for cunning. He is alone now, essentially. And within himself the psychological conflict now rages. He is spirit facing a consciously selected or repolarized matter. The inadequacy of the latter strikes him pitilessly. Then is born real "intelligence"—or the defeatist evasions of a soul too weak to face the mental pressure and no longer able to return to the low-tension field of tribal or collective living.

Then the concrete philosopher, the scientist, the experimenter, are born. Then also the creative artist, whose inspired works are essentially recorded patterns of integration—as for instance Dante's *Divine Comedy;* in other words, tales of successful psychological adjustment. Then the Great Mind is truly the Initiate. He stands between the two columns, his arms upraised. Spirit and matter become for a moment harmonized within him. He dies; but as an Examplar he lives in his performance wherever distracted souls cry for knowledge and yearn for that creative intelligence which can open vistas of divine splendor. Through intelligence the past is made into the future during moments consciously and lucidly lived.

Humanity now stands at the crossroads of the mind. The old physiological ideals of the first birth—the call of the blood to glorification of racial purity and blood-sacrifices, the tribal instinct—are spasmodically yet most widely re-energized. They have never died, and will not die for ages. The minds of most men today are as yet rooted in their blood; and when the blood gets heated the mind boils and "sees red". The scientist, the artist, the author, the inventor are yet too often like youths in a clan trying by cunning to get the better of their relatives. Their ideal is technical excellency and the formation of more perfect automatisms to further the ends of their groups. The intellect is used *against* something; to allay fears or safeguard for the ego his possessions. And so there is no peace among men; for mind is the slave of possessions and the ego is as yet identified with what he owns.

This war is not only between men, but within man the individual; for even though he begins to emerge as an individual, yet is he bound to the sense of power which possessions give to him. And the intellect is a tool to keep, solidify, and increase these possessions. Therefore it is "the slayer of the real"—as occultists say. Because the real is the ceaselessly new and the eternally creative. It is the ever-changing present: that "intelligence" which makes every performance nearer to the ideal of the spirit that is the Self. And in "intelligence" there is no cunning and no fear; but the joy and ecstasy of being born always and anew. For this is the mystery of the second birth, that it occurs in every moment fully lived in utter freedom from the thralldom of the past and the cravings of the blood.

How remote from such a creative, exhilarating "intelligence" is the "intellectuality" of our age, boasting of its glorious mechanical achievements! Such an intellectuality is not any more *spiritual* than the primitive efforts of early manhood living at the level of the soil and using its primitive tools for the fashioning of objects of beauty as well as of utility. Spirituality has not primarily to do with the level of efficiency of the intellect in mastering the forces of nature, but with the power in the individual to transform creatively his response to life and to use what his collectivity produces for nobler and more vibrant purposes.

In intellectuality there is no *inherent* nobility or vibrancy;

because there is no real spiritually transforming purpose. The average scientist of today, and the readers of popular scientific magazines, are making no use of creative intelligence. They merely operate as collective beings at the level of the intellectual achievements accumulated by past generations and by the anonymous research of thousands of craftsmen in intellectual analysis. They are just as ready to make their high intellectual gifts operate at the command of national and tribal passions as the savage of old, fighting cunningly with sticks and arrows for the satisfaction of his instincts. Thus the intellectual level of a race has very little to do with the intensity and purity of the intelligence demonstrated by its individuals.

"Intelligence" is a quality of the free and creative spirit in man as an individual. It is not dependent upon the amount or nature of racially inherited intellectual possessions, but upon the use to which these possessions are put. Its true nature is revealed only as it integrates and synthetizes knowledge for the purpose of the Soul's development. And if the term "Soul" means anything, it is the free and spontaneous play of the total nature of man, of that essential wholeness in which spirit, mind and body are united in the joy and beauty of creative living: a wholeness not limited to the individual's boundaries, but rather geared to the glorious ascent of Man-the-whole toward that stage of perfect integration in which humanity is revealed as the microcosm of the universal Whole.

In intelligence we are whole, and yet parts of the greater Whole; because in it a quality of perpetual adjustment to life is shown at every moment. And in this adjustment there lies the secret of true freedom and of real joy; the secret of the constant adaptation of means to purpose, of becoming to being, of possessions to selfhood, of substance to spirit. It is this power of adaptation alone which raises us from our natal environment to a greater environment, which after having made us fulfill the brotherhood of blood leads us to enter the brotherhood of individual souls, and eventually to move through patterns of cosmic relationship which sun-like beings only may know, whose lives are poems of ever-radiating light. It is knowledge lived in perfect adequacy of form to function. Such a knowledge transcends all dualities of knower and known, of subject and object. It is life fulfilled every moment according to the purpose of the Soul and in consideration of the materials at hand. It is life glowing forth as pure and radiant "intelligence".

Fourth Mansion
To Establish

THE FIRST THREE MANSIONS THROUGH WHICH THE INDIVIDUAL proceeds in his long journey toward the goal of fulfillment and personality-integration constitute the first act of the drama of individuation. Within these mansions the "I am" becomes aware of being what he is. To breathe—to own—to know—are the three basic stages of this awareness of self. Everything that occurs is directed toward the building of the realization: "I am". Every value is subjective. Even possessions, while they are objects, are seen merely as means to project or consolidate the sense of self. The world is really a dream dreamt by the eternal dreamer, the "I". It is a dream because everything that appears in it is apprehended as a confirmation of or an obstacle to the sense of being "I". It is a purely subjective world, apparently made for the self and by the self—even when, as a hindrance to self, it serves to test and consolidate the power of the self.

In every human life this is the cycle of early childhood; for the child is absolutely rapt in self, even though his is not yet a formed selfhood. His toys, his parents, his comrades are things with which to prove his own sense of being "I". The child has absolutely no intrinsic morality and no real sense of objective valuation. He acts and reacts only in terms of how much of his self the present moment allows him to become aware of. All his actions and reactions are tentative questions he asks of life: What am I? How much do I own? How can I know what "life"—all that causes me pleasure or pain—will do to me when I act one way or another? How can I get what I want?

Then, around the crucial seventh year, a new phase begins. A new mansion opens its gates. The "I am" has become quite aware of his selfhood, of his powers, of the means to extend them in the neighborhood of the body. He must now go a step further. He must *establish* himself. The fourth mansion is characterized by the urge to establish, to build foundations, to become a concrete manifestation.

Every abstract idea has the tendency eventually to become a concrete objective reality. The abstract "Word" must ever become "flesh". This is the fatality of the Spirit, that it must take embodiment in some earth-substance. All Spirit tends toward the condition of Body. All concepts yearn to be formulated into sentences. Everywhere the supreme power of life is that power inherent in Spirit which compels it to become "form and name"—as the Hindu philosophers used to say. This compulsion is the essence of life. It is the desire-to-be, the eternal Eros. And it is also the desire to remain permanently what one is. It is the urge to become established.

At the normal human stage this urge leads man to build a home, to establish a foundation for his activities as an individual self. It is the urge to take root; to found a family; and, at a more mental level, to establish a doctrine. It is the spiritual striving toward the formation of an immortal Soul that will be the permanent shrine of the "I am"; the effort toward personal immortality, whose shadow is the fear of death, of ceasing to be. Until this urge asserts itself all living is only dreaming, and outer circumstances are mere stimuli which stir the imagination of the dreamer. The self awakens only as he contacts the earth and marries objectivity. The true "waking consciousness" is consciousness established in a body and operating in an objective world.

"Reality" is that in which consciousness can establish itself and prove itself to itself. In "reality" the self can actually experience. An experience is distinct from a dream insofar as it is something in which the self can establish itself. The dream may mean increased awareness of self; but the experience is always a deeper, broader or more steady establishment of self in reality. Reality, objectivity, experience, self-establishment are all correlated terms. Insofar as dream is opposed to reality, reality is always objective and dream always subjective.

But there may be various levels or types of reality, of objectivity, of concreteness. Spirit always tends to formulate itself in and through a "body". But there may be various levels or types of "bodies". A great symphony and a great poem are "bodies", as much as any physiological organisms—provided they can reproduce and perpetuate themselves in the minds of men. If they are merely the dreams of a youthful "I am", they have no objective reality. But if the "I am" that created them is actually established in them, if they have become his home and their foundations are solidly built into the soil of the race, then the symphony and the poem are to be considered as "bodies" of this creative "I am".

Here we must differentiate "body" from "form". The term form denotes merely an abstract pattern, a concept which has become exteriorized so as to be communicable to other minds. Form, organizing substance under the impact of a central will, or self, becomes body. But substance may exist at various levels. One should not apply the term only to physical substance perceptible to our normal senses. "Substance" is that which is a basis, a substratum for the objective manifestation of life in and through "bodies". This substance for self-establishment in a body is found in the second mansion. But it is only in the fourth phase of development of the individual being that it reaches a relatively permanent identity. Man's body is what he, as an abstract self, has made out of his heredity under certain conditions of environment. It may be a success, or a failure—at least a relative one. The self, as a divine Idea or archetype, may be a wondrous formula of being; yet the race may not offer either hereditary materials or an environment adequate for its successful *incorporation*— and so the "body" may be a poor objective manifestation of a great but premature or belated Idea.

For the man of the first birth, centered at the physiological level, to be established in objectivity means first of all to operate in and through an integrated physical body. This does not occur at birth. To be born means only to have developed a mechanism of self-awareness through independent breathing. In these studies we are not considering the human being from the standpoint of the biologist, but from that of the psychologist. We are dealing with the growth of consciousness from mere awareness of self to total fulfillment of individual selfhood—which really means universal consciousness.

It is only around the seventh year that the conscious ego establishes itself in the body. It is only after some months or years during which the ego yearns to find himself established, and thus powerful, that this ego actually becomes the dweller in the body. To own hands and feet by means of which one may become aware of an objective world and of limitations to the instinct of flowing outward in space (which is the primordial instinct of every self) is one thing. To be established and concretely conscious in and through a body is another thing. Inherited possessions constitute merely an aggregation of energies to be used; but a body—or later a home—is not a mere aggregation of energies. It is a centralized organism in and through which the "I am" can be positively and powerfully active. A body is selfhood become concrete. It is a base for operations. It is the foundation for self-expression; the foundation for release of power.

He who does not realize this significance of "body" has not realized as yet the meaning of power. Identification with "body" is necessary if self is to be powerful and creative. A self not thus identified is a dreamer. It has not yet taken root in objectivity. It is Spirit unmarried to Substance: unestablished Spirit.

But it is only for the man of the first birth that "body" signifies no more than a physiological organism. He who has passed through the portals of the second birth finds himself established in a new type of "body": an individual soul-organism. *The symbol for such a soul-organism, at our racial level, is the home.*

What is the home? The interaction of a masculine and feminine polarity made concrete and operative within a structure of earth-materials. While a physiological body is polarized, that is, either male or female, the home is the projection of a nexus of bi-polar (that is, male and female) psychic energies. The home thus requires three things: a male and a female center of life-radiations, a constant rhythmical pulsation between these two psychic poles, and a projection in concrete materials of this pulsation. If these three things are present a home is established, whether it is a palace of marble or a desert tent.

The home becomes thus a symbolical "body". It is symbolical, and not absolutely real, because the pulsation of two inter-related psychic poles, man and woman, is not a constant and indissoluble one. Thus the significance of monogamous indissoluble marriage. It is an attempt to transform the home from a symbol into an absolute reality. Yet it is not absolutely real, for the union can be broken by the death of one of the partners, or by psychological changes in the individuality of the partners. It is as a result of the yearning—conscious or subconscious—to make of the man-woman union an absolutely real unit, that the concept of "soul-mates" has arisen. Through it the pulsation between the two psychic polarities is seen as an immortal and transcendental reality. Because physical and biological polarities are obviously as impermanent as the flesh of our bodies, the absolutely valid "mating" is transferred to the psychic level. "Soul-mating" thus can be understood as a subliminal concept, a border-line realization—just as, in another sense, the devotional self-surrender of the devotee to the Christ-image (or the Oriental Guru) is a transitional process. Both are attempts at objectivating a reality which eventually the individuated human personality must find at the core of his selfhood. Thus the true mystic experiences Christ within, and the teachers of old India said "Thou art that" . . . "Thou art Buddha". Thus also the Sufi wrote of the "Beloved" that is known in the inmost chamber of the soul.

The home is a symbol and a prophecy: the symbol and the prophecy of the individual soul-organism, of the immortal Christ-body. The latter is also the projection of a rhythmical and constant pulsation between two psychic poles; but these two poles are active *within one single individual*. They are the psychic man and psychic woman to some extent operative within every human being who is more than a mere human male or female; in other words, within every individual who is a partaker in some degree of the quality and reality of the second birth of selfhood. This means, within every creative individual.

No individual can be creative as an individual if a rhythmical—if not constant—pulsation between the two poles of his psychological nature is not established. This pulsation begins to manifest in the third mansion through the operation of the formative energies of the intellect. The typical intellectual operation, the Aristotelian syllogism on which all logic is based, is a sort of pulsation between two conceptual poles. All intellectual thinking is based upon such an oscillation between thesis and antithesis, which finds itself harmonized in the synthesis; even though in some cases the oscillation is so rapid that the act of synthesis appears to be instantaneous. Whether it can ever be absolutely instantaneous is a problem difficult to solve; yet one of great interest, because on its solution depends the possibility of a type of thinking beyond ordinary logic.

The psychological soul-organism may be said to pattern itself upon such an intellectual framework. It is a dynamic synthesis of "soul-forces" which pulsate rhythmically and eventually release power in creative works—just as the rhythmical sex-pulsation established between the man and the woman eventually releases the child, who becomes the center of the home, the seed of the man-woman flower.

Thus the home is a symbol and a prophecy—and marriage is a sacrament. It foreshadows (and, in the present biological and psychological condition of mankind, may help to produce) the formation of the individual soul-organism—that great reality of the truly *human* level of being to which all ancient Scriptures symbolically referred.

Such an individual soul-organism must not be confused with what modern writers call the "astral body" or "mental body". These are not actually "bodies". They are rather phases in the gestation of the soul-organism. They deal as it were with the embryology of the soul-organism, but are not "organisms" in themselves. The soul-organism is a true "body" because in it the self establishes itself at the psycho-mental level, and, through such an act of establishment, gains relative immortality. In this soul-organism the second birth is fulfilled. It is the true "home" of the Individual, the body of the indwelling God.

The Bible refers to it in the symbolism of the Temple of Solomon; while the "Ark in the Wilderness" represents the phase of psycho-spiritual development during which only the "seed" of true individual selfhood is objective and manifest. The "Wilderness" symbolizes the state of chaotic being and of homeless wandering when the soul-forces or component energies of the psyche are not organically correlated, and not even completely subservient to the central will of the self— to the integrative "law" or pattern of individual selfhood. These soul-forces are the substance, or rather the raw material, of the future soul-organism. They have been in the past parts of the psyche of many men, just as the molecules composing our bodies have been parts of the bodies of trees, animals and men. Each has a will of its own; each strives for power, for the possession of the "Ark of the Covenant", trying to usurp the authority of the true "Priests of the Most-High", until Solomon, son of David—the overcomer of the giant—succeeds in bringing all the unruly elements under the sway of his power and wisdom; until the Temple is built from materials gathered from all lands, an organic synthesis of being, a "home" for the sacred Ark, the "seed" of individual selfhood now fulfilled as a majestic tree.

What comes after this fulfillment of the stage of the second birth is not so clearly definable. But we know that with the coming of Jesus the Christ—of the house of David—the gates of the third birth open. This coming leads eventually to the descent from heaven of the "New Jerusalem". The Holy City symbolizes the reality of the fourth mansion at the third level of being. It is an organism of spirit and of light. It is more than individual, in the sense that it comes down from the universal realm, from heaven. It is a celestial host focused in and through a man acting upon this earth. It is a complete manifestation of deity in and through personality.

Fifth Mansion
To Release

From the foundation symbolically built in the fourth mansion, from the home—be it a material or a psycho-mental home—the established individual is able to operate. The energies wound up in the concrete structure can now be released as efficient power. To release, to express, to create: such are the basic key-notes of the fifth mansion. And as the energies which man can release are many and varied, the fifth mansion of the self is apt to be a field for the bringing forth of strange and wondrous powers, but also at times of very queer and nefarious ones. In all cases it is the field for self-expression, for the pouring forth of self in pure spontaneity of being.

Here we find expressed whatever has been built in the fourth mansion. It is a place of emanation, also of emancipation. The free man expresses the freedom which he has gained through mastery of the laws of form and through an understanding of the nature of the materials he is to use. The homeless one expresses the psychological tensions produced by his homelessness and instability. The dreamer sings his "castles in Spain", which sway in the breeze like colored soap-bubbles. He who has built his home as a dungeon releases his inhibitions as complexes or vices. The arrogant lord of the castle flaunts his pride and gambles his wealth away. The fool speculates on his folly. He whom society has deprived of home and soul executes his crimes . . . While all the time mothers, here, bear children; great geniuses create immortal sons; and the Universal Mind gives birth to the First born, the "Flames" that are, in ancient mythologies, the Spirits of men.

This mansion is the creative mansion; and as all creation presupposes a release of power through the formative agency of the mind, here we find the creative mind in action—from the Universal Mind to the most insignificant human minds housed in frail bodies of clay. If the fourth mansion can be characterized by the term "focus", the fifth carries the symbol of the ray. It is the realm of the sun-ray. It is the realm of the pulsating flow of the life-force. It is the mansion of the heart and of the photosphere of the sun. It is the symbol of "operative wholeness"; for that which is whole must needs be effulgent. The saint cannot hide his halo of sanctity. The devil cannot hide the scorching exhalations of his destructive homelessness; for he is the destroyer of souls and of spiritual homes, the disintegrator of all foundations.

There is a close connection between this and the first mansion. Here is revealed objectively and actively the selfhood of the individual. The abstract has become, not only concrete, but active. And activity is the one quality of Life. We are alive because we act. We act because we find, in our body, the basis for action. And if it is often said that the body is the negative counterpart of the highest spirit (*atma*) in man, it is because all activity is founded upon a "body", of this or that type, at one level or another of substance.

Fundamentally, the individual self is a pattern of activity or, in modern terminology, of behavior—provided we extend the boundaries of the field of activity usually covered by this last word. That is why the first mansion was called the mansion of the breath: breathing being the first *independent* activity of the organism. But at a later stage the breath must be made to release the rhythm of selfhood hidden therein. Thus, in the fifth mansion breath becomes expressive and modulated tone. It becomes song and melody. The birth-cry unfolds as the symphony. At the same time the ancestral possessions of the second mansion become working capital, to invest or to speculate with; the intellect becomes the word which goes forth in command; and feelings become emotions.

There has been a great deal of confusion caused by not sufficiently differentiating these two words—feelings and emotions—and that which they represent. To feel is to receive upon an integrated foundation of selfhood impacts from total life-situations. I must have an organic body to feel what is attempting to disrupt the organic quality of this body. I feel hungry. I feel cold. These are organic bodily feelings; that is, the ways by means of which a situation that may disrupt the wholeness of my body (viz., lack of food, insufficient heat, etc.) is registered by the conscious "I".

Likewise I feel sad or exalted, at the psychological level of being, if the life-situation in which I find myself as a soul decreases or increases the integral quality of my psyche. Wherever there is feeling, there a concrete and organic entity is becoming impressed by a life-situation as a whole. Feelings arise always from a total situation, and differ in that from intellectual judgments, which tear the situation into bits in order to analyze it. Feelings originate as the whole personality meets the concrete world as a whole.

Out of this meeting arises from the center of the whole personality a reaction: a going toward some object in attraction, or a going away from the object in repulsion. Thus love and hatred. This reaction, and all the mechanisms by means of which the feeling is exteriorized into some sort of muscular gesture (direct or indirect), constitute an *emotion*. E-motion means "a moving outward". Often, however, the movement outward is inhibited; and so there is emotion without apparent muscular motion. But the modern psychologist has shown us that even where there is no apparent motion, very small, normally undetectable contractions of inner muscles may be revealed by sensitive apparatuses.

It is because of this normally unperceivable character of most emotional muscular reactions (at least in civilized societies) that the terms "emotion" and "feeling" have been used so indiscriminately. But a "feeling" is always an organic or psychic impression or realization caused by a particular (or a diffuse and vague) life-situation. It is that which causes us to react, not as a finger or a leg or a partial organ, but as a total being, whether it be predominantly at the physiological or at the psychological level. From the basis of this total being, from the basis of our conscious or unconscious selfhood, we move. We release ourselves in an emotion. And if this release is inhibited, an accumulation of psychic energy is started, which leads to psychological or physiological disturbances—or to a definite change of attitude toward life. The nature of the disturbance or change of attitude varies with every individual and every situation. These variations lead to certain processes which belong to the realm of the sixth mansion.

The fourth mansion is the mansion of feelings; the fifth, that of emotions. The latter is a fiery mansion, because emotions are eruptions of the fire of individual selfhood. It is a mansion of power, because through it the power initiated in the breath and made concrete in the body or the soul-organism is made manifest and released. To each type of breath corresponds symbolically a type of release of power—therefore of emotions: emotions released through the engine of the body; through the engine of the soul organism; through the (to us quite incomprehensible) engine of the spiritual organism.

In the man of the first birth—the ordinary man of today —emotions arise, more or less obviously, from the self that finds in the body his engine for the release of "I am" power. These emotions are reactions to organic feelings. They are racial and collective. They deal with hunger, with sex, with the desire for self-aggrandizement, with anger and jealousy, with fear. They are rooted in the three great organic instincts: self-preservation, self-aggrandizement, self-reproduction—also, to some extent, self-realization in objects or persons that we transform into mirrors wherein we contemplate and narcisstically adore ourselves.

These emotions, being reactions to organic feelings—sublimated, as they may appear in civilized society—are rooted in the blood, the symbol of organic wholeness. Psychologically speaking, they are closely connected with the activity of the endocrine glands. The hormones of the latter blend in the bloodstream, which, under impulsions originating from the heart and from various secondary nervous and muscular reactions, stimulates or restrains the activities of our organs of action.

There is nothing basically individual in these emotions, when they are allowed to release themselves naturally. It is only as their release is inhibited that the individual self is able to use, along new channels of expression, the repressed physiological and psychological energies. The manner in which this transformation will operate is dictated by "soul-images", which in turn are the results of abstract concepts, of ideas and ideals.

Here is a point of great significance, the understanding of which is essential for a proper evaluation of all methods and techniques of spiritual development. Ideas and ideals are abstractions which belong to the first mansion. They acquire power only as they are converted in the fourth mansion into "soul-images", that is, into definite representations, symbolical in character and susceptible of arousing feelings and a resulting release of psychic power. This release, occurring symbolically in the fifth mansion, is the true creative expression of the individual self.

While the racial self could express itself through the physical body, which belongs to the race rather than to the individual, every truly individual mode of expression requires as a foundation a psycho-mental organism (at least in a rudimentary stage of development). Such an organism is developed through the operation of "soul-images". In other words, the soul-organism is the product of the creative imagination, of the power of visualization—what the Hindu philosophers called *Kriyashakti*. It is the product of the individual's ideals and ideas, once these have been precipitated into the psyche in the shape of "images of power", images that compel psychic reactions. Such images as those of "the Buddha in meditation", "the crucified Christ", "the Virgin-Mother and the Christ-child", and many others less linked with religious symbolism, are psychically potent. They have been the sources of feelings and emotions for millions of men. They have actually formed the souls (the psycho-mental organisms) of millions.

These images are of course collective, in the sense that they have the power of generations back of them. Yet the individual who makes them his own is able to give formation therewith to his own psychic energies or "soul-forces". This is spiritual creativeness. The creative artist acts in the same manner. In the great cultural periods the images used by the creative artist are strongly collective and born of the needs and experiences of the racial or national group as a whole. The artist fulfills the aspiration of his collectivity and is impelled by ancestral forces finding in him a focal point for their release. During periods of transition, such as our nineteenth and twentieth centuries, the creative release is more strongly conditioned by the individual artist's own realizations as a spiritual being. The creative action is a descent of power from spiritual sources into the individual, who becomes thus an exemplar of the future rather than the fruition of a long line of ancestry. In the first case we have a Haydn and a Bach; in the second a Beethoven.

With such types of creative activity we come to the level of the man of the second birth who has transcended mere physiological action. At the first level of human development the fifth mansion is that of the physical progeny; man does not project his own individual pattern or image of being so much as he becomes a transmitter of a racial pattern. His children are the progeny of his ancestors, through him. This fifth mansion is also that of education, which is a kind of mental-psychological giving birth—the true educator being, at least potentially, the father-mother of the psychological organism of the child. If, however, we come to the level of the second birth, the child being brought forth in this mansion by the man who has built his bi-polar soul-organism is ultimately the Christ-child within, the "Living God". The works of all great creative artists are progressive symbols of such a psycho-mental birth; symbols for the use of the race at large, especially in the great periods of religious and classical culture—but also symbols that reveal the progressive soul-integration of the artist as a representative personality whose inner (and possibly, but rarely, outer) life can serve as an example to others similarly polarized.

What the fifth mansion means to those of the third birth is necessarily clouded in mystery; for to very few indeed is it given to know the significance of the "body" of light which is the "home" of the spirit. At this stage the individual and the collective become one. Life is then a progressive series of illuminations and of identifications with ever more universal realities. Man then reaches beyond the individual stage, even though in so doing he acts even more truly from the core of his Selfhood. The "soul-images" through which he releases the power of his "light" must be vast and cosmic Archetypes with which he has identified himself; and, as the mystics have said, he is "taken up" by his God. He acts, yet God—or the collectivity of his spiritual Predecessors—acts in and through him. And his path is effulgent with the glory of cosmic harmony.

Sixth Mansion
To Improve

Just as "it is only as the ego senses the inadequacy of that which he *owns*—his body and his inherited mechanisms of action—in his attempts at expressing what he inherently *is*, that the need to *know* the whence, how and whither of these possessions is made imperative", so it is only as the *release* of creative power seems inadequate to the *soul* that attempted to express thereby its feelings, that there arises the urge for *work* and for becoming the disciple of a "master of expression".

In these six italicized words is told the entire story of the first series of the mansions of the self. In this series the self is entirely preoccupied with himself. The whole horizon is filled by the needs and the wants of the ego. And if in this sixth mansion the element of human relationship enters, it is only as the result of the realization of a lack. It is still the result of a self-centered want, even if it manifests as the very finest and noblest desire for self-improvement and self-absorption in a life greater than the ego's—even if it leads to utter devotion and martyrdom. For the devotee who surrenders self acts still from the basis of self. He denies self and thus is yet bound to self—as we are as much bound to what we hate and deny as to what we love and identify ourselves with.

The keyword of the sixth mansion is *improvement*. Negatively, it is the field for self-deterioration, for the disintegration of the organism built in the fourth mansion. As already said, no release of power, no creative act, appears fully adequate for the soul which is not altogether emotionally drunken with self. Every emotion ordinarily falls short of the feeling which gave it rise. There are of course exceptional cases, cases in which the soul is merely the terminal of a greater cosmic entity and may thus be weak in self-consciousness though powerful in its energy-releases. But even then, after the glow that follows the rush of creative power is passed, the conscious soul is left with a ghastly feeling of emptiness. At such times it is the release which appears greater than the feeling, the effect more intense than the cause, the torrent mightier than the apparent source. And there is still the same sense of inadequacy, merely reversed. It is as if the wealth of possessions (second mansion) to be used by the self (first mansion) was infinitely greater than the capacity of the self to conceive the utilization of wealth. In this case also the result would be a more or less deadly sense of emptiness leading to a search for knowledge—or for self-forgetfulness in ever renewed thrills and travels creating a constantly changing environment (third mansion).

In the sixth mansion the search is for self-improvement, if the emotional release was greater than the consciousness of the soul—or for improvement of technique and performance, if the means for expression were inadequate for the exteriorization of the "soul-image". In both cases the "work" done, or the "service" rendered, is conditioned by the realization of inadequacy, either in *being* or in *doing*. Where the inherited possessions or the psycho-mental values assimilated during early youth are scarce, the lack may be in the doing. In other words, the self has poor instruments to work with. On the other hand, where much has been inherited and acquired during childhood, the lack may be felt in the realm of being. What comes out of the personality is greater than the individual self. The being is as it were a "medium" through which great collective, racial or universal powers flow.

The latter case is always the case where animals are concerned; in fact, with regard to all truly instinctual actions. The instinctual act is a perfect performance; but there is no conscious self back of it, at least in the particular entity that is performing. The true performer is the Race-soul. In proportion as the Race-soul overshadows and overweighs the individual soul, in such a proportion the performance is greater than the individual who is the apparent performer.

On the contrary, with the typically "human" being, whose life is focalized around the development of an individual selfhood—the only absolutely *human* factor—the performance falls usually short of the ideal. This is true even of normally instinctual activities—as feeding, mating, etc. In such cases, physiologically speaking, the brains and the cerebro-spinal systems have developed at the expense of the cerebellum and the great sympathetic. Individualized consciousness has drawn too much power away from the centers of instinctual and automatic organic functioning.

In the first of these two alternatives the soul, sensing deeply its inadequacy as an individualized consciousness, is easily led to consider devotional self-surrender as the only way out. It searches for a "Master" or Guru; that is, for a greater being, a spiritual Father-Mother, within whom it can feel big, powerful and secure. Feeling its weakness, it desires protection. In exchange for this soul-security, the person is ready to give his "performing power"—his inherited and acquired wealth of possessions. He is ready to serve in utter self-surrender as well as surrender of possessions . . . and emotions.

Strange as it may seem, the devotee and server is actually surrendering to the protector and *guru* his emotional powers. He has rooted his "feelings" in the soul-organism of the guru and he therefore reacts to feelings (that is, experiences emotion) at the initiative of the *guru*. Similarly, his own spiritual "home" has become absorbed in the *guru's* soul-organism, which at its best is of almost cosmic proportions. He dwells no longer in his own abode but in the *guru's* spiritual "temple". He reacts, therefore, to life-situations from the point of view of that "temple". The resulting emotions are thus no longer his own.

Then the psychological situation is reversed. The perfect devotee has identified himself in soul-consciousness with his Master's soul-organism. He "feels with" his Master. His being thus has been prodigiously intensified. But his physical body has not changed—or at least has changed relatively very little. Therefore, now it is his performance which has become terribly inadequate in expressing the soul-nature of his Master, which is now his own by psychic transfusion—or even by proxy. Therefore an intense urge for improving his technique of living arises in the devotee. And that urge may be so great as to produce apparent miracles.

We speak of "miracles of faith"—but faith, in the devotee, precisely analyzed, is the result of the identification of his feelings and of his psychic nature with those of the Master. It is actual self-surrender, which has necessarily as consequence a sudden enlargement of the psychic sphere. The erstwhile individual soul is flooded with the psychic contents of the Master's soul-organism. The effect upon the devotee's physical body is often cataclysmic—frequently involving tuberculosis; an indication of the inadequacy of the physical structure in coping with inrushing psychic energies.

If, now, we take the second alternative, that of a human being centered in his individual selfhood whose ability to express his "soul-images" is inferior to the inner reality of these "images-feelings", we see another story unfolding. The sixth mansion will not mean for him *service* in self-surrender, but *work* for the mastery of technique.

Realizing the insufficiency of his means for self-expression, he will have to go to a teacher; that is to one more proficient than he is in the technique of self-expression. Such a teacher may be called a "master of expression" or an "adept"—one who acts perfectly, or a master-engineer who can control perfectly, through an understanding of materials and of form, the release of natural energies. But the individual who wishes to learn how to better exteriorize himself and his feelings, how to handle emotions so that they shall be more powerful and more significant releases of selfhood, will not approach this "master of expression" in the way in which the devotee approaches his guru. The approach will be that of pupil to teacher; not that of psychically insecure soul to an incarnate god, dispenser of salvation and sole path to spiritual perfection.

Work and devotion are the two aspects of this sixth mansion of the self. In and through work the individual, established in his own physical or psycho-mental "home", will strive to fortify his position and improve his behavior as a creative personality, secure in his own power and his own right. This will mean not only intellectual knowledge—as in the third mansion—but deliberate and constant practice; for here we are dealing with activity, with the probing of self by self. The teacher is the "Elder Brother" who has more experience, has worked harder, and possesses the qualities and faculties which can only be developed in one who has passed through the second series of mansions centered in relationship, and no longer in self.

Such a teacher will be especially careful not to bind his pupil and disciple emotionally, not to accept any self-surrender or total surrender of possessions. In fact, he will often accept nothing at all, save work and the proof of work done in a spirit of dedication to the ideal of the perfection of the work itself. What the disciple must learn in this sixth house is the respect of the apprentice for the master, the utter consecration to a task, once the task is accepted deliberately, the steady discipline of emotions, thanks to which no wasting of power is allowed, no maudlin sentimentalism, no self-indulgence or self-pity, as the task grows harder. He must learn also precision, sharpness of outline, unblurred edges—everything which deals with engineering skill, with the perfect adequacy of form to function, with the inherent logic and inner necessity of an organic release of power.

He must also understand the lesson of "purity". But here, to be pure means to be exclusively that which one is. Pure water is water free from any extraneous substance: pure H_2O, chemically speaking. Likewise, the individual must learn to be nothing but what he is, as an abstract formula of selfhood; to cast away all that is not his own; to repudiate all alluring byways of destiny, all fashionable or even traditional attachments save those which he has deliberately invested with his own significance and valuation.

Work and devotion: two words which, of course, in themselves do not convey all the meanings which these paragraphs detail; yet which are symbols of two mighty *directions* of consciousness. The devotee will obviously work, often with terrific and utterly self-sacrificing intensity. The worker-disciple will need also utter devotion—but better still, consecration—to his self-imposed task, even if under the guidance (inner or outer) of a "master of expression". Yet the self-surrender of the devotee, and the methodical operative concentration of the apprentice, stand out in sharp contrast.

This essential contrast gives the key to the nature of the sixth mansion, just as the contrast between the integrating mind and the disintegrating formalistic intellect, between intelligence and insanity, is the basic reality of the third mansion. In the man of the first birth, the sixth-mansion contrast is that between working independently for a living (to "keep body and soul together") and being attached to someone of greater social prominence and power, as his "protege". At the level of the second birth this contrast opposes the apprentice in the art of individual life-mastery to the devotee radiantly absorbed in the "household" of a great spiritual Personage, or in a monastery where a divine Incarnation is being worshipped.

In all these cases so far considered the sixth mansion has been seen in a positive light, as a successful manifestation of being, as a direct path to attainment. Oftentimes, however, in this mansion life teaches through repudiation and chastisement. The profligate who wasted his powers in senseless dissipation, the homeless dreamer who refused to build for himself a foundation in concrete reality, will experience illness and poverty, or enslavement to forces over which he has no control. In this mansion the cycle of pure individual selfhood ends. It may end into super-individual realizations, either through surrender of personality to a greater personality, or through identification of the personality with a Work; but it may also end in the disintegration of body and soul. Emotions which could not be released may choke the soul-life and produce "complexes" which thwart the full development of the psyche or lead to split personality and abnormal mental states.

Therefore the sixth mansion is often one of retribution. But here it is not society punishing the individual for violation of ethical or social laws. The individual is his own judge and his own chastiser. And even illness and psychological disturbances or repressions may serve a great purpose. For in this sixth mansion we are still in the realm of the individual; and at times the individual has to be sacrificed to society or to the vaster collectivity of spiritual mankind. It may even be that this sacrifice is a deliberate offering, made in utter consecration to a work which must needs break down time after time the organic wholeness of body—and possibly even of soul. For there may indeed arise great eventualities when a man may be needed as the focus for a great release of power of collective significance. And the power may shatter the man. Yet there are sufferings and deaths which are tokens of immortality.

Seventh Mansion
To Relate

IN THE SIXTH MANSION THE CYCLE OF INDIVIDUAL SELFHOOD closes. It ends either in surrender of self to a greater Self, or in fulfillment in a work through which the self may reach relative immortality. Farther than this, for the self as a purely individual and unique self, there is no way to go; for in this last mansion the singleness of the individual is surrendered— or else exalted to the point where the individual ceases to be a one, and becomes *the* One. Should the cycle of individual selfhood have been a failure, then illness or slavery would be the result. In such cases also the self becomes dependent upon other selves; or it loses its hold upon the materials and the organism through which alone it is ever able to actualize itself.

As the seventh mansion is reached one meets an altogether new world. Gone are all values based on individual selfhood. Forgotten is the uniqueness and integrity of that divine spark which sought only to make itself patent and effective, which had no goal save that of demonstrating its powers to itself through alternate series of expansions and concentrations. Vanished is the pride and the singleness of the soul established in the magic circle of its own focalization. In the strange and baffling world that is the seventh mansion there is an eternal wind that fans sparks into flames leaping beyond their singleness; leaping to where they merge and withdraw, and merge again, as if yearning to be what they are not—as if by blending with other flames something miraculous, unutterable, divine were to occur—as if all that had been built through many mansions not only was forgotten, but was passionately left behind as encumbrance and ballast staying some wild ascension through realms that alone were true, alone were radiant, alone held value in their winds and their storms and their amazing mirages.

The magic of love . . . The great mystery which makes the known and the secure worthless, and forces individuals into wild ecstasies in which all individualism, all unique qualities, all originality may be lost—in which ancestral values and universal yearnings alone remain, majestically and meaninglessly tossing upon their vast tides the dissolving remains of what once had claimed to be individuals! The magic of love . . . which kills all separateness and all uniqueness, all purity and all focalization. An ocean that has no peace, no stability, no form; but which moves on from mergings to mergings, blindly, powerfully, eternally . . .

The ancient Hindu philosopher, centered in pure selfhood, named this the mansion of the not-self; the ocean of existences; *Samsara*, the Great Illusion of ever-renewed desires and ever-renewed embraces that belong to the love that is death. And the formula given to characterize the great Wheel of Life, the drama unfolding through the twelve mansions of being, was: "I am not the not-self". To which the God of the Bible added His majestic pronouncement: "I am that I am".

But the age of such a focalization of consciousness upon the Self, the "I am", passed away, and after the beginnings of our era a vast tide of the ocean of Love swept over the whole world. Vaishnavites in India, Sufis in Persia, Christian mystics in Europe, sang the intoxication of utter surrender of selfhood to the magic of love. The not-self—now seen as the "Other", or as all the others together—came to be recognized as the greater self. In and through the Beloved the whole world was to be reached in an ecstasy of fulfillment, and boundless powers were to surge from the communion of the lovers with eternal Love.

Thus love began to conquer the world of ideals and human dreams. Its ecstasy transfigured saints and lovers, who gave up self to love in joyous abandon. What is the meaning of this ecstasy? What part does it play in the great twelvefold cycle of being? Which attitude holds the greater key to Life's mysteries?

If we follow the trend of thought which considers the individual self as the beginning and the end of all, we might say that as he who would storm a gate draws back to gather momentum, so relationship follows selfhood in order that selfhood may become more truly, more powerfully, more universally the supreme jewel of being that it essentially is. "Lose thyself that thou mayest find thy Self." Surrender the lesser in order to gain the greater. Die to the first birth, in order to be re-born of the second birth. Love is the death of singleness, that out of this death of the lonely one may be born a greater and immortal One.

What is love, relationship, communion, save that which brings together two or more selves? And what can be the meaning of relationship, save that it serves the ultimate purpose of the selves which are related, that each self may emerge more radiant from the relationship? What can be the value of love, save in function of that which love brings to the lovers? The one positive factor is self; from self to Self through love and relationship—such might be the formula. But selfhood is the first and the last, the *alpha* and the *omega* of being—and relationship, a crisis of growth.

And yet—such an attempt at resolving the fundamental dualism of selfhood and love into a sort of monistic emphasis upon self seems to leave something unsaid. Is the setting less basic than the rising of the sun? Is the sense of relationship less basic than the sense of selfhood? Has an organism more reality because it is a unit than because it is composed of the inter-relationships of many cells which themselves are living entities? And what is a unit?

Questions like these can be asked indefinitely. Philosophers, in their eagerness to escape the fallacy of postulating two absolutes and two infinites, have attempted to reduce all fundamental dualisms to positive and negative, self and not-self, reality and illusion. And men have never ceased to extol alternately one or the other of the cosmic polarities. Surrender love to the self. Surrender self to love . . . Men have lived and died to proclaim either alternative as the only one possible, true and divine. What a foolish game, after all!

Polarities are not to be called good or bad, reality or illusion. They are to be integrated. Reality is in their integratedness; illusion, in accentuation being placed upon one or the other. In the magical Cross of Being symbolically formed by horizon and meridian and by horizontal and vertical, power, significance and life surge neither from right nor left, above nor below, but from the integrated wholeness of the Cross, whose ceaseless swastika-like whirling alone is the source of the livingness of right and left, of above and below. Spirit is a whirling motion, and all motion presupposes two poles: self and relationship, being and becoming, space and time.

In the first mansion the spatial "form" of the self—the magic formula, or "name", of the individual—is intuitively known. In the seventh mansion, the manner in which this formula will, in time, be fulfilled through cyclic becoming is progressively revealed to the experiencer of sensations, and eventually to the thinker. In the silence of the innermost the individual knows what he *is*. In the constant turmoil of experiencing relationships of all sorts, at all levels, the living Person finds himself fulfilled, slowly, step by step. The fulfillment of this living Person is the becoming of God. God *becomes* out of the fulfillment of relationship. This is the mystery of the seventh house; and it is the mystery of love.

Before love comes to the individual, life is merely the

demonstration by the self to the self of the powers (the "name") of the self. There is no *real* becoming, no real unfoldment or growth. What occurs is merely the concretization and demonstration of an abstract idea. When an engineer, after thinking out a formula, makes it concrete in the detailed blue-print of an engine, all that he does is to demonstrate to himself the exact workings of the formula. But when he attempts actually to build the engine, a new process begins. He has to get materials, money, a place to build in, and probably the cooperation of other people. Then things begin to happen; if not to the formula, at least to the blue-prints. Changes, compromises to satisfy the financial backer, to adjust the idea to the demands of customers, etc. This is real becoming. This is the living of relationship. Psychology enters upon the stage, with the fact that ideas and selves must be put to the test of usefulness, of service; that they can only be fulfilled through *fulfilling the needs of other men*, and in general of human society.

Fulfilling the need of other beings; fulfilling the need of the human race . . . Is this the core of the mystery of love? Is true love always rooted *unconsciously* in compassion, that is, in encompassing elements and values not one's own; elements and values which, in ultimate analysis, will be parts of a greater synthesis of living, of which one also will be a part?

We should not forget the message of the sixth mansion. There the individual either surrenders himself to a greater Person, or through mastery of technique identifies himself with a Work. These two alternatives constitute the background of the mystery of the seventh house. In the act of self-surrender the individual sees himself as a part of a host. The greater Person—the Christ-being, or in a more concrete sense the "Church" or apostolic "group"—is not merely a great individual Self. It is a host of selves, a communion of beings. The devotee, through self-abnegation, joins this host, participates as one among many in this mystic communion. This henceforth will constitute his "becoming", his growth through relationship and through love—but a relationship and a love of a psychic-spiritual kind.

He who learns to be an accomplished Worker finds soon that technique is not enough. His accomplishments are stillborn unless they serve a purpose, unless they are stones of some great racial temple. And, on a more biological plane, of what use is the perfected body of the youth except it serve to maintain the actual presence of the greater entity that is the Human Race?

A small cellular organism, like the amoeba, is an individual unit. But millions of such cells, differentiated through relationship, become a human body. In these words "differentiated through relationship" is the key to the mystery. The will to improve and to be more than one is, flaming forth in the sixth mansion out of the relative failure of self-expression in the fifth, becomes in the seventh mansion the will to play a part in a great drama: the drama of the birth of the greater Person that is God. God is always the "greater Person", at whatever stage of being, the greater Whole. That greater whole is constituted out of the fulfillment of relationship—which is love. Love is fulfillment of relationship. Love is, universally speaking, the birthing of God; the gathering of the host.

At the level of the first birth—the biological level—this host is the tribe, the host that grows through time, generation after generation. It is a host centered in the primeval Two: the first father and first mother. Each tribe is a psychic and biological unit, with its own mode of living, its geographical environment, its religion and culture. It is founded upon biological love and the procreative urge.

At the level of the second birth—the psycho-mental level—the host that is to be gathered through fulfillment of relationship is the greater Person, whom some call God, others the Seed-Manu, others still, Civilization. The devotee speaks of God, or of the Prophet of the Dispensation, because he sees the greater whole, of which he is becoming a part, as a greater self. The worker speaks of Civilization, because what he contributes to the greater whole is his work, rather than his psychic energies. The distinction is one of level of focalization. Ultimately, man will always have to operate at both levels.

Through such contributions the needs of the greater whole are filled. The individual ceases to act as a single self and assumes a functional part within the greater whole, building, as it were, in cooperation with his companions, the mind, soul or body of the greater Person. Thus that which was a whole (individual) acts as a part. In most cases, men act as parts of a greater whole, which they but dimly conceive, only under the compulsion of inner (biological) or outer (social) necessity. When this action is undertaken as a conscious determination, there is conscious love; also conscious partnership of work.

In true love, as well as in true partnership, the individual overcomes the pull of his own exclusive selfhood. He goes willingly into the unknown and the dark—as, symbolically, the sun is seen to set into the underworld. The whole becomes a part; and in this there is a real death. But there is also a radiant birthing of reality. For reality is neither in the whole nor in the parts; neither in selfhood nor in self-surrender to a greater Person or corporate body. It is to be found in the eternal commerging of whole and parts, in the sacrifice of the greater and the communions of the lesser. And this commerging of all there is is life itself—wholly lived.

To be a self while loving; to love while realizing one's innermost selfhood. To be, without the fear of becoming. To become, yet remain always true to one's own being. This is the play of the opposites; of day and night, of spring and autumn. The "magic of love" can only be used by him who is, in his own selfhood, a magician. In true "personality" and in "mastery", an immortal self plays on every string of his being a song of love. Only the string taut with the intensity of self can release the tonic power of a love that will be a birthing of God.

Eighth Mansion
To Renew

THE EIGHTH MANSION IS REACHED THROUGH PORTALS WHICH often appear illumined by the ghostly light of deprivation and death. But these portals reveal, for whosoever dares face the mystery of relationship and the magic of love in freedom and purity, the great temple of reality. The world understands little of this feared and darkened mansion; because the world understands little of the wondrous equation of destiny in which selfhood and love are linked and integrated by him who can wield the power of creative significance.

With the seventh mansion we began a new cycle or hemicycle, the keynote of which is: *Relationship*. In a sense, every mansion of this new pilgrimage of the self will appear to oppose the corresponding mansion of the first cycle. Considered therefore from the point of view of individual selfhood, the new mansions appear negative and spell deprivation. Love often means the loss of the integrity of the self, passionate formlessness. Likewise in the eighth mansion the individual is often seen to lose whatever he had owned in the second; indeed, the very substance of his being, the very materials and chemicals which gave him concreteness.

This is so because, in the eighth mansion, love finds its own substance; relationship, its own material for subsistence. Who can furnish this substance, save it be the individuals now commingling in love or deep partnership? Thus the love becomes substantiated at the expense of the lovers. Love has two parents, who are the lovers. And the parents must endow the child, Love. Thus, deprivation of substance for the individuals who enter into relationship; just as the gestation and birth of a child means physiological and financial deprivation for its parents.

What is lost by the individuals is more than substance per se; it is all that they had built to give weight and dignity and earth-solidity to their abstract selfhoods: the habits, the privacy, the pride which had been the daily support of their very sense of I-am-ness. Love cannot gain substance and concrete power unless it be enriched by the sacrifices and the gifts made to it by the lovers. Every lasting partnership likewise demands a more or less complete pooling of the resources of the partners, the sacrifice of their absolute individualistic control over their own possessions. And for the individual who is thoroughly identified with his possessions and his habits of behavior or traditions, this means "death" indeed.

Thus love may seem often to cause the exhaustion of the resources of the individual. The very act of love may have such a meaning for its participants—especially for the male, who (in the lower stages of biological development) loses its very body as the result of the mating, and serves as foodstuff for the female. Its substance is utterly consecrated to the rearing of the progeny. Thus love becomes insubstantiated, incorporated into the progeny—at the expense of the very being of one of the lovers, sometimes of both of them. Wherefore love and death have often been seen in close conjunction. Death is the food of love. The eighth mansion follows after the seventh. Relationship often absorbs and feeds upon the related individuals.

It may seem strange that an abstract thing such as "relationship", or a state of experience such as "love", can absorb and even kill individual beings. But we must not forget that individual selfhood also is but an abstraction. This abstraction gains substance in the second mansion, and becomes fully concrete in the fourth mansion as a psycho-physiological organism. This substance, however, needs always to be replenished. It is a portion of the earth, a mass of earth chemicals (or, at a higher level, of racial and ancestral elements), *assimilated* by the individual. The individual must keep assimilating constantly this substance. He needs constantly to build it into his own personality.

The relationship, or the love, that conjoins individuals must also find its own substance and assimilate it. And it can find it only as the related individuals provide for it out of the substance of their own beings. Moreover, this substance assimilated by the relationship takes the form and grows into the likeness of the relationship. Eventually it may return to the individuals; but not until after a long series of transformations which may make it unassimilable to them.

This is, obviously, the way in which the eighth mansion and its fatality appear to the individuals, and to those only, who have become profoundly identified with the substance of their own being as well as with their possessions. It is thus only a negative attitude, a negative approach to that stage of the process of development of the wholeness of being which the eighth mansion represents. But it was the approach which had to be emphasized in a period of the world-history when possessiveness and identification with ancestral or family traditions were such powerful factors in the development of the personality.

On the other hand, wherever the mystical ideas of higher Christianity have been emphasized, a positive meaning should have been given to the eighth mansion of the Soul. For if Love is the fulfillment of the Law, and if self-abnegation is the means to reach holiness and perfection, then the eighth mansion becomes the mansion where holiness and love find their own sustainment. In it, love becomes real through the lovers' sacrifice and renunciation of all that does not carry the seal of this love. In it, the individual frees itself from the shackles of individualism and is reborn as a servant of omnipotent Love.

Thus, rather than being seen as the mansion of death—as was usually the case throughout the Middle Ages—it should have been understood as the mansion of regeneration. Its keynote should thus be: *to renew*. Through the magic of love all things and all men are made anew. The separated lives, united at last, willingly throw their treasures of selfhood into the all-consuming fire of love, all-encompassing. And the portals of death are transfigured into the gates of omnipotent love: the gates of the greater Mysteries, in which men learn how to act as functional parts of the greater whole in which thenceforth they live and have their being.

Here, everything depends upon the willingness of the individual self to give of the substance of his being to the relationship—or to the partnership, at a more material level. His resistance to the law of love brings upon him the judgment of death. His half-hearted acquiescence to the demands of the partnership, curtailing as it does the efficiency and power of this partnership, may mean the loss of his individual resources. From him who is willing to give but little, much shall be taken. To him who deprives himself of all for the sake of love, for the sake of that commerging of values which builds a culture and a strong society, much shall be given, and his name shall be immortalized.

If, however, we refuse to accept the emphasis which the Christian altruist and the devotee put upon self-surrender to love, if we believe that selfhood and relationship are to be balanced and integrated, instead of either one being utterly sacrificed to the other, then we shall have to modify somewhat this last interpretation of the eighth mansion. It may retain its meaning of "renewal", but in this renewal there shall be no death of selfhood—rather *a transfiguration of the contents of personality*. The "form" of personality will remain the same, generally speaking; but the "light" that shall illumine the contents of personality will be indeed new. The dark of selfhood will become the radiance of love.

Selfhood is of the darkness, because it is abstract and it antedates manifestation. It antedates God's command: "Let there be light!" It is the Idea before it becomes the living Word. Relationship, by the fact of its bringing two or more entities into close contact, generates tension and the spark that is light. The integration of selfhood and relationship is the integration of Form and Light. It is therefore symbolized in the Gospels by the Transfiguration. The body of the Christ-being is made to shine. Light emanates from every facet of the Christ-like Person. Not that the human organism is destroyed. Not that the form of selfhood of the man Jesus is destroyed. But the Christ-light is seen to pervade, to suffuse, to shine through all the purified earthliness of the man Jesus.

This obviously applies only to the realm of the third birth, when the mystery of the seventh house is that of the union of personality to its divine complement—the Christ-light. But even in the biological realm of the first birth, the miracle of love transfigures the dullest creature. It paints ecstasies of color on the wings of birds as on the petals of flowers. It gives vibrant tone to inarticulate throats. It makes the humblest earth-being glow with a light that overcomes the earth and transfigures the heavy flesh. And in the strongly individualized man of the second birth, a creative radiance overflows his harsh sense of uniqueness and his jailed-in self-sufficiency. Romance brushes his mind with emotional wings that stir imaginative flights. The roots of self flame upward, burning all dross, to add to the pure light of love transubstantial.

To him who is strongly centered in individual selfhood love may come as a storm that shatters the deepest seclusion, as an earthquake that throws into confusion all the contents of the home. Relationship may indeed bring the strain of dissonant harmony; and the gates of the eighth house may witness the death of selfishness, of all that is crystallized, harsh, stubborn in self. But, how beautiful the trees and flowers after the storm has fled into the abyss of mere memories! How pure and liquid the air, crystalline with exquisite freshness! Every blade of grass is renewed, and nature is made whole.

The Beloved becomes increasingly an Image of the life within, as the cycle of the second birth runs its dramatic course. It is extracted by the self out of many loves or the one love of this cycle. It builds itself within as the mystic Complement, as a Presence of Light that suffers to be born in the midst of all trials, and lightens the weight of self that is but self.

And at the last comes the final scene of the long drama, the transfiguration of all the separate vital forces of personality into a transcendent flame—a tree of light—crowned by the thousand-petalled flower, the mystic Lotus of the *yogis*, the halo of Christs and Buddhas alike. Here the drama of love and relationship is concluded within the personality experienced as a perfected microcosm. What is celebrated is the marriage of *Kundalini* and of selfhood, of fire that has become light, with the pure form of being and of cosmic destiny. The individual self has become identified as personality with a Work, with his own function as a cell of the greater Whole. And this Work receives, as a result of such an identification, the vital substance which the "blood of Christ" symbolizes. It is indeed the "blood" of the greater organic Whole vitalizing the cell that *has fully experienced its personality as a cell of the Whole*. This inflowing "blood" is the Holy Ghost—and it is *Kundalini*. The two are one, as above is one with below, and right is one with left, in the consummation of the mystery of Operative Wholeness.

To experience personality as a differentiated cell of the greater Whole: this perhaps is the best way of stating what is underneath this mystic transfiguration. We know that the term "personality" has become extremely ambiguous as the result of its special use in modern theosophy and related philosophies. But what else can be used to signify that which is not only individual selfhood, but also the perfume or quintessence of all the relationships fulfilled through the process of living? That whole of behavior, feeling, thinking, intuition; that which is being in becoming and becoming as actualization of being; that in which heaven and hell unite, and God becomes through constant fruitions and integrations of opposites—what else can it be called save: personality—or, perhaps better, the Living Person?

Personality experienced only in terms of individual selfhood is an organism of darkness; but personality experienced in terms of being a cell in the greater Whole becomes an organism of light. "To live in Christ" is to have "Christ living me". It is to have Wholeness operating within the part, thereby transfigured by the "blood of the Whole". This transfiguration is the deepest reality of *Initiation*.

Thus motherhood is a true initiation for a woman; because during pregnancy it is not she who lives, but life (the Race) who lives her. In other words it is Relationship living in and through Selfhood. This permeation of the separate and single individual by love is the reality of the eighth mansion. Love, there, is being clothed with substance within the magic circle of selfhood. It is therefore the mansion of the bearing of seed. And the seed will grow and expand through the ninth mansion, and be born at the mystic Mid-Heaven: a birth of light —while the birth of the body of selfhood was a birth of darkness, deep in the eternal midnight.

Ninth Mansion
To Understand

IF THE THIRD MANSION BRINGS TO THE UNFOLDING SELF THE realization that it is only through knowledge that the abstract "I am" will ever succeed in integrating and assimilating the many substantial elements of heredity and environment, the ninth mansion will render to the human consciousness matured by relationship a similar service. In it man discovers that only through understanding will the mystery of love and the need for sacrifice or rebirth ever be linked in a vital and glowing synthesis. The keynote of this mansion is thus: *to understand*. And through understanding the individual soul expands. It soars toward regions opened by the magic of love, deepened by the power of renunciation and sacrifice.

Every new step in understanding is a climax to a relationship and the result of a sacrifice. In understanding, relationship proves its worth—just as in knowledge, selfhood demonstrates its power. But more than this, in understanding alone can ever be solved the awesome conflict between love and death. Love which claims the death of the lovers, so that it may gather itself into the Seed; love which demands sacrifice and renunciation of the selves it links in supernal ecstasy— what is the meaning of that cruel and fateful power which so haunts the souls of men that they willingly give themselves with garlands of smiles to the insatiable and the inexhaustible?

There is no solution, no answer possible save that which takes the form of understanding—from the most elementary realization of the simple soul confronted with the riddle of love and death, to the wondrous meditation of the Buddha, which opened to him, the Enlightened, the gates of *Nirvana*: the absolute of understanding. It is because spirit (the Self) is never adequately expressed by matter (the body and all ancestral tendencies) that man becomes thinker and knower. And the search for knowledge is endless; for there never will be any material aggregation which will satisfy the needs of the spirit; no material organism will ever be an absolutely adequate vehicle for the "I am" who is to dwell therein.

Likewise, there can be no sacrifice and no renunciation final enough to satisfy the demands of love. There can be no seed which will be full enough with life and substance to gather within its hallowed shrine all the energies roused by a relationship into which the participants have flowed with the irresistible sweep of great rivers as they near the sea. How inadequate the substance and the possessions of love to lovers touched by the magic of union! What caresses, what spasms can ever fulfill, can give body to ultimate love? What words or images can ever convey the ecstasy of the soul in rapture of divine Union? There is never enough. The lovers' flesh and souls cannot give enough, sacrifice utterly enough of their substance to feed love. And because of this yawning dissatisfaction of love, because of this perpetually unfulfilled thirst of entranced bodies and souls, there come the endless array of perversions, of stimulants—of all the means whereby love attempts to get more and ever more from the lovers.

Just as intellects will ever search feverishly for the eternally elusive secret of the perfect adequacy of matter to spirit, and just as out of this "divine discontent" is born intelligence—so relationships and loves will ever reach for a supreme quality which shall bridge the mysterious abyss between love and death. And this quality is understanding. It is the power to "stand under" all loves and all deaths; to gather them into a circuit of intelligent realization, into a chain of causes and effects and again causes. It is the power to place oneself as it were outside of the irreducible dualism of self and not-self, of individual selfhood and all-consuming love; and from this point of vantage, to "see" indeed—to see with the "open Eye" of the Enlightened Ones.

In this act of self-removal from the wheel of birthing, loving and dying resides the deepest secret of understanding. It is because of it that understanding may be said to be opposed to knowledge. For knowledge is the assimilation by the self of that which is outside and yet which must be made subservient to or be polarized by the self. Knowledge can always be referred to a self that needs to solve his problems and to integrate his conflicts in order to operate as an integral and efficient whole. But in understanding, the self effaces itself and, as it were, "jumps beyond its shadow". It has known relationship and sacrificial death at the hands of love. And yet, neither love nor death are solutions; for they do not really include the new factor, the cause of love and of the need to self-sacrifice: the "other".

The self and the "other". Why should there be an "other"? Why should there be the ceaseless tension between self and the whole outer world? Why should there be sensation, and why should there be relationship?

Now, it is no longer that the self must correlate and use intelligently the substances by means of which he is to build his body of manifestation. That, he could do—and he had to do—by remaining centered in himself. But after the self has united in love with the "other", and has readily given of his substance to the fulfillment of love, to remain centered in self becomes meaningless. He who has known death of self in the eighth mansion can no longer demand of mere intelligence and of knowledge the key to a problem that must of necessity transcend the self, the "other," love and death. He who has died to self can only be satisfied with understanding; for in understanding, self, "other", love and death are transcended—and yet they are linked, integrated, chorded into a supernal Tone which has the quality of silence. And in that Tone there is liberation. Liberation from self and liberation from the poignancy of love; liberation from the "other", from sensations, from the passionate bondage of touching, seeing, hearing, smelling, tasting; liberation from death and the need of death.

Yet such a liberation as that experienced by the Buddha, the supreme Understander, is not mere freedom: freedom to act according to the will or the impulses of self. For, in understanding, the self has united with the "other"—with all "others"—in utter compassion. And what is liberated then is not the self alone, but all the "others" that now the self "sustains". He who understands all things is the sustainer of all things. For to understand is indeed to "stand under". More accurately, it is to stand at the center of the "earth"—that point where all the "unders" converge; that point toward which all human feet and all vegetable roots are directed, and which sustains them all. It is the neutral point, the "laya" center of Hindu philosophy, the mysterious "Empty" of Chinese philosophy, the Vacuum upon which are poised all destinies.

These may seem very big words to describe such a common term: understanding . . . A common term, but how rare a faculty in its higher reaches! Understanding is the polar opposite of knowledge, inasmuch as the latter must always be concrete and related to the matter of utility—however transcendent this utility may be. To know is to accomplish something useful for the self who knows. But in understanding there is no sense of utility as far as the self is concerned; only a sense of fulfillment in which individual selfhood itself is absorbed. For there can be no perfect understanding where there has not been first of all perfect union in love and a perfect readiness to die as a self in that love.

Therefore the supremely Enlightened One is seen also, and

first of all, as the most Compassionate One—and as the perfect Renouncer of all possessions. One must leave behind all that fed the ancestral nature, before there can be understanding. One must leave behind knowledge and its compartments, before one can integrate the conflicts between love and death, the self and the "other", in understanding. And understanding alone can ever be the true soil from which are born philosophy that is real sustainment, wisdom that is equilibrium, and religion that gathers all true devotees and servers into the group-consciousness which is the abiding place of the greater and more encompassing individual Whole that men have named God.

There are indeed many degrees and levels of understanding; just as many as there are degrees and levels of relationship. Every fulfilled and substantiated relationship always gives birth to understanding. The quality of the understanding depends upon the quality and inevitability of the love—or even upon the quality and intensity of the sensation; for sensations are the outposts of love, and he who is afraid of sensations can never know the fullness of love.

There is an understanding born of fullness of sensation, just as the first stage of intelligence is cunning and competitive intellectuality. When the eyes see intensely, the hands touch with utmost vibrancy, there is something that flows between subject and object, between him who sees or touches and the thing seen or touched. In that flow there is communion, and there is death. Some "virtue" or essence in the man leaves him, dies away from him, into the thing sensed so acutely. And some "virtue" also leaves the thing and penetrates into the man through the gates of his senses. A mysterious, subliminal communion; yet real indeed. And as it is real, it bears progeny—which is understanding. There is in the man with such full sensations a curious "sensing" of the reality of the thing seen or touched, a communion under the appearances. The beautiful flower vibrantly seen by the Japanese artist acquires "meaning"—a reality which makes nature and man one in a communion of beauty and of taste; yes, a "sensing" of what the flower is there for, an intuition of "significant essence" which is the foundation of all true philosophy and of the deeper types of religion.

In the man of the first birth, rooted at the physiological-emotional level, relationship means primarily sensation and that love which is the synthetic summation of an aggregate of sensations and impressions centered around the loved one. Whatever understanding he may reach depends mostly upon his power of living in sensations to the full, in self-denial; sensations of love, sensations of death, pleasure and pain. He must therefore expand through increasing the range of his sensations, of his pleasures and his pains. This is what culture does for man; and also travels. One learns to see more objects, and these objects more deeply. The individual self thus is really pulled outward into variegated communions with many "others"—which become "symbols", because relationship with them is "understood" more and more deeply.

After being "born again" as a truly individual soul, man faces in the seventh mansion the single relationship which is called "marriage" or "companionship". As an individual he meets another individual or other individuals. The understanding that eventually arises from such unions is also individualized. It partakes of the quality of Soul and of conscious intelligence. In it, the element of *meaning* blooms forth. Understanding becomes regenerative. It opens new doors. It cleanses old racial deposits and "complexes" which developed during the first life-cycle. It becomes the foundation of the true work of destiny.

When man has opened himself to Spirit, understanding becomes fully creative. It re-creates the universal within the transfigured particular being. Then man and God meet in understanding, and God gives to the man Moses the tables of the Law—to the man Gautama, the supreme realization of the technique of Liberation, the Noble Path . . . which is understanding.

Tenth Mansion
To Achieve

In the tenth mansion the individual self realizes the full and vital significance of *power*. Power, when actually in operation, real and fulfilled power, means always a demonstrated ability to achieve definite results. Moreover, in order to achieve results the Self must of necessity deal with elements, materials or other selves outside of himself. He must deal with those masterfully, bringing the many elemental or separate wills into a harmony of which he is the center and tonic.

There are two kinds of "outside": the first is that outside which is called at one level the body and at the other the psyche, if this term is given its widest possible significance; the second kind is represented by the "outer world" composed of objects and of people. The first type is so peculiarly related to the self that it is identified but too often with the self: as when we say "I am ill," or "I am angry." Actually, what is ill is the body, and what is in a state of anger is the psyche.

Now, both body and psyche (that is, the sum total of physical cells and of psychic energies, tendencies, faculties) are composed of elements or materials which come within the zone of influence of the self, either through parental inheritance or because they have been absorbed from the environment (from the physical as foodstuff, or from the psychological as traditions, habits, preconceptions, and the like). If the self manages to control, organize and integrate these elements of his body and of his psyche—that is, if he has power over them—he achieves "personality integration". He becomes a wholesome, harmonious and efficient personality. This comes to pass in the fourth mansion.

A somewhat similar process occurs in the cycle of development which begins with the seventh, which becomes consolidated (if all goes well) in the eighth, and expanded through understanding in the ninth mansion. Through these mansions the Self gathers to himself elements and materials which no longer will become the substance of his body and psyche, but which instead will build his *place and function in the greater Whole of which he is then learning to become an efficiently functioning part.*

This "greater Whole" means, first of all, human society. It may be a very limited "human society"—a small racial group and a village. Or it may be a vast nation; or the whole of mankind, visible and invisible as well. In any case, it is a whole composed of units more or less similar to the self, and to which he relates himself on the basis of a give-and-take operation (seventh mansion key-note).

It is a whole which may not as yet be considered as a real organism, but one which eventually and ultimately should reach the state of organic wholeness. A tribe is an organic whole of a kind; so is a nation which is the possessor of a well established culture and national spirit. Humanity will become some day, in an even more definite manner, a planetary organism. Each human personality will be then a cell of this organism, which we have named elsewhere the *Synanthropy*.

Ideally speaking, the message of the tenth mansion for any human personality is this: Find your place and function in that Greater human Whole which you are able realistically to envision and in which you are ready, by birthright, efficiently to participate. If you can actually see no farther than a small tribal or economic group, then that for you is the "greater Whole". If you can conceive clearly and act efficiently in terms of humanity-in-the-whole, then that should be for you the "greater Whole". The important thing is not to confuse an intellectual dream with an actual reality; not to consume yourself yearning for an unattainable ideal, and thus fail to participate efficiently in the only "greater Whole" in which you are able to function with competence.

The crux of this tenth-mansion problem is the matter of "power"—actual, real, operative power. The scope of your participation in any human whole composed of units similar to you is determined always by the "power" which you can marshal and put to efficient use. It is wise not to yearn for attainment beyond your power to achieve. Yet it is most unwise to bind yourself to narrow ranges of power-operation out of false modesty, psychological inhibitions and fears. It is true that "all nature's powers are there for you to use: take them." But it is also true that "it is better to fulfill your dharma (or inherent capacities); the dharma of another is full of danger." Self-inflation, imperialism, auto-hallucinations and ideas of grandeur do not pay. But to shrink from fulfilling the greater purpose of your life, because of an inferiority complex and fears, pays even less.

What then shall guide our judgment and the scope of our attempts at establishing on true bases and in true proportions our participation in the "work of the world"? Obviously, the only guide is understanding. It is this understanding, gained in the ninth mansion, which will enable us to evaluate the nature and scope of the "greater Whole" in which we are to function as an efficient part. As the gates of the tenth mansion open, the final revelation of the purpose of our destiny, in terms of whatever represents for us *by birthright* the "greater whole", should come upon us. It may come to us by the force of circumstances—as a job, or as the nearly unavoidable choice of a profession. Or it may reach us in the form of a vision of a Work of Destiny that will compel us to grow beyond our *apparent* limits—this according as we are men of the first or the second birth. But, whether with the sharp intensity of a release of power from on high, or with the matter-of-fact compulsion of social necessity, it will come, at the threshold or at some critical moment of the phase of development which we now symbolize as the tenth mansion—the mansion of power, of achievement and mastery.

What is achievement, and what is mastery? To "achieve" is "to become chief". The word "chief" comes from the Latin *caput*, which means "head". Achievement signifies therefore "coming to a head". But what is head without body? What are the best brains without the vital organs contained in the trunk of the human body—organs which feed and sustain the brain? In what, moreover, resides the "power" of the master, save in the unanimous allegiance of those over whom he rules, as chief or head? In other words, what is the great individual without the collectivity of which it is the fruition and seed? There comes a time when the seed leaves the plant which gave it birth, when the great individual leaves the collectivity which fulfilled itself unconsciously in and through him as chief and master. But as this occurs, the collectivity disintegrates, and the great individual finds his place and function in a still greater collectivity or Whole, to which he brings the fruition of that from which he arose. He goes as a plenipotentiary; that is, as one who has assumed the power of his collectivity.

This all means that power is not of the individual, but of the collectivity or group; even though it is the individual who, as chief and master, wields and manages this power. He wields power because he has achieved social recognition, because he has fulfilled—through relationship, sacrifice and understanding —one aspect of the *culture* of his social group, the aspect which was his by birthright. "By birthright" may be interpreted at the level of outer social functioning; in which case it refers to an inherited trade or a traditional professional or aristocratic duty. It may also mean the fulfillment in a personality of a long trend of spiritual endeavor. In such a case the united powers of a host of ancestors descend, as it were, as a regal mantle upon the man who, as "son of his fathers," becomes the spiritual fruition and seed of his genealogical Tree.

"Humanity is composed more of the dead than of the living," wrote, a century ago, the French philosopher Auguste Comte. A true statement indeed. The focalized power of the dead is what makes of a man a chief and master. "A buddha is the flower of his race," wrote a great adept. Buddhahood is humanity meeting a man and investing this man with the power to be MAN. In this same sense, Christ is "Son of Man" and "Son of David", as well as "Son of God"—God who is always at any stage of development the next "greater Whole", "in whom we live and have our being". And it is in this tenth mansion, which is symbolized by the noon-point of the Sun, that this power which has been accumulated by the ancestors descends upon the man who has been fulfilled in understanding, after having died the death of selfishness.

Thus the man becomes a consecrated chief—and as such is invested with the power to achieve his destiny: to fulfill his part within the "greater Whole" to which he belongs by birthright. This power is what the Hindu philosopher named *shakti*. It is the power of culmination of all life-processes. More than this, it is essentially and at whatever level the term may have to be understood, mastery. Mastery is the power of culmination, and yet it is more. It is not only the apex of the pyramid of man's successful efforts toward his goal, but just as much the descent of the Fire from Heaven upon this apex. A man does not entirely *become* a master by his own efforts. He qualifies to become a master through his own efforts; but to qualify as, and actually to become a master are two different things. What happens is that, in some mysterious way, mastery descends upon the would-be master and consecrates him a master. And this, which may be true of those great Initiations during which the disciple is invested with the magic power of the "Word" by the One Initiator, is also true in lesser ways in every case when a man emerges as a leader, a true chief, and is given public recognition. Such a recognition is an elusive thing; but it is at best only the outer reflection of an interior happening, a real consecration of that man by the invisible unity of his community: a mastery investing a ready personality with the power to act as a master.

In order to realize the meaning of the foregoing we will have to remember that in the fourth mansion the *individual* foundation, the roots, of power and achievement are built. The self must first build inward a soul foundation, or a "home", before he is able to meet the challenger, the loves and the many deaths of the life of relationship. The physical body, the house of earth, stone and wood,—such are the roots of the individual. They are foundations whence power starts on its long journey upward and outward. The culmination of this journey—the fabled rise of *kundalini*—takes place in the tenth mansion, at the noon point of individual selfhood. There power is released, and man as a social personality achieves. And the achievement consists in this, that he who has understood his place and function in the "greater Whole" not only assumes henceforth the responsibility of operating outwardly as an organic part, or as an agent, of this "greater Whole", but actually receives from the "greater Whole" the very power of mastery.

This ascent of power from the "midnight sun" to the "noon sun" occurs along the Meridian of the man. It links the roots to the seed, the base of the spine where "*kundalini is coiled, asleep*" to the center of the head, which is the "house of the creative". This "house of the creative" is *the very form of the individual's participation in the "greater Whole"*. It is his *cell-form* within the cosmic organism which tribe, nation, mankind, and even more universal collectivities, in turn represent for him.

Thus in the tenth mansion the archetypal form of man is revealed: that for which he emerged out of the inchoate earth, his form of destiny, his Work of destiny. But it is not only revealed as a form, as an abstract structure. It is made an actual and concrete experience. It is lived and made a reality for all to behold. Thus in this mansion man experiences his "birth of light". He is born in the open, as a solar chief invested with the mastery which is the active, effective and permanent reality, beyond all masters who have come before him and will come after him. And this is true, *potentially*, at whatsoever level he is operating.

In the cycle of the first birth, the individual's achievement is fundamentally one which not only results from, but which repeats his or his ancestors' achievements. As man emerges into the full realization of his individual selfhood, he reaches toward his individual Work of destiny. To what he has received from heredity and environment he adds the seal of his own present mastery. And as the wide horizons of the third birth are opening, the transfigured personality, now fully participating in uttermost consciousness as a cell of the "greater Whole", becomes a fully commissioned agent of this "greater Whole". He becomes an *avatar*, a Christ. The "Son of Man" proves himself "Son of God" by the eternal, ancient and veracious proof of works.

Eleventh Mansion
To Transfigure

AFTER THE INDIVIDUAL HAS ESTABLISHED HIS PARTICIPATION in the activities of the greater whole—be it his village-community, his nation or total humanity—after he has become able to perform a socially significant work, he can expect to receive a reward for such a participation and such a work. Likewise, the cell of the leg muscle which participated in the work of carrying the whole body from one place to another will receive from the whole body a reward—in the substance of a new blood supply. This new blood supply means both new building materials to repair the wear and tear of cell activity, and a new charge of the mysterious energy which the Hindu philosopher calls *prana* and to which the modern scientist vaguely refers as electro-magnetism, vital force, bio-chemical action, and the like.

In astrological symbolism this energy, which flows from the heart of the whole to those parts who have fulfilled their organic destiny (karma), is represented by the mysterious "Waters" which pour from the urn of the Water-bearer, symbolizing the zodiacal sign Aquarius. The urn may in a sense stand for the left ventricle of the physical heart and the great artery, the aorta, through which the red blood flows into the body. In a more occult sense, it stands for certain cavities or sinuses in the head from which drops the mysterious "nectar of the gods"—the Hindu *Amrita*, the Greek *Ambrosia*—which revivifies the psycho-physiological organism of the man who has surrendered the flower of his individual fulfillment, in a total and spiritual sense, to, and for the benefit of the "greater Whole".

This fluid or *"liquor vitae"*, more mysterious still than the mysterious blood, is truly the polar opposite of this blood—just as Aquarius is the polar opposite of Leo in astrological symbolism. And while blood is the result of physiological integration, which it in turn sustains and makes permanent throughout the span of life of the organism, so the Aquarian "Waters" are the products of psychic and mental integration, and in turn sustain the life of the immortal or "Christ" body mentioned in Christian as well as in Oriental esoteric philosophy.

In and through blood the body as an organic whole exerts its creative activity upon its many cells and organs. At the beat of the heart, man as a concrete personality goes forth as lover, creator and conqueror through the gates of the fifth mansion. This takes place in the hemicycle of purely individual expression. But after man has been initiated into the mysteries of love and of sacrifice and, on the foundation of the understanding thus gained, has established himself as a socially potent and significant *citizen*—then, as he goes forth through the portals of the eleventh mansion, it is no longer in the capacity of lover, creator and conqueror. He has now assumed a different—yet complementary—role. He is friend, civilizer, reformer.

The tenth mansion is that of "achievement"; but in the eleventh, man is confronted with a new mode of activity, which may be best expressed by the word "transfiguration"—or perhaps as well, "metamorphosis". What this signifies must be clear to one who realizes that in the tenth mansion the individual reaches fulfillment; this, because his individual selfhood is now solidly established, not apart from the whole, but as a part of the whole. There is thus nothing more for him to do *as an individual*. But there is much indeed to do as a part of the greater whole to which he now rightfully belongs and in which he functions as a vital cell.

What is to be done is no longer to be done as a separate individual, but as a responsible citizen of a community. He must, first of all, prove himself a good citizen, a good neighbor, a good friend. And this is self-transfiguration—which means that he must "figure out" things differently, from a communalistic, and no longer from an individualistic basis; also that he must "cut a figure" full of social implications and guided by a social or group purpose. This indeed is nothing short of a metamorphosis. Out of the chrysalis the butterfly now emerges. And the butterfly feeds upon the nectar of flowers, the ambrosia of the gods—of those who live fully in terms of the cosmic or planetary whole.

The erstwhile individual personality is now seen in a new role. He is the "friend of man"—the friend of all creatures, the compassionate One who encompasses in his love all his *companions;* that is, all those who "eat of the same bread" (etymologically speaking), the bread of participation in the greater whole which is, cosmically, the Body of the cosmic Christ in whom "we live and move and have our being". A friend of man; a companion in the midst of all companions who form the sacred apostolic brotherhood. Indeed—but also at the more ordinary level a clubman or clubwoman active in cultural and social affairs, keeping and improving the standards of class and culture, helping to reform old conditions and abuses; a crusader for the right, a man or woman of ideals who attempts to mould his or her group—small or large—into the likeness of his or her vision. In the real sense of the word: a *civilizer.*

Civilization, rightly understood in its positive aspect, and not as perceived by a Spengler and by many contemporary thinkers seduced by his facile ideas, is world-metamorphosis in terms of the recognition of the reality of a planetary whole.

Culture proper is always bound to racial and geographical differentiations, to particular customs, particular environments, and particular ancestral characters. Culture is born of earth and blood—and thus belongs to the realm of the fifth mansion. It differentiates and individualizes human collectivities. It creates or develops national languages, traditions, and religions, which lead to misunderstanding and enmity between races. Culture creates compartments and relatively narrow forms. At its apex, in the so-called *classical* periods, it is only understandable by those born within a particular cultural race-unit. It creates solid barriers, which only world-communications and world-wide travels can slowly thin out and eradicate.

It is true that for the single personality, man or woman, the culture of his or her nation constitutes at first the greater whole within which he or she has to function as a responsible citizen and as a trustee of racial and cultural traditions. And the boundaries of this cultural whole are indeed as far removed from his narrow selfhood as he can possibly see or experience vitally. But beyond the cultural and national whole there is a still greater whole, planetary in scope. This greater Whole is the world-brotherhood of Man. It is organic Humanity—what we have named already the *Synanthropy*. Civilization, in its true sense, is the great effort toward a planetary organization of mankind.

A magnificent effort, and a tragic one; one which, in proportion as it is successful, "transfigures" the face of the globe. Indeed, civilization will *eventually* lead to the metamorphosis of Mankind. It will reform, change the form of human ideals and human relationships. It will make of all men friends and companions—this, through the glorious portals of the eleventh mansion; for all will then participate in the great planetary Whole which will be the culmination of this physical earth. A great, a distant ideal.

But such is the reality of the eleventh mansion: that men therein make ideals, see great visions, become aflame with the noble determination to transfigure themselves and their world.

And the power that compels them to do so is the electric Aquarian "Water" which is the gift of the whole to those of its parts who have well achieved; who have received the mantle of power from the collectivity of their great ancestors. It is that collectivity of the liberated thinkers and doers of the past which inspires the man of the present to work toward the future. Some call such a collectivity the "Council of the Great Ancestors"; others, the great "White Lodge"; still others, the "Church Triumphant" or the "Assembly of the Saints". Names matter little. What such names veil is the reality of the successful past of planetary Man—the living memory of great moments of civilization, which sands and storms may obliterate in their physical evidence—yet which can never die spiritually.

In every one of us that is born to this earth such a vast planetary pan-human Memory operates—that which the psychologist Jung calls the "collective unconscious". Our own individual thoughts, feelings and endeavors emerge as faint sprouts out of this vast and vital soil of instincts, of collective and unconscious urges, which force us toward goals often mysterious to ourselves. And it may very well be that this vast soil of the "collective unconscious" is not left to operate unguided; that there is also what might be called a "collective conscious", or better a "planetary conscious", a multifarious yet unified Power which guides the cyclic efforts of human races, in all times and in all climes, toward the great world-civilization which is the end and the purpose of human life on this earth.

This is the reality of the "White Lodge" to which so many thinkers now refer and toward which ever more searching souls are irresistibly and gloriously drawn. And it is this "White Lodge" which must be called the transfiguring agency of mankind. For it bestows upon man illumination; such an illumination as came to the man Jesus on the mount of Transfiguration. Because he had achieved as a flower and as a trustee of his race, because he had become heavy with the seed of a future era, Jesus became transfigured by the power and the light of Holy Spirit. And this Holy Spirit is the spiritual blood of the greater whole, the divine *Ambrosia*, the Aquarian Waters that are "light and life" for those who have become Companions—civilizers—in the brotherhood of the great dreamers, the great idealists, the great friends of mankind.

Yet many are those who dream, yet whose dreams are not founded upon the rock of social-cultural achievement. Many are those who make wishes without end, yet who have not captured by inner will the power to fecundate wishes into actualities. And many also are those who merely go on wishing and dreaming traditional and superficial images, merely repeating the worn out patterns used by their parents and grandparents. Because participation in what is to them the greater whole has been merely a matter of routine behavior, they have not been quickened by the *living* waters of the Great Ancestors, but have merely followed after the patterns, the classical forms and traditions from which this living substance departed long ago.

Also there are those who cling to their individualism and refuse to be renewed by love, sacrifice and understanding. What they achieve, but too often, are those accomplishments which spell out spiritual death. They become the cancerous cells of the body of mankind. They feed on noble dreams which they twist and thwart to satisfy their greed and to maintain at all cost the structure of their glorified egoism. If they have achieved social power, they waste it. If they are great thinkers, their thoughts may poison the race atmosphere and make of civilization a dreary death. They too, as imperialists and ruthless *conquistadores*, may transfigure the world of man. But the result of the metamorphosis is ugliness, crime, world-misery and war after war.

Alas! that our vaunted Western civilization should have known so many "chiefs" of destruction, so many dreamers of materialistic dreams! Yet even such a kind is playing its part in the great ritual of the world-life of man. Man at the level of the first birth is too immersed in matter to dream much beyond his material instincts; and the man of the second birth has often too much individual pride willingly to surrender his achievements to the service of the greater whole. Therefore men must learn the sacred and unselfish use of achievements by seeing these achievements caricatured or pushed to their most extreme nefarious consequences.

Thus they learn, by imprinting upon the "collective unconscious", which is the vast Memory of the race, the tragic remembrance of failures and of lost ideals . . . While, serene and secure in the realization of the divine Pattern of Perfection which is the immortal heritage of Man, there are Those who everlastingly dream and fashion ideals after ideals for the generations of men to embody in their sand castles on the beach of time. And their mystic Waters ever flow upon the souls of men who, having won the solar Crown of the tenth mansion, can now go forth into the night and darkness of the ages, bearers of Light, seeds of civilization, exemplars for lesser man.

Twelfth Mansion
To Transcend

...AND NOW WE TURN TO THE LAST PHASE OF THE CYCLE OF selfhood: the phase which seals the book of the past and which may open a greater book for the soul to decipher . . . or perhaps it will be the same old book once more to be read, because the soul failed to grasp the meaning of the twelve chapters. This phase finds its positive key-note in the word: transcendence. More precisely, it refers to the ecstatic union of the far and the near, of the universal and the particular, in the great sea of spirit-born Light. It brings to the transfigured mind the bliss, the pure joy of the true mystic state.

The personality which, after having reached achievement as a cell of an organic whole, became "trans-formed" by the downflow of the Waters of Inspiration, finds itself now "beyond the pale" of mere cell-life. The cell enters the bloodstream—there to find in a mysterious manner its divine counterpart; and both swim now in utter bliss within the tides of this cosmic Blood which is light, ecstasy, *Samadhi, Nirvana*—liberation from the need for being rooted in one particular place and being the product of a particular set of conditions.

This is the transcendental life—which men so often misinterpret by calling it "formless" being. It is the life of the mystic Wanderers who move from place to place, linking races and continents with the subtle threads they weave by the magic of their mere presence. Of such men there has been none greater than Gautama, the Buddha—the great planetary prototype, for our humanity, of the transcendent life. His life is shown to us as a great mystery-ritual of overcoming. The perfect and radiant fruition of a culture which glorified the most beautiful aspects of earth-life, the young Hindu prince, moved by compassion and by the need to solve the poignant enigma of suffering, left behind all this perfection, social power and achievement. He "transformed" himself into a wandering seeker after Reality, received from Teachers and Yogis all the inspiration they could bestow; then at last, after meeting the simple heart of a woman who gave his starved body food and the treasure of child-like wisdom, he reached the transcendental state which he named *Nirvana:* life within the "Blood" of the Universal Whole; that is, life not in terms of a particular condition but as an agent of universal wholeness.

Such a life may appear "formless" to the cell which is utterly defined structurally by the fact of its being a cell of the liver or a cell of the kidneys—in other words, by the place it occupies in the organic whole. It appears so because it is a life of ceaseless adaptation to the needs of the particular and structurally rigid organs and cells of the whole; a life of protean service conditioned only by the will of the whole. Yet this whole has form, and the tides of blood have rhythm. Therefore formlessness is only a relative term. What is spiritually formless to the lesser entity is formed through its activity within the formed greater being of which the lesser entity is a part.

To transcend is to *pierce through* nature and nature-born conditions. It requires an act of will and spiritual courage. Thus the twelfth mansion, if it is seen in its positive aspect, brings to man the message of heroic effort—but an effort which does not mean the kind of work and devotional self-surrender characterizing the sixth mansion. It is an effort which does not manifest as the personal ego doing some definite particular type of work, but rather as a still and steady, almost effortless, gathering of psychic energies around certain Images or Symbols held fixed within the consciousness of soul and body.

In a sense, one might say that the process is one of *creative imaging*. The image of the universal whole (or some potent symbol of its activity) is held steadily within the consciousness of the fulfilled personality. This image or symbol has come to this personality by inspiration or through the teachings of some true spiritual Brotherhood during the span of development of the eleventh mansion. Of such images or symbols the true living Civilization is made. The personality, transfigured by the vision and the dream experienced in the eleventh mansion, must now transcend its entire cycle of particular earth-born selfhood. And it does so by becoming the likeness of the image or symbol.

This requires, if not effort in the ordinary sense of the term, at least a deliberate steadiness of mind and emotions which might be defined as "meditation", provided this much-abused word is well understood. Meditation is the process by means of which a particular earth-born personality turns away from the sense of being in bondage to the conditions of its earthly birth, and re-polarizes the energies derived from heredity and environment, so that they serve to energize a universal or archetypal image with which the transfigured personality wills to identify itself.

This image can be said to be the "Father that is in Heaven" of whom Jesus spoke when, having reached the transcendental stage, he said "I and my Father are one." Meditation is then a process aiming at a transcendental union with one's spiritual Archetype.

It is, however, a union which occurs within the sea of universal Light, and during the first stages of the final process the personal consciousness may be so blinded by the intensity of this ubiquitous, intoxicating Light that even the archetypal form is lost in it, together with all the familiar appearances of this world. Thus there is a "piercing through" the Light—just as there is a "piercing through" the moving phantasms of that darkness which closes in upon the man who, having seen the supernal Vision, dares to become that very Vision. And for both there is need of will and courage; need of steadiness, poise—and faith.

Transfiguration and transcendence—these two last stages of the cycle of selfhood are transitional stages which lead from the perfect personality which has achieved in the tenth mansion, to the "new birth" as a "babe in Christ"—if the cycle has proven wholly successful. This "new birth" is the first mansion of a greater or higher cycle; and Life moves on, and ever on, from birth to re-birth through self-organization (IV), love (VII), and achievement (X).

Alas! Very few are those born of the earth who, having perfectly achieved, reach the glory of rebirth in the Light. The vast majority of men, having failed to attain complete fulfillment, dream dreams that are but of the earth, reach for ideals which are destructive of spiritual integrity—and thus find in the twelfth mansion but more or less potent forms of bondage; bondage which means the necessity for a new birth in the blind embrace of material elements.

Thus the commonly understood idea of *karma*. Where there is lack of perfect fulfillment there is *karma*. The unfulfilled selfhood, the imperfect action, leave residua ("karmic deposits") which become the inchoate substance of a new cycle of manifestation—at more or less the same level of being. The deed left undone forces him who should have been the doer to face a similar need for accomplishing a similar deed. Life, instead of becoming a spirallic ascent, becomes under the fateful pressure of *karma* a monotonous wheel of birthing and dying—meaningless, in the sense that perfect meaning arises only out of perfect fulfillment.

In the twelfth mansion the man who does not pierce

through the shadows and into the beyond must witness the onsurge of all that has been unfulfilled, inhibited, repressed, thwarted in his life. Thus it is the symbol of what Freud calls the "unconscious—what Jung more accurately terms the "personal unconscious", to differentiate it from the "collective unconscious". Yet in a sense, both personal and collective unconscious are aspects of the mysterious something which we name "memory". It is the whole of a cycle gathering its energies and its experiences into a last moment, either of perfect remembrance (in the case of a "buddha") or of haunted obsession by the unachieved and the repressed.

Now, in this last mansion, memory is not the foundation or inspirer of new ideals. It is the past to be transcended, overcome—this through meditation in understanding—or else it is the past which rises to force the consciousness into a new birth in the world of suffering and crucifixion.

This confrontation with the past may take many and varied forms. It may be deliberately faced by the perfect soul who has naught to witness but the light of his noble deeds, or by the daring soul who, though his failures be many, has grown through all and never lost the realization of his cyclic Identity or archetypal essence. It may be forced upon man by life itself in the form of a fateful confinement—as in a hospital. It may also be forced by society upon the individual who either has broken collective laws or has tried to bring forth ideals and reforms which were too far beyond the inertial stability of his community.

In this last sentence the often tragic conflict between individual and collectivity is briefly outlined: a conflict which makes criminals and anarchists; and which also may cause great geniuses to starve and suffer, only to be glorified after their death by a new generation.

This conflict is born in the tenth mansion, develops in the eleventh, and comes to a culmination in the twelfth—the symbol of imprisonment and retribution, the place of expiation and repentance, the place of martyrdom and of serene acceptance of a fate to which only the future can give full significance.

These last two mansions are full of mysteries and of complexities, because they tell tales as varied as the individual lives which here succeed or do not succeed in their attempts either to adjust themselves to the requirements of society, or to fecundate the collectivity with the Vision which it is only the individual's privilege to behold. No collectivity ever steps into the "new life" as a collectivity. It is always impregnated by the Vision and the Dream of one or of several individuals. And, as is the case in many species of insects, to fecundate is for the male often to meet death.

The criminal rapes society. The genius fecundates society and gives to mankind a radiant progeny. The former is a throwback, a resurgent image of past social and individual failures. The latter is the agency through which the future calls to the present, urging it to transcend itself. Both suffer. Both, in a broad sense, are maladjusted.

As to the difference between the perfect adept or mystic and the creative genius, it lies in this—that the former overcomes the race within himself and makes of his whole personality a work of transcendent significance, whereas the creative genius does not usually bother much about overcoming the race in his personality, but instead projects into the consciousness of his generation a plan, a model, significant forms, colors, or tones which reveal the archetypal structure or power of the cycle-to-be.

According as man operates at one level of being or at another, the twelfth mansion presents one task or another. In the cycle of the first birth man transcends the race and the soil which conditioned his physio-psychological development. Later, man, become truly an individual, finds that at the close of that cycle of individual selfhood there comes a moment when individualism must be transcended. Then he emerges into the realm of the third birth, which is the realm of Light.

But even that Light which man may reach in his highest culminations is but a pale reflection of a Reality more sublime and more transcendent. The greater whole is not a static God whose boundaries are marked by the stars' orbits or the tides of expanding and contracting space. It is that timeless and spaceless "More" which ever urges on toward more transcendent bliss and more ultimate unions.

And yet—all these mansions, and all these stages of the eternal journey toward that which ever eludes the quest, are but phantasms of our scattered being. Wholeness is absolute in every moment and every point of space. It dwells in the fullness of every whole. To experience this is to know that there is no "lesser" and no "greater"; that in the individual alone can there ever be perfection and truth; that it matters little whether it be man or God, if man or God be fulfilled and made perfect in the ineffable NOW.

Music of the Spheres

Prelude

IN LANDS THAT ARE VEILED IN THE LURE OF DISTANCE AND mystery, in Java, in Bali, men listen throughout deep tropical nights for the music of native orchestras; orchestras in which sets of gongs of all sizes, played in various manners, occupy the most conspicuous place. Throbbing with wondrous resonance, the big gongs scan the periods of the music as it flows evenly, flows like a deep river, releasing into the silence of towering forests myriads of tones. And the tones resound incessantly, fluid, alive. Quickly they drip from the hands of brown-skinned performers wrapped in batik "saroengs"; quickly, without break, yet also without haste, measured and solemnized by the soft throbs of the big gongs, which to these men are the very voices of their gods.

Unlike our highly individualistic and emotionally strained Western music, this music of gongs is the image of life itself, as it flows serenely, universally, rhythmically. It is music that is cosmic indeed, pure and full as the music which men of exalted realizations, like Pythagoras, named "the Music of the Spheres". Well may we compare the two; for to the awakened sense of those great dreamers, whose dreams at times interpret for us the meaning of celestial mysteries, the planets which circle majestically round the Sun can often be perceived as vast gongs, huge discs vibrant with hosts of energies centered round a core of flaming power, before which the seeing human soul fain would bow in awed reverence, calling it a god.

Modern minds, caught by the glamor of scientific analysis, may dismiss the vision as mere mythological fancy—even though science itself has come to describe in similar fashion our still mysterious Galaxy. Little does it matter; for whether the image be endowed with substantial reality or not, the pure significance nevertheless remains. And it is with this significance that we would deal, without being afraid to veil it in poetical symbolism, for after all, the deepest core of life is poetry and symbol.

Wherefore we shall attune our ears to the gong tones of the orchestra which our eyes see as the solar system. In this orchestra there are two solo performers, which ancient astrology called the "Lights"—Sun and Moon. Their performance is a twofold song—song of days and of nights; and the tones thereof are vibrations of light and of life. The bright Singers intone melodies throughout the earth, and as they sing, all beings are stirred, moved to become what they are. And in every living organism sympathetic resonances are aroused, a reflected song which to these organisms is light and life.

Through the greater heavens the solar song of light flows. It strikes the planetary hosts. Like huge gongs they resound to the impact. Their tones mount to a climax, boom forth through space. These tones are power. For they are words and they are commands. They circle through space. In appointed circuits of power, they revolve. Their revolutions stir —in every atom, every cell, every living whole—activities which, blending with the songs of light and life, of Sun and Moon, constitute the warp and woof of organic living.

The significance of this celestial orchestra resides in this, that in every living thing of the earth there is also, hidden behind the opaque veils of materiality, a cosmic orchestra. And for those who have retained the vision of poets and seers, these orchestras, the one in the skies and the myriads of those in all living wholes, are synchronous. Each organic entity is a little watch timed to the vast clock of the solar system. Life in the many microcosms can be interpreted in terms of the music of the orchestras they contain and which are their living souls—the breaths of Life. For Life is a moving harmony of functions. Organic activities are rhythmical and periodical. Their pulsations can be measured by the beating of invisible gongs; gongs which are hidden within the body, and cosmic ones also which man beholds in the sky.

Modern biologists are prone to refer all life-activities to endocrine glands, and to their infinitesimal secretions which hold such a magic power over the functional behavior of the organism—a power tremendous in relation to their size. Yet it may be that these glands are themselves but the concrete bases of operation for vibratory streams which emanate from more hidden or more deeply symbolic centers of force. These, in their totality, we would call the "life-gongs' orchestra" within the body: the "Planets" within every living whole.

Each whole, insofar as it is a living whole, partakes in the activity of a few basic streams of energies which operate through the greater and more universal Whole of which it is a little part or cell. The essential *functional structures* of every whole, the smallest as well as the vastest, are analogical. Life performs in a few basic modes in every organic whole. These modes are set by the life-gongs which throb in all living things of the earth, as they boom forth through the vast spaces of the solar system.

We shall therefore attune our ears to the music of the planetary gongs, to the songs of the "Lights" whose circuits in our skies measure the reality of Time; Time that is Life creative and Life singing; Time that binds all gongs into a vast symphony of planetary voices; Time whose silence itself may become Tone—the small, childlike, pure, simple tone of our innermost self; a tone that vibrates through the whole of us, and is the wholeness of us; a tone so translucent, so clear, and so simple that no one may hear it save those who themselves have become silence.

That tone is the blending of all the overtones of life; yet in a curious, inexpressible way, the source of all that is "I". It is that which men of other times have named *Tao*; realizing which, great Sages and Saints and Poets have known God. Not the flaming triumphant divinity who sits on a throne of glory amid the paeans of celestial cohorts; but that mystic Presence which is humble and tender, radiant and pure—which is the song of Silence and of Love; which is nothing, yet without which there is nothing; which has gladdened the hearts of all mystics, and given to men the peace "that passeth understanding".

The Song of Light

THROUGHOUT OUR EARTHLY YEAR, MODULATED WITHIN THE range of the Sun's octave of motion as it spreads from solstice to solstice, northward and then southward, light sings its cyclic melody—the source and being of all living melodies.

The melody of light! We who bathe in its radiance and its eternal wonder, seeing this light centered in the moving majesty of the Sun, believe that knowing the light, we also know the Sun. Yet mystics and occultists of all ages have taken pains to show that the brilliance we behold is not the reality of the Sun, but only its outer glory. And scientists intent upon penetrating celestial mysteries speak of the various layers of the Sun's surface, especially of the photosphere which is the source of light; yet few would be bold enough to claim that they know what lies beyond the effulgent solar veils: what has been called "the Heart of the Sun".

The "Heart of the Sun" is the unknown Deity; the photosphere, His "Robe of Glory"—as the Gnostics said nearly two thousand years ago. Light is the effulgence of this Glory. It is the song of the Multitudes that are the cells of the divine Body. It is the song of the celestial Hosts conveying to the outer world the inner reality of the One who is the beginning, the middle and the end of all there is in the solar system, the

One who is drawing all things to Himself that they may partake of His divinity, the One who is the supreme Integrator, the All-encompassing and Compassionate: Whom men call God.

Light is the compassionate gesture of God toward matter, the flow of His love which ever "redeems" the residuum of past failure, gathering the chaotic elements, the ashes of ancient worlds, into living organisms. Light is the call to renewed life, and therefore the command "Let there be Light" resounds as the creative evocation. It is a command; but it is even more an act of compassion—which means an act of integration.

After the end of any cycle of manifestation, be it the cycle of a man or that of a galaxy, all that was "spiritual" in the once living being is indrawn into the supreme unity of Spirit, and all that failed to reach that condition of unity is in a state of chaos, of extreme divisibility and elemental materiality. Thus there is an emphasis of duality and non-integration, even though at the time being there is no *active* conflict between spirit and matter—the two polar opposites within the universal Whole. But, we must not forget, conflict is relationship; hatred is relationship. It is only in utter indifference and utter oblivion that all relationship ceases. And after the end of a cycle of life-manifestation, spirit has completely forgotten matter, and matter is utterly indifferent to spirit.

It is only as spirit and matter are correlated within a living organism that relationship between the two opposites is possible; even though such a relationship means uninterrupted conflict. When the body disintegrates, spirit goes its own way, and so does matter. Then organic life ceases—life, which is the ceaseless interaction of spirit with matter, of positive with negative. Consciousness or soul is drawn into spirit—or at least whatever of it was at all spiritual. The materials of the body decompose and become mere chemicals, manure or food which lower organisms in turn will assimilate.

What could draw together once again spirit and matter, if

not the will and love of Him who is the supreme Integrator, wholeness ceaselessly operative and compassion absolute? It is that divine One whom men call God and whose celestial symbol of active power is the "Heart of the Sun". Within that eternal Heart surges boundless compassion for matter, the strong desire that all inchoate cosmic elements be once more made to interact with spirit, so that out of the interaction and the conflict consciousness and soul may once more sound the majestic chord of universal Being throughout the fields of Space.

And this compassion that surges from the "Heart of the Sun" is light. It is light that thrills through Space, arousing Spirit from its dream and stirring the "dark waters of chaos". This light is the eternal power of integration, and it radiates everlastingly from the "Heart of the Sun". Men whose eyes may see only the radiation and must ignore its mystic source, believe they know the Sun; yet what they perceive is only the gushing torrent of the light. And the light flows from the Heart of divine Fullness into all the potential seeds of living organisms—be they universes, or men, or plants. That light is absorbed by the seeds, and it becomes, *in them*, life. To the song of light answers—faintly at first, yet ever more strongly—the song of life.

This distinction between "light" and "life" is a basic feature of esoteric philosophy. Medieval philosophers, following after still older teachers, spoke of *Natura naturans* and *Natura naturata*; which mean, Nature as an active principle and Nature as a passive acted-upon element. They spoke of the former as the "astral light"; of the latter as the sub-lunar realm, of perpetual flux and passionate change. Light, thus, is always the active, universal principle; Life, considered as a manifested essence in living organisms, is the reflected, particularizing element whose tides regulate the growth and decay of all organisms. Life is the fluidic essence in the body, that mysterious elixir whose potency may be due to the presence of secretions from the endocrine glands. But, beyond the life-giving fluid, there is what some occultists have called the "body of light" or "sidereal body". The terms are unfortunate, in the sense that such a "body" is not really a body. It is rather an orchestra, a relationship of creative, light-radiating whirls—which are indeed like vibrating gongs.

These gongs are set vibrating by the mystic "Sun" within the human organism—the leader of the orchestra; nay more, He who plays upon the gongs; who plays not with hands and mallet, but with Rays of light. This Sun is said to be a very mysterious little blue Flame which can be perceived by the seer at the center of the heart, where the four cavities thereof meet. There is to be found the immanent Christ of the Christian mystics, the living God; Ishvara-in-the-body, the incarnate Krishna of whom the *Bhagavat Gita* speaks.

"There dwelleth in the heart of every creature, O Arjuna, the Master—*Ishwara*—who by his magic power causeth all things and creatures to revolve mounted upon the universal wheel of time. Take sanctuary with him alone, O son of Bharata, with all thy soul; by his grace thou shalt obtain supreme happiness, the eternal place." XVIII

We may not see this Sun in us, but we may sense its light. It flows through the great nerve systems of the body: the great sympathetic, the vagus nerve, the cerebro-spinal system. It is the electric fluid which passes through the nerves, now found by modern science to be indeed like electric wires wrapped in a protective sheath. It is that, and possibly more than that. It is the *organic resonance* of the body as a harmonic whole: the source of all vital activities and at the same time their synthetic vibration; the *alpha* and the *omega* of all individual being.

Light is a song—not because it changes of itself, for the Heart of the Sun is changeless; but because the Earth—symbol of the individual's consciousness—orients itself differently to it, season after season. The Earth revolves around the Sun, and, because its axis is inclined and not perpendicular to the plane of the revolution, the light of the Sun strikes most of the Earth's surface at varying angles. Therefore light is not a single tone, an unchanging diapason; it is a melody. Likewise man's attitude to his spiritual source varies throughout the span of his life; and the light within him is also a melody—at first clear and pure, then tumultuous and torrid, lastly softer and more tender, like the light which caresses the yellowing trees before the coming of the great white snow.

In the fully-developed human being the song of light is heard three times, each time in a different tonality. Each time the melody unfolds from a Winter-solstice "tonic" to a Summer-solstice "dominant", then back to a new "tonic"—or perhaps it is the same original "tonic", if growth is made impossible. Each melodic cycle takes twenty-eight years. The song of light is a song of selfhood—flowing northward, flowing southward—from purity to passion, from passion to purity—from illumination to heat, from heat to greater brilliance.

It is a song of Will; for Will is that which ever flows from the center of the living being. Will is the result of the polarization of the multitudinous energies of being to the abstract Source of that being. It is energy directed by purpose according to a pattern. The pattern may be the inherent pattern, or archetypal Form, of the being as an individualized spark of the Universal Fire—a Monad; or else it may be a pattern imposed upon an immature and unpolarized organism, or organism-to-be, by a coercive, outer ruler or discipline. Saturn is the symbol of such a pattern—be it that of inherent Destiny and Dharma, or that of collective compulsion rooted in the species or the group, but not differentiated through individual consciousness.

Energy directed by purpose according to pattern. In these words we may find the key to the basic relationship linking Sun, Jupiter and Saturn. For all energy flows forth from the Sun, but Jupiter makes the purpose of this outflow operative in terms of organization, and Saturn symbolizes the pattern through which the purpose is established as a formula of being. All energy flows forth from the Sun—and the source of the energy itself is the "Heart of the Sun"; and the source of the purpose likewise is the "Heart of the Sun". Jupiter reveals this purpose, makes it operative; just as the Hierophant reveals the Mysteries and establishes the rituals of Initiation. But behind the Hierophant is the Supreme Presence in whom —nay, *through* whom—is known the Mystery.

The Sun, as we know it, is not the Mystery—though men have worshipped its glowing countenance as God. Even the "Heart of the Sun" is yet a veil upon the Mystery. That God who has been called the "Unknown God" is but an atom within the Mystery—as the Sun is but a pin-point of light within the inconceivable immensities of Space, the unfathomable Ocean in which galaxies move and have their being, fulfilling purposes beyond any possible knowing.

Who can ever reach even the fringe of the Mystery! We witness the pageant of stars that are suns like our own, circling within galactic wheels for incommensurable eons. Haltingly we measure with our frail minds, strained toward infinitude and dizzy with eternity, realms which extend beyond realization. Our Sun-god nearly vanishes into insignificance when plotted against nebular vistas. Nevertheless, in Him is our Source and from Him we must receive our direction through the mediatorship of Jupiter, the Hierophant within or without. As we link ourselves in realization with Him we may sense our purpose as a compelling force, as that innate instinct of being which is even older and more primordial than life itself—for it is the source and reason of embodied existence. As we link ourselves with the Sun-god we live in terms of will; and the directed energy, which is will, polarizes the many impulses of our little organic selves, in conformity with the significance of our true being as a unified whole.

It is often easy to become lost in the ecstasy of light, swirling from sun to stars in waves of galactic bliss. Men have been drunken with cosmic consciousness, shipwrecks on the high seas of light. It is not man's destiny to be a thing floating in the sea of light or pulled toward shores beyond the reach of the Sun. Even though our Sun be not the only sun, yet it is our Sun, and though there may be paths reaching far beyond, yet are we all of one progeny. His strength is our strength and his path our path . . . until this earthly fulfillment.

He who worships stars through paths of identification which avoid the direction of the Sun, may forego his human destiny and become the fantastic devotee of some strange cosmic god. Dark indeed may turn the way to the Mystery; dark even with the blindness of overwhelming light. The Universal Person, in whose abysmal wholeness stars and galaxies circle for incomprehensible eons—how can we speak of this unfathomable and this absolute, bounded as it were by light, yet as far beyond the level of light as Personality is beyond mere physical characteristics?

Yet, it has seemed to many that the most universal Deity is also the nearest presence in this strange world where atoms seem made in the likeness of solar systems. The God of the occultist may be awesome in His inclusiveness and His space-body spread over billions of light-years; but the mystic knows an immanent God, a Living God who is born within the heart of fulfillment of the Eternal Now, a God smiling within a space which gives the lie to astronomical distances and within an immediacy of possible union which disproves hierarchical structures erected by the mind bent upon cosmic vivisections.

God the intimate, and God the remote, all-encompassing Mystery—God the immanent, and God the universal—the Living God answering to the macrocosmic Wholeness—the divine Person one and identical with *Parabrahman*—Man, the Son of God, made in His own image: such a wondrous identification of the smallest with the vastest, of atoms with stars, gives a strange and adorable beauty to that union of two opposite attitudes to life, of mysticism and occultism, which remains forever unnamed, though every cycle attempts to crystallize it under a terminology soon to become ready for the morgue of histories and dictionaries.

Light is the substance of it all. The divine Person in human form is an organism of light, just as are galaxies. Light is the beginning and light is the end. Dark bodies and planets, by reflecting light to each other, lead to the slow rise of objective consciousness through relationship, through hatred as through love, through greed as through sacrifice. Until the time comes when light-reflecting objects, having assimilated fully the energy of light-radiating entities that shone in their own skies, emanate also, at the last, light. Then the illumined Ones become the Light-bearers, the Shining Ones. Personalities become divine Persons. Bodies which could only reflect sunlight shine with a glow in which may be distinguished the radiant outlines of the long-imprisoned god. They too will sing the song of light, for they will have become "solar heroes"—their lives "solar myths" indeed, and paeans of blessings.

This song of light is a universal song; but each living being sings it with his own tone color. Because each one of the gongs which throb under the divine melody is made of an alloy the composition of which varies; because each object that reflects the light is made up as yet of unregenerate and diversified past, there need be many types of being. One Light, but so many lamps; one Sound, yet so many tones. Illumination comes to those who hear the song of Light unchanged, unflickering, eternal—Light that is one though the lamps be many.

The Song of Life

As the compassionate ray of light surging from the Heart of the Sun plays upon and penetrates a portion of space "set apart" to become the magnetic field within which a future living being will be born and will grow, a "current of induction" is generated within that space, the first manifestation of life in a particular mode.

Space is substance, and substance is the reason for space's being. Substance must always have space to be extended in; and were it not for the fact that there must always be matter left over from some solar or cosmic cycle of manifestation—that there will ever be substance to oppose spirit, there would be no space. Spirit, being pure unity, is symbolized by the mathematical point, without dimension or extension. Matter, on the other hand, is the manifested reality of space and has in itself the potentiality of an infinite number of dimensions. We do not see space; we see only matter in extension, matter of various densities—and what seems to us "empty space" is merely the expanse of a type of material relatively less dense.

This matter of extremely small density is, at the origin of any cycle of manifestation, what has been called the "great Waters of Space" or "primordial Chaos". It is abysmal darkness—utter indifference to spirit. But when under the compulsion of God's command: "Let there be light!" the spiritual

Essences of the past are aroused from their condition of bliss and unity, and the song of light begins to thrill through the infinitudes, then upon the face of the dark Waters of Space rays of light begin to play.

Deep vibrations are aroused in response within the bosom of these Waters. Motion throbs throughout the abyss. Waves begin to swell, agitating the quiescent substance. To light answers life. The waves of the "Sea" answer to the waves of the light. Vibrations echo vibrations. Cosmic relationship is being established. The cosmic antiphony of light and life sounds out; two songs in a cyclic counterpoint; major and minor tonalities weaving tone-patterns; the warp and woof of the universe. Upon those will be woven the fabric of organic existence, the brocade of consciousness and of soul. What people call imprecisely "life", what more exactly should be named "cyclic becoming", is this eonic, ever-changing relationship of the songs of light and life; a vast duo between the Sun and the Moon, going on and on throughout the ages. The harmony needed to sustain the two melodic strands in their interaction is provided by the planetary gongs. Saturn sounds the fundamental tone, the Root-sound.

. . . Out of the dark Waters of Space wells up the song of life; and this song is born of the past. It is born of unfulfillment. All life springs from unfulfillment. This is the true meaning of the "original sin". That which is fulfilled has no need for life. It is pure being; bliss. But life is suffering; because it is striving; because it is the attempt to overcome the memory and the pull of the past. Light is the compassionate gesture of God providing another opportunity to neutralize or redeem the relative failures of the past. This opportunity is what is meant by "living in an organic body of earth-substance". The Earth is the new field of opportunity. The Moon is the song of the resurrected past.

Because the Moon vibrates to the echoes of the past, because it is a ghostly presence summoning from forgotten depths memories of failures or unfulfillments, men have called the influence of the Moon evil. But is it really evil? Is the cleansing passion that arouses all repressed unregenerate desires, the hand of the housewife that forces the hidden dust to rise to perception, evil? Is disease evil? Is it not rather the way of redemption and purification, Nature's effort to reestablish harmony and health, to free the organism—be it psychological or physiological—from the subterranean pressure of racial subconscious *karma*; yes, from the ancestral sins of mankind . . . or the ancient perversions of the reincarnating Soul?

The Moon is not the past as mere dead weight. Rather, it is the striving and the struggling of embodied man away from that past; his yearning for freedom from that past; his willingness to face it and overcome. The solar light provides the energy and incentive for the overcoming. The lunar life-tides measure the phases of the effort toward fulfillment. They beat the rhythm of overcoming. They energize the periodical currents of the life-flux, which mould themselves upon the root-pattern of destiny, or *karma*,—over which rules Saturn, the Lord of Boundaries.

Nothing that is a part of organic living can be evil. The body is the one field of opportunity provided by God in His great compassion for the unfulfilled and the imperfect—so that it might become fulfilled and perfect at the end of the cycle of living. And by "body" here is meant every living organism—from the atom to the solar system and the vastest galaxies. The whole manifested universe is the "pattern of redemption". The body is the one and only divine Church, in which light officiates. The song of life—the Moon song—is the answer of the congregation. It is the faith and the prayer of men; and also their indifference and their hypocrisy. It is the inchoate expression of the crowd which is the raw material to be organized into a society, a harmonious group, by the supreme leader that is light. It is the barbaric impulses to be civilized.

The Moon therefore represents all raw materials, all elemental or psychic energies not yet organic or individuated. But it is not only the inorganic as such. It is the inorganic striving to become organized. It is the "woman" yearning to be fecundated and to become a mother, longing for her "home". It is not chaos; but rather, the response of chaos to light; an unsteady, changeful, moody response, now waxing, then waning—yet it is light nevertheless; as much of light as the resurgent past may mirror and reflect. And the Earth and all living things thereon are the temples where the song of light and the song of life resound. Light gives to men the will to be whole and integrated. Life gathers their chaotic soul-energies, churns them up, dissolves and boils them in the alchemical vessel in which may be generated the gold of consciousness and of individual selfhood.

At the physiological level this alchemical vessel is the mother's womb, the place where life gathers its momentum in answer to the call of light, the place of the Moon, the "sublunar realm" of ancient philosophy. At the psycho-mental level the alchemical vessel is the "psyche", the womb of the Self, the "place" where the inherited ancestral and racial soul-energies are churned by the rhythm of the psychic life, and whence, perhaps, a god-like Individual will be born.

The formation of the child's body within the mother's womb is a mysterious operation; yet still more mysterious is that other process of psychic formation which produces, if successful, a truly individual soul. The former is the process of gestation; the latter, that of individuation. Both depend upon the rhythm of the Moon's song. This rhythm operates following a four times seven phrasing, twenty-eight being the synthetic number of individuation as well as of gestation. It may be divided in many ways, as for instance the 40 weeks of pregnancy, which become the 40 years of wandering in the desert, or Abdul Baha's 40 years of imprisonment in Akka—meaning the womb—in Bahai symbology. Considered from the point of view of solar light—and no longer of lunar life—

the number becomes 9, the sacred number of the Bahai movement, which can be considered as an expression of *planetary gestation*, the gestation of a new Era seen from the planetary standpoint of power, rather than from the human standpoint of consciousness.

The processes of gestation and individuation are based on analogical operations; only, the former is an entirely *set* process at this time of man's evolution, with a relatively small percentage of failures, whereas the latter is not at all well established at present, and carries a vast majority of at least relative or temporary failures. We may easily believe that there was a time when physiological pregnancy was also beset with failures, and many monsters were born; when mating between incongruous types or species was most frequent and led to hybrid and short-lived stocks. This is no longer true, now that our planet's life and the life of its main biological types are quite definitely set and relatively crystallized; that is, now that the planet has reached physiological maturity. But Man as a species has not yet reached psycho-mental maturity, or let us say, stability. It may be said that humanity, while physically past the mid-life point, is in the throes of an early "change of life"—with all the resulting problems of psychological readjustment.

Such a readjustment, when truly understood, can be seen as a process of psycho-mental pregnancy. Humanity, as a whole, is attempting to set a process of individuation which would be valid and successful for the race at large, and which would result in the formation of *true individuals*. In order to do that, mind must have reached a high point of development; for the formative Powers of individual selfhood are mental. The mind is the formative instrumentality of the soul. Without mind, the soul is a field of conflicting psychic energies which can be controlled only by an autocratic Will, itself the product of a dominant desire. Thus the process of individuation in the past was a process of forceful initiation, which meant the assumption of power over the psychic nature by an entity superior to this psychic nature. This meant, in short, the need for personal subservience to a *guru*, or spiritual ruler (not really Teacher), in whose hands was placed the key to the psychic nature. Initiation therefore implied absolute self-surrender and obedience to the *guru*; and eventually a complete transference of will from the *guru* to the disciple (*chela*) ready for initiation.

Such a process, however, cannot possibly apply to the whole of mankind, for the relation *guru* to *chela* being a personal one (however spiritual in essence and purpose), the number of those admitted to initiation was obviously limited. It is only when mind can be made the basis of the whole process of individuation that this process can become valid for the majority of men. Mind as a *basis*; not of course as the whole structure. But just as certain agencies of physical nature have control over the formative process of biological development in the womb (or in any seed), so the somewhat analogical process of psycho-mental formation (individuation) is to be put under the control of mental agencies of a definite type. These agencies are now being developed in a planetary way, through the spread of logical (that is, formed) thinking, objective mentality and conscious metaphysical understanding of man's relationship to the powers of the "collective unconscious".

In a planetary sense, such formative agencies may be considered as those exalted Beings who constitute the "White Lodge" and its differentiated branches, one of which dominates especially during each racial cycle—as for instance the "Blue Lodge" of the original Aryavarta (Greater India) during the Aryan great cycle. They have taken the place of those celestial Hierarchies who at the dawn of human evolution projected into Man their "emanations," and thus sowed the seeds of the complete human being. What these Hierarchies accomplished *in and through the unconscious*, the human Adepts of the last few millennia—especially since the time of the Buddha—are now achieving *in and through the conscious*.

Thus the celestial Hierarchies and the "Planetary Spirits" were the ancient Sources of all instinct and of those "Primordial Images" or "Archetypes" (in Jung's terminology) which have ruled men's behavior for long cycles. But today, the new method of development is through the "conscious Way". It operates primarily from the level of the conscious individuality; not through a process of compulsive direction by overshadowing, but through one involving the steady and relatively slow building of the formative powers of the individual soul; the building of a psycho-mental structure which parallels at a higher level the bone structure of the physiological organism. Logical thinking is the builder of this psycho-mental structure. It is spiritual calcium.

Such a structure is necessary so that the individual Soul may *assimilate* the psycho-mental food it needs, without losing its form or individual character, just as the embryo assimilates nutritive substances from the mother's blood. At the psycho-mental level the "Mother" is the *Nirmanakaya*: that synthetic "being" that is the summation of all civilization. It is the "Collective Conscious", the fruition of all that the race has felt and thought. Of this mysterious being Goethe spoke to some extent when he made Faust reach the realm of the "Mothers". Yet he who knows how to differentiate between the "race-Mothers" who are the souls of cultures born of the soil and bent toward physical fulfillment, and the universal "Mother" whose soul is the Light of integrated humanity beyond racial and physical boundaries or religions—such a one is on the path to the higher mastery. It is a mastery based on intelligence and love, rather than on mere will. It is conscious mastery consciously won through synthesis—not through exclusion. It is an *incorporation of the Spirit*. Wholeness made operative through a man; Deity transfiguring Personality; Man corporifying God.

This development means that the song of life is being sounded at a higher level. It means that the Moon is becoming trans-substantiated. A "hidden" Moon is being revealed, and its vibrations are stirring a new layer of the dark Waters of Space. A deeper layer. A past more ancient, more cosmic, is being resurrected, to be redeemed by a will to integration more profound and more absolute. A new Sun-call is arousing a higher song of life. This Sun-call was heard last century by those who had ears to hear. Now the song of life is answering. Pluto opens the gates to the formative powers of a new Order of life. A new Root is conquering the depths of Man—depths as yet never truly conquered and civilized, depths the denizens of which could only be forced back into dark dungeons of the planetary Unconscious by the Will of planetary Rulers. And this conquest is by Love and Understanding. Such is the reality of the "Second Coming".

A New Moon—an eclipse, releasing a new song of life. The old song was conditioned by the chord of Mars and Venus. The new song is born of the harmony of Jupiter and Mercury. And beyond it, souls that are illumined may behold a new Ray shooting forth in glorious splendor from the cosmic depths: the Ray of the "Glory of God", whose source may be found in the mighty star, Betelgeuze—Beth-el-Ghazi, the "House" of the Lord.

Saturn:
Lord of Boundaries

OVER THE SONG OF LIFE RULE TWO MIGHTY POWERS. THE pulls of their opposing forces sway the living tides hither and thither, and the motion they induce and regulate is cyclic and constant. Two currents of motion; ebb and flow of the great cosmic Sea that is life—systole and diastole of the universal Heart—from which are born the two great life-currents within every organism. Venous and arterial circulations at one level, become the nerve-flow of the afferent and efferent nerves at another; and still deeper currents could be mentioned.

Saturn is the symbol of all systolic—Jupiter, of all diastolic movements. The former contracts, the latter expands. The circulation of life is regulated by the interplay of these two universal and ubiquitous Powers.

In the fabric of European music this "circulation of life" is conditioned by the two great centers of tonal attraction and repulsion, concentration and modulation—the "tonic" and the "dominant". All melodic and harmonic movements, in classical tonality, sway around these two centers. Interestingly enough, in Europe, all classical melodies end on the Saturnian "tonic"; while in most Oriental types of music, they close with what is an approximate equivalent of the Jupiterian "dominant"; because Asia has always moved in devotion toward the greater Whole—while Europe has worked toward an emphasis of the personal, limited and materially focalized "I".

The graphic symbols used to picture the two universal Powers reveal the truth of their essential natures, as well as the relation they bear to the Moon, whose phases represent accurately the tidal ebb and flow of the ocean of Life. All New Moons are Jupiterian in ultimate meaning; all Full Moons, Saturnian. In the sign used to represent Jupiter the lunar crescent is above the *horizontal* line of the cross; with Saturn, it is attached to the lower end of the *vertical*. Moreover, in the Jupiter sign the curve of the Moon points outward to the open space, suggesting a counterclockwise rotation; while in the Saturn sign it closes in, as it were, upon the cross, suggesting a clockwise motion, thus:

Jupiter: ♃   Saturn: ♄

The Moon-crescent here symbolizes the motion of the life-flow; its relation to the cross and the suggested direction of the rotation indicate the polarity of this flow, whether outward and diastolic, or inward and systolic. The cross is, as ever, the mystery-sign of the Incarnation; the quartering of spirit into manifested space; the crucifixion of the One, that is the "Heart of the Sun", into the ebb and flow of Life, into polarities, into sex, into within and without, "I" and "the Others". The highest of all Light-Rays—the first and most mysterious, the *Sushumna* Ray—becomes crucified into the two antagonistic Powers—vertical and horizontal, symbolically —which control the tides of life. The path of its descent, the Way to the Cross down from the Center of the Sun, is also the path of return for all the living individuals that arise from the Sea-depths. Saturn forces the Spirit down into polarity, into form and gender. Jupiter is the compensating Power that brings the incarnate ego to the realization of all there is in the world besides himself, and thus helps him to assimilate the non-ego, so that he may grow into universal awareness and, ultimately, into conscious participation in the life of ever larger Wholes.

Another way in which this dual process could be graphically represented would be by picturing, in the case of Saturn, a spiral whirlwind closing in upon a cross (involutionary process); in the case of Jupiter, a similar spiral moving away from the central cross (evolutionary process). But the lunar crescent shows us in a luminous manner that the whirling Power which draws toward or away from the cross is that same Power which, striking universal substance, aroused therein the great tidal "song of life".

This whirling Power is also symbolized by the *svastika* with its two possible directions, counterclockwise and clockwise. These two directions are represented by the two letters Z and S; the former symbolizing the outward expression of the spirit through "works", i.e. through action—the latter, the inward concentration or meditation of the incarnated soul reaching to its central Source. The counterclockwise motion in astrological symbolism is that of the Houses, while Planets rotate on the chart in clockwise direction. The Houses define the "works of the individual Self" as it expresses itself outwardly. The Planets are essentially the energies of life reflecting the outward rays of the light back to its Source, the "Heart of the Sun".

Another interesting analogy can be established between, on one hand, the sign for Jupiter and the number 4, and on the other, the commonly made sign for Saturn and the number 5. The analogy is correct, for the number 4 symbolizes the in-

卐　Z　—　symbol of Persia — ♃　4

卍　S　—　symbol of India — ♄　5

corporation of Deity into Personality, of macrocosm into microcosm. It is the number of avataric descent. This is shown also in the fact that the number 4 (Personality), by Kabbalistic analysis, gives the number 10 ($1 + 2 + 3 + 4 = 10$) or the number of Deity. 4 is the number of wholeness operating as an organism of substance. 10 represents the emanation of the universal whole, as Light: God projecting himself, focalizing himself into his own creation, man (4).

As man reaches back toward participation in the life of the divine Whole, as he returns to his celestial home, then he is seen as the pentagram or five-pointed star—whose mystical name is Sanat: the highest aspect of Saturn (5). He ceases to be overshadowed by God. He becomes active *in* God. From being a medium, or at a higher stage, a mediator (4) or hierophant—a Door into the Kingdom of God—he becomes an Adept: one who acts within the divine Whole—an atom of divinity. Saturn and Jupiter are the two aspects taken by the Power emanating from the core of the Sun, when it manifests as the ruler and controller of the universal motions of life. No one can reach the "Heart of the Sun" who fails to stand the tests of Saturn-Jupiter, the Two-in-One. These cosmic Twins are the great Lords of Life; and they are lords over the souls of all of us in whom the yearning to reach the "Heart of the Sun", our divine Home, is aroused. They are indeed the very symbols of the "individual soul" in every man: this soul that the old Vedic seers once named "Yami-Yama"—significant names indeed, which find curious phonetic equivalents in our modern "I am I"—to which we should add "I am That".

"I am I"—such is the great *mantram* of Saturn, Lord of Boundaries, Lord of Form. In the beginning, the Saturn-power proclaims through the spaces encompassed by the solar Rays, the command: Let there be Form! And as these great words resound, gonglike, through the spatial substance of the universe-to-be, behold! a cosmic ploughman traces a circular furrow round the fields that are to become, in distant eons, the new "City of God".

Thereafter the within is differentiated from the without.

There is that which stands within the pale, within the precincts of the light, and that which lies beyond the pale, beyond the gates: the eternal outcasts and barbarians of the then dawning cycle of life-manifestation.

Saturn traces the boundaries: the "Ring-Pass-Not". He traces a furrow, just as in olden times a furrow was ploughed around that space of earth which had been selected to be the site of a new settlement. This furrow is the "magic circle" traced by the medieval magician with the point of his sword. It is the "sacred enclosure" of all temples—even the temple of the human soul. Within this enclosure—the city-walls, the walls of the living cell—the law of Saturn rules supreme. And this law is rhythmed to the beats of the *mantram*: "I am I".

The rod of Saturn, symbol of his power—the rod of the Initiator also—is the magical axis of man's individual selfhood: man's polar axis—the spine. Saturn is said to rule from the occult center at the base of the spine, the "Root-center" of Hindu occultism. From this point the entire body-structure is balanced. This truth is being recovered today by some physicians who, instead of adjusting dis-arranged vertebrae, work with the muscles of the sacro-iliac region, from which all the muscles holding the upper body in alignment are controlled. The lower regions of the spine and the coccyx constitute therefore the power center of the human organism, the mysterious place where *kundalini* is coiled. It is Root-power, and this Root-power, ascending upward under the urge of Self-renewal and spiritual rebirth, is that very power which gives existence to "flowers" (the Golden Flower in the head); the number and quality of the roots being shown in the number and quality of the flowers—a fact in horticulture.

The basis of the spine is the Dragon's Tail; because Saturn, like the latter, refers to the past; and the coccyx is the symbol of the past of the human animal, being a vestigial remains of the animal's tail. Why does Saturn refer to the past? Because the individual structure of the new manifestation is necessarily conditioned by the unfulfillment of the past; by the remains, the failures of the past—preserved in the Records of Nature, in the memory of universal substance: the "astral light" of the occultists.

The Moon is the song of the resurrected past, striving toward delayed fulfillment, struggling toward the "Heart of the Sun". The Moon-tides scan the cyclic efforts of the human soul, reawakened from its spirit-intoxicated dreams to fulfill the "pattern of redemption" which the Compassionate One provides, so that the unregenerate substance left over from the past universe may become integrated with Spirit. This "pattern of redemption" is the very "pattern of destiny" of the individual life. It is the *form* of the individual. And the Compassionate One . . . yes, indeed—it is Saturn, Lord of the Golden Age, in Greek mythology.

The Golden Age is the first period of any cycle; and it is called the "Age of Innocence", for throughout its duration men are completely dominated *from within* by instincts which, as instincts, are unfailing and absolutely true to the inherent nature of man. To be "innocent" is to be true to one's own nature, to be purely what one is—and nothing else. Pure water is water unmixed with anything that is not water. A man is pure who is entirely and solely that which he is originally and according to the law of his own nature. This law is the law of Saturn, the law of form and of purity—or integrity. He who fulfills completely his particular form and character, and never oversteps his own boundaries—in thought or feeling any more than in action—such a man is pure and innocent, whatever his destiny may be. Saturn therefore, the lord of destiny, is rightly the ruler over men who are *inescapably true* to their respective destinies.

Inescapably true. There is no escape from Saturn in the Golden Age; and no one wishes then to escape, any more than the animal and the tree wish to escape their own destinies, to be different from what they inherently are. The power of Saturn, in the Golden Age, is the power of instinct. It is life acting from within the organic being, with absolute control: life the autocrat—the benevolent and compassionate All-Father, the primordial image of whom is still the background for many of our modern concepts of God.

He is compassionate, just because he is an autocrat. At the beginning of any life-cycle the formative powers of Spirit face inchoate substance left over in a state of chemical disintegration (symbolically, of manure) or else the highly specialized substance "saved from the deluge" in the seed—the seed that is indeed an "ark of Noah". Leaving aside for the moment this seed-substance, we will easily realize that unless an absolutely dominating "will to formation" can be exerted upon the chaotic substance gathered within the "walls of the city-to-be", there can be no growth, because no order. Therefore every first phase of organic growth requires the absolute subservience of the chaotic elements to a ruling principle of organization and form. This principle is Saturn, the Autocrat. But this autocratic rule is benevolent and compassionate, because it is necessary; moreover, because acting from within, as instinct, it is not challenged; there being no principle of individual selfhood to challenge or to rebel against it.

Men of the Golden Age, generally speaking, are not individuals. They constitute a crowd, soon becoming a tribe by inter-marriage "within the pale". The tribal law is the law of Saturn. It is the law of the Father-God (or tribal God), who is a celestial and mythological transposition of the Great Ancestor of the tribe. This law is instinct. It is bred into the new generations as soon as the tribal unit is established within its "land of destiny", within the "sacred precincts" of its Holy Land.

The god of the Jewish people was the last planetary manifestation of the Father-Saturn idea; and the Old Testament is the symbolical story of the birth of a race, a birth made more difficult because it occurred not during the physical Golden Age of mankind, but in preparation for another type of era—the universalistic psycho-mental Age of which Christ is the initial symbol. The tragedy of the Jewish race consists in this, that it refused to recognize the dim beginnings of this new Age, and that it clung to the Saturn-ideal, to the law of Saturn —the law of form and of particular selfhood. At this time of the earth's evolution such a law *has to* operate at the psycho-mental level, where it enhances both intellectual brilliancy and the crystallizing power of Saturnian feelings and concepts.

At the psycho-mental level Saturn is the power of logical thinking through which the psycho-mental organism of man acquires a relatively permanent form: a spiritual skeleton. Real individual selfhood depends upon such a "skeleton". What occurred in the far distant past of mankind when, according to occult traditions, men acquired solid bones and began to operate as ever so little self-conscious beings on the physical plane, has been occurring at the higher psycho-mental level since the time of Gautama the Buddha, and particularly since the Greek period. Mankind has been learning intellectual logic, objective thinking and structural ideation to the exclusion of almost everything else, in Europe, and this focalization has given to the Western world its peculiar characteristics. The struggle between Persia and Greece was a struggle between Jupiter and Saturn. Magianism and Greek intellectualism are the two forces which underlie the entire development of European civilization. Ritualistic Christianity derives from the former; the Universities from the latter.

Saturn is the logician; because logic forces us to think objectively—to think *straight*. Logic sets up a type of thinking based on unanimously accepted processes of thought. It therefore provides a foundation necessary for the next stage of human development. Nevertheless, as its rule becomes tyrannical it must be overcome. Thus when the period of the physical-instinctual domination of the Saturn-principle has run its natural course, the complementary and compensating Jupiter-principle begins to wax in strength. Men begin to look "beyond the pale"; they begin to yearn for the open spaces. They begin to break the law of their tribal nature—because another urge is born within them. The urge to expand; to come in contact with other races, other horizons; to assimilate new materials, and to become broad and fluidic—such a Jupiterian urge slowly increases in power. Then the "confusion of castes" becomes a fact. Purity and innocence die with the Golden Age.

Then Saturn, the once compassionate and benevolent formator and fecundator of chaos, begins to take an altogether different meaning. Where men find themselves bound into an air-tight, age-old tradition, the law of Saturn becomes the enemy of progress. Saturn becomes Satan, in one of his aspects, as the symbol of racial pride. Yet transgressions against the law of Saturn cannot be ignored, as long as humanity still lives within the larger cycle, of which the Golden Age was the first phase. Saturn becomes known as fate. Man, as an individual, tries to turn his back against the tribal law and the passions generated by blood-relationship in all its aspects—which include sex, jealousy, greed, etc. As he does that, he begins to raise himself to the station of the "second birth", to shift gears, to give up self-focalization at the physiological level. But before he completely refocalizes his energies and his consciousness at the psycho-mental level of true individual selfhood, the old physiological appetites haunt him—no longer as pure and innocent instincts, but as mentalized cravings. They take a fateful, perhaps sinister meaning. Saturn avenges himself. He becomes the tester, the "Dweller at the Threshold"; the symbol of the old, symbol of utter weariness of soul and body. And this is true at any level, even at those heights when, as occultists say, the body of individual selfhood—the "causal body"—has to be given up.

. . . Until the time when the individual, completely focalized at the higher level, becomes a *seed-being*. As such, he arises, at the last stage of the cycle—vast or small—as this cycle's ultimate fruition. And all together, these "seed-beings" gather as the vast collective Seed of the entire cycle; as that protected grouping of specialized cells whose destiny it is to bear witness to eternal life, even during the long fall and winter. Out of this Seed new life will be born; a new Fatherhood, to project into being a new race. And upon the life of such seed-men Saturn once more holds sway; a glorified Saturn, not less severe and not less compassionate; a Saturn who is a poem of formative light. Of him it can be said that his symbol is the perfectly cut diamond: pure geometrical splendor, supremely formed radiance.

Jupiter:
Organizer of Functions

THE REAL SIGNIFICANCE OF THE GREAT ASTROLOGICAL SYMBOL, Jupiter, will be fathomed by those who understand the deepest and most universal implications contained in the terms: *organic function*. The idea of "function" is closely related to ideas of unfoldment, of development and of growth. Even when used in algebra, the word conveys these same dynamic meanings. Always, function stands as the opposite, but even more as the complement, of the concept of structure. Structure refers to Saturn; function to Jupiter. The former is static and relatively permanent; the latter, dynamic and unfolding. The contents of the structure are symbolized astrologically by the Moon; the substance of the function, by Mercury.

Jupiter complements Saturn. Function, in order to be organic, must be contained within and related to structure. Thus Jupiter cannot be understood apart from Saturn. To attempt to do so, as the astrologer often does, is to miss the central point in an interpretation of the Jupiter factor. One may say, loosely speaking, that function determines form; but here the term "function" is misapplied. Purpose, rather, is what determines form; and form in turn determines function. Purpose is the Sun—or rather "The Heart of the Sun"; form, Saturn; function, Jupiter.

It is the solar purpose which initiates the cycle of manifestation. Before there is systolic and diastolic motion of the heart, there is a solar outpouring of light and a stirring up of the lunar "Waters". It is the solar Will which emanates and projects the purpose of the organism-to-be, in answer to a cosmic need conditioned by a past yet unfulfilled. This purpose becomes a pattern of organization in operation through and as Saturn, lord of form and structure, lord of bones.

Within that structure, which at first is only a "magic circle" isolating a portion of space and of substance as the field for future development, Jupiter, the organizer of functions, begins to operate. But there can be no organic function, no organism indeed, unless there is first of all a "magic circle", a wall or boundary line, to separate the within from the without. Jupiter—in his first and basic role—can only operate in the within. His work is to organize the substance within the pale, "the faithful"; to keep it coherent, harmonic and glorying in its differences from all that is outside. Thus, in terms of historical development, Jupiter, the High-Priest of the tribal religion, acts within the structure set by Saturn, the Great Ancestor and Leader, the conqueror of the tribal "sacred land".

Organic function means therefore unfoldment within the boundaries or structure of the life-unit: unfoldment of the purpose willed by the Sun. To work out this solar purpose, Saturn projects a structure; Jupiter then begins to *differentiate* the chaotic materials contained within the Saturnian framework. He gives to each unit of substance its most congenial task, the task which answers best to its need for redemption. As he thus builds a "hierarchy of functions" from the most central to the peripheral units, Jupiter is often called the Hierarch. As he sets a schedule of operation and oversees the work of the many departments, he is also organizer, overseer—and efficiency expert. Finally, in order to be sure that the protective walls of the organism do not give in, and later, that whatever the outer world can contribute to the within may be properly accepted, and the refuse of organic activity may be evacuated, Jupiter is made ruler of the walls and of the gates— of the skin and of the senses.

This work of "organic differentiation" transforms the inchoate chemical elements—which, in the beginning, filled the walled-in space of the organism-to-be—into cells having varied and well-determined functions in terms of the total operation of the organism as a whole. In this work, Jupiter—as always— operates in association with Saturn. Both constitute the *imaging power* of the solar system, the central will of which is the Sun. Solar will transforms itself into the Saturn-Jupiter imagination. The spiritual Monad—the "Heart of the Sun"—operates through the formative, differentiating and cohesive agencies of Saturn-Jupiter, the Twin-builders of the organic whole. The raw materials they work with are symbolized by the Moon —the unorganized crowd, the public as an inchoate mass, the lymph of the body (mostly sea-water, and therefore still subject to the lunar tidal rhythm).

Organic differentiation of itself would not lead to proper organic functioning. Cells, and groups of cells as organs, must be given well-defined works to perform; but these varied types of work must be closely inter-related. The sense of the unity of the organic whole must be ever patent and absolutely compelling to every single cell and organ—lest these units become too separative and self-centered, and thus turn into cancerous formations. This "sense of unity" is *religion*: that which, etymologically speaking, "binds back" the cells to the constant realization of the unity of the whole.

Jupiter is the master of religion; and he makes of Saturn the Great Ancestor, and of the Law of Saturn (the Law of Manu of the Hindus, the Mosaic Law of the Jews, the Bible of the Protestants) a God to be worshipped by every cell within the pale of the organic whole. Tribal religion is always twofold. It is Jupiterian, as faith in a beneficent God, the All-Father; it is Saturnian, as an observance of set and formal life-regulations and rituals derived from the Law of Saturn. In the universalistic religions which have been slowly superseding the tribal religions, since the great planetary turning-point of the Sixth Century B.C.—when Gautama the Buddha lived and taught—the tribal law of Saturn has become transformed into an *ethical law* which applies mainly to the individual. Thus Christian ethics superseded the Mosaic law, just as Buddhistic ethics and codes superseded the complex rituals of Hinduism.

The transformation, however, not only failed to affect the Jewish race and the Hindus; it even failed to remain true to its own spirit, both in Christianity and in Buddhism; and the Law of Saturn reappeared in other forms, both in the Catholic and Protestant churches, as well as in the Buddhistic churches. It took form also in medieval "ceremonial magic". Truly, the Jupiter-Saturn Twins cannot be separated, and the inertia of Saturn always tries to pull back to old forms and to old techniques the Jupiterian flights toward the beyond and the vaster wholeness.

Indeed, there are periods of sharp, crucial conflict between the Twins. These are the great crises of life, the great transitions between the several levels of being and of consciousness. These crises are caused by *changes of solar will*. A solar purpose having been worked out, a lunar need having been fulfilled—the two things are always inter-related—then a new purpose is projected by the solar will in answer to a new and deeper lunar need.

Such a process does not take place all at once. First the realization that the purpose has been potentially worked out comes to the Sun at the symbolical Full Moon; then the feeling that a need has been fulfilled is felt by the Moon, at the New Moon—even more accurately at a typical solar eclipse. As this occurs the solar rays release from the innermost core of the obscuring Moon a new need: an ancient and forgotten unfulfillment or failure is projected into active being. The new cycle will be devoted to the fulfillment of this new need for redemption, to the neutralization of the ancient *karma*.

The relative position of Jupiter to Saturn then conveys to

the spiritual Interpreter an idea of how the new cycle will unfold. If Jupiter and Saturn are in conjunction, then an entirely new and virgin start is possible. Life is brimming full with potentialities, unburdened by memories of the past. If they are in opposition—the first period of the cycle will be much obscured by the unconscious memory, by the *karma* of the past; then quite suddenly the tide will turn and the veil will be lifted. Life will seem to bloom on a new continent. If Jupiter and Saturn are in square (90°), the new cycle will see many trials and many tests. It will be a sharp, perhaps brief cycle of readjustment and self-transmutation. There will be strain and forced soul-activity: a purgation of the spiritual organism. A trine aspect between the two planets (120°) will show the unfolding of a new vision and the revelation of solar purpose; a sextile aspect (60°), the practical application of purpose through harmonious cooperation between "form" and "function".

From the point of view of individual selfhood and destiny, the relationship between Jupiter and Saturn is the basic factor. Great crises of transition occur when the Twins are in square formation. The soul is being released from the dominion of Saturn, and the Jupiterian urge breaks open the gates, or tears through all walls. The without is being absorbed by the within, or else the "I" is being lost into the chaotic immensities of the "not-I". When these things happen we must look to the "messengers of the beyond" (Uranus—Neptune—Pluto) for indications as to what is actually taking place. If the walls of the Saturnian ego collapse, the amorphous overcomes the formed. Man is lost in the "astral sea", in its phantasms and its deceptions. But where the walls of consciousness are strong, the Jupiterian urge opens the gates, that caravans loaded with Uranian gifts from the farther lands may enter. Slowly, steadily—through commerce, through the growth of knowledge and of a love that ignores boundaries—the conscious self expands and grows richer and more mellow with wisdom.

Then Jupiter is the beneficent power of expansion—but

only if balanced by the steady restraint of the Law of Saturn. This Law is the law of caste and tribal purity, at one level. It is the law of logic and of intellectual honesty, at another; the law of spiritual integrity, at still another. On the other hand, Jupiter, as he marshals his forces *against* Saturn's crystallizing inertia and pride, becomes the "Soul": that which compensates for intellectual limitations and the hard shells of logic and routine reactions, that which reaches the consciousness through feelings, through love, through religious yearnings and the thirst for universal truths unbounded by creeds and authority. In such a mode of action, Jupiter is seen in union with Venus and the Moon. Jupiter gives warmth to the Moon's waters which have been sweetened by the Venusian mellowness, fruitage of experience and of love. Through Jupiter the most distant planets (beyond Saturn) operate in answer to the will that reaches them directly from the "Heart of the Sun".

Jupiter becomes thus the pathway of liberation: the spiritual *guru*—the mediator between the solar will and the blind Saturn, now seen as "devourer of his own children"—as was shown in the Greek myth. The help of this Jupiterian *guru* (or spiritual Teacher and Guide) is needed to offset the power of Saturn. Through the *guru* all that is beyond the walls of the ego, all that is universal, is focused as through a lens. The guru is universal Space focused into a Person become absolutely transparent to light and to solar purpose: a lens indeed. He is the dispenser of spiritual food. He conveys safely to the unsteady ego the essence of the dangerously vast beyond.

However, he who needs the help of a personalized guru will receive the solar will colored by the quality, tone, or coloring of the *guru's* former path or Ray of development. For this must be said: neither Jupiter nor Saturn reaches to the "Heart of the Sun", abode of whiteness and of wholeness. Only the great "messengers of the beyond"—Uranus, Neptune and Pluto—know the "Heart of the Sun". Only the infinitely far knows the infinitely near. This is the truth conveyed dimly by the fact that, from the Earth taken as a pivot, the outer planets Mars, Jupiter and Saturn are seen to balance respectively the inner planets Venus, Mercury and "Vulcan" (or rather the photosphere of the Sun). Only the three outermost planets beyond Saturn's orbit find their spiritual counterparts in the "Heart of the Sun"—the triune "Heart" that is creator, preserver and regenerator.

Jupiter operates always and only in relation to Saturn: this is one of the greatest of all life-truths, symbolically expressed. It operates *with* Saturn within the boundaries set by Saturn. It operates also *against* Saturn, compensating the latter's exclusiveness and crystallizing logic; but even then, Jupiter's action is merely producing the exact reverse of Saturn's operation. He compensates for Saturn. He neutralizes Saturn. Yet his power is always conditioned by his polar opposite, Saturn. The *guru's* guidance and teaching are conditioned by the pupil's limitations. The former impersonates what the latter fails to see. Likewise, racially speaking, the great Artist or Seer brings to the race what the race lacks.

Such is the great law of psychic harmonization, the "law of compensation" so clearly expressed by the old Chinese wise men, and today by Jung. He who understands this law understands indeed. But such an understanding must ever be renewed by fresh experience, for intellectual knowledge ever formalizes and crystallizes it—and so Jupiter must operate over and over again, always adjusting his action to the new need of the personality.

This is true of the *guru.* It may be true of the mate, at the spiritual or psycho-mental level, when the realm symbolized by the dualism of Mars and Venus is transcended: thus the idea, so basely materialized most of the time, of "Soul-mates"— which complements and in some cases may supplant the *"guru-chela"* relationship. The latter refers to vertical alignment (meridian); the former, to horizontal polarization (horizon). In the positive *"guru-chela"* relationship the pure ideal of spiritual Son-ship operates—in the negative aspect of it, a sense of devotional self-surrender which negates true individual development. In the positive "Soul-mates" relationship Consciousness is the goal, rather than happiness or the reconstitution of the primordial Egg before polarization—the negative aspect, leading to the search for sexual *Nirvana*.

At a time when the individual is attempting to reach beyond the tribal order and its rigid psychic and social walls, Jupiter is called the "Greater Fortune". He vitalizes the quest for the Grail, or that other quest for gold and riches which opens to the individual all roads and all seas, which makes him absorb—or lose himself into—the vastness of an ever greater social or planetary whole. Thus he is the expansive power of wealth, of fortune—that which, but too often, makes man reach greedily beyond his capacity for assimilation and digestion. He desires the greater whole—and loses his own "I", blurred by the frantic reaching out. He over-eats, be it physical or psychical food. He becomes fat, distorting his own form, rounding out his belly in an inglorious attempt to reach the perfect form of wholeness, the sphere!

Jupiter makes the little self yearn for participation as a cell in the cosmic organism of the greater Self. Yet through over-confidence and an exaggeration of self-importance, often turning into paranoia, he sacrifices the integrity of individual selfhood to a "God" who is often but a mirage or a fraud. Even compassion, the yearning to die for the whole of mankind, is ordinarily a Jupiterian escape from a sour Saturn and its oppressive influence. Jupiter is still bound to the lunar realm and to the solar radiation. He is still working in reaction to the past. And to react against slavery does not mean freedom. To hate hatred is not—love; and to yearn for the greater Whole may be shirking the immediate task of fulfilling one's own individual destiny.

Beyond Jupiter and Saturn stand Uranus and Neptune; and through them the promise of a New Order. But none may reach the actuality thereof who has not fulfilled his own Moon, who has not learnt the lesson of form and of functional organization—and that of Martian initiative and creativeness. Let no one dreaming of Jupiterian hierarchy and expansion forget that, first and last, there must be form. Wherever there is Moon, there must be Saturn.

Nevertheless, form must always be seen from two points of view: from the inside and from the outside. Let us consider a bronze statue as it emerges out of the plaster cast which envelops it. That cast had an inward form; it was formed space. Into that space the bronze was poured, and only as the cast is removed is the *outward* form revealed: which is formed substance. Inward form is Saturnian; it is a mold or matrix; the shape of a hollow. Outward form is Jupiterian; it is substance ready to function and reveal a message—reflecting light. In this illustration, the original clay figure fashioned by the sculptor represents the solar archetype.

Likewise, man's outer being is Saturnian. The body, however final and of itself significant it seems to our superficial vision, is but a plaster cast. Through Jupiter, soul-substance is poured into it and ultimately man shines in his "glorious body", in his Christ-body, which is substantial light vibrant with consciousness and significance. The Saturnian mold must be dissolved—rather than broken up—before the golden substance is revealed in the perfection of its form. This substance is generated constantly by Jupiter during a noble life; by our aspirations, our faith, our participation in the work of the world. Thus Jupiter is the point of emanation of Soul. It fills the limitations of Saturn until, at the date of fulfillment, the binding power of Saturn is no longer necessary—because the Jupiterian Soul-flow has become solidified and formed. Then the solar Purpose shines, revealed in the statue; made substantial and permanent; made corporeal. Spirit has become Soul —Soul that is an organism of spiritual substance. Man is fulfilled.

Mercury:
Weaver of the Threads of Life

THE SUN SETS THE PURPOSE AND RELEASES THE WILL-TO-BE that is to energize the new life-cycle in answer to the need once more to integrate spirit and matter, the One and the Many. The Moon arouses and gathers the inchoate substance left over from the past cycle, within the boundaries and the structural pattern provided by Saturn. And Jupiter directs, inspires, leads into paths of ordered development and harmonious functioning the substance that answered the Moon call and became "set apart" within the Saturnian walls. This substance is a crowd of unrelated units of matter. It is true that all these units had been linked in the far distant past. But they have now forgotten this fact. They have lost the memory of their inter-relationship—and this loss of memory is the very foundation of the state of chaos, the state of absolute materiality and separateness.

Now that a new life-cycle has begun, a new opportunity is given to the scattered units of matter to learn once more the great lesson of relationship. This lesson can only be learned progressively, step by step. And this is the reason why there needs must be Saturnian boundaries. A *limited* number of units of a *particular* type are "set apart"; and the lesson of relationship is to be learnt by these units among themselves. The lesson could not be learnt well if new and strange units were constantly being met. This constant incoming of unfamiliar units would disturb the establishment of deep and permanent relationships between the units constituting the original group. It would create confusion, dissipation of the energy of relationship, a break-down of the growing sense of unity in the group. Therefore the Law of Saturn must establish a strong barrier between the "Elect" who are within the pale—and the "barbarians" who stand outside of the pale.

The "Elect" thus isolated and left to themselves are compelled to become closely inter-connected, inter-bred, inter-woven. This inter-weaving produces "patterns of relationship" which in their totality constitute the tribal Soul, the tribal Culture, the tribal Tradition. And this Tradition is nothing but the race's memory: the memory of the deeds accomplished together, of the images perceived together, of the feelings born from constant interaction and interdependence. The many beings inter-related within the definite structure of the Saturnian Law come to realize that they "belong together"; that they are multiple aspects of one total Reality which is the tribal Whole.

This Whole finds its symbolical representation in the tribal or national God, in the Church, in the King-Hierophant who becomes the "Center of the Covenant", the "Son of Heaven" —Heaven here meaning the archetypal pattern of relationship which is finally perceived as the spiritual reality of the tribal Whole. The weaver of this pattern of relationship is, in astrological symbolism, Mercury.

Here we should at once clarify our thoughts as to the difference existing between Saturn's *structural frame-work* and Mercury's *pattern of relationship*. The former is—as far as the men of the tribal group can see or experience—imposed *from without* by the Great Ancestor or First Ruler. This beneficent God of the Golden Age (Saturn) must always appear to the tribesmen as belonging to a level of being far transcendent. He was indeed a God incarnate on earth; and they are his seed. Because of this, they are "noble men", true Aryans (Arya means "noble"), true "Celestials", truly the Elect.

Likewise, the Law of Saturn is God-given. It is a direct Revelation from Heaven—that is, it is a projection of the Archetype, of the Plan which God had for his most beloved children, a Plan which He moreover, in His great love, traced in the skies through the ordered movements of the celestial bodies, so that the Wisest among these children could constantly witness His decrees. Even in modern America, the Constitution is endowed with an almost similar meaning. Even more so was the Law of Manu in India—the Koran in Islam—the Bible in the orthodox Protestant Churches, worshipped as a Divine Law imposed (benevolently imposed) from the outside by the Great Ancestor or Son of God.

On the contrary, the "pattern of relationship" woven by Mercury, the Master-Worker, is growing from the inside, as the result of the ever more complex and more complete interrelating, commingling, commerging of the many cells constituting the tribal Whole or national organism. This pattern must evidently *conform* to the general structure determined by the Law of Saturn; yet within this framework it may grow with at least relative freedom.

In terms of physiology, Saturn represents the skeleton—truly a frame-work which is generic, depending upon the form of the species, and thus, we might say, imposed from above. Mercury refers to the nervous system, which follows the generic bony structure, yet is susceptible of quite wide individual variation, as it is conditioned by the growth of the organism as a whole. It is in a condition of emergent evolution; and the result of this emergent evolution is individual consciousness. Individual consciousness is to the physiological organism what culture and tradition are to the racial Whole. It is an ever accruing synthesis of the vast number of relations which constantly integrate the myriads of cells into a personality.

The nervous system is the objective form assumed by the totality of inter-connections established within the living organism as every cell relates itself, directly or indirectly, to every other cell. It is therefore both the symbol of organic interrelationship and the actual product of such a constant interweaving of cellular behavior. The nervous system grows more complex as the organic commerce between cells increases in activity, in speed, in significance. And the same is true as we consider the national Whole. Roads, canals, railways, telegraph and telephone lines, buses, and finally radio broadcasts, constitute the nervous system of this national organism. They are all lines of communication, growing out of men's desire to associate, to travel, to become related through commerce and through all cultural and social activities. Truly, they are conditioned by the geographical structure of the land (skeleton); yet man succeeds in overcoming natural obstacles as his engineering ability develops. Likewise, in the perfected physiological organism, the nervous system covers the whole organism, and lines of organic communication subtler than the nerves may develop; lines which are no longer limited by the Saturnian frame-work—just as radio communication is not limited by the geographical lay-out of the land.

This progressive liberation of Mercury from Saturn, of lines of communication from the structural frame-work of the organic Whole, occurs when the authority of Saturn becomes challenged by Uranus and the most distant planets; in other words, when world-civilization begins to supersede geographical and racial cultures. As this occurs, Jupiter, who had been operative under the Law of Saturn, changes his rhythm. Then tribal religion is superseded by universal religion. Jupiter becomes the truly expansive power which sends men upon the quest for a universal—and at the same time a "personal" because immanent—God; or else upon the quest for gold, wealth, and markets ever expanding. Jupiter, the tribal High Priest, becomes then the *conquistador* and the imperialist, the colonizer and builder of empire. Mercury follows the lead, for he weaves patterns of relationship as Jupiter bids him do so.

Jupiter is first the power of organization of functions; then the power of expansion and assimilation. Therefore Mercury, being the servant or messenger of Jupiter, is first the power of organic inter-relationship, which means the power to receive impressions or sensations and to transmit them through the entire organism by means of the afferent and efferent nerves. At a later stage of evolution, Mercury becomes the power of thought-association and generalization; the substance of the activity of the mind. Through the agency of the mind, man expands his range of activity. He overcomes the physiological Law of Saturn and weaves patterns that link him with the greater Whole—with the Planetary Being.

When such a linking has become definite and deliberate enough, the individual man finds himself reborn at a higher level of selfhood—the psycho-mental level. He experiences a new "Golden Age". He becomes subject to the law of the *planetary* Saturn, which transcends his own personal Saturn as much as the complete metabolism of the whole human organism transcends the chemical reactions of one single cell. But before this transfer of level can become a *reality*, and not a mere intellectual concept, man must pass through the forbidding gates of Uranus, Neptune and Pluto. He must be "initiated" . . .

In Tibetan astrology, Mercury (*Lhagpa*) is symbolized by a "Hand". In Blavatsky's *Voice of the Silence* it is written: "Behold the fiery aura of the 'Hand' of *Lhagpa* extended in protecting love over the heads of his ascetics". This symbolism will be easily understood if one considers the fact that Mercury has dominion over the zodiacal sign Gemini, which refers to the lung region and to the brachial plexus controlling arms and hands. But the symbolism of the Hand goes much deeper. It is the Hand which gives birth to all culture, because it is through the Hand that the forces of super-personal and social integration operate. The five-fingered Hand and the Mind-ego symbolized by the five-pointed star are completely connected. In a sense, the latter is Jupiter and the former Mercury.

This is so, at least as long as mental and cultural processes in man are controlled by the power of tribal or group integration—and thus are not individual and conscious as much as collective and unconscious manifestations. Archaic man used his hands in order to exteriorize the dictates of the tribal Spirit and of his instincts; not as a means to manifest the powers of conscious intelligence and personality. Workmen and artisans of the ancient past created under the inspiration of a religious faith and of traditions based on occult-magical realizations. Their hands were indeed guided by Jupiter. Their hands were moved by the influx of "Primordial Images" through the gates of the solar plexus; not by the formal or rational concepts issued from the brain. The same is true even today of most types of "automatic writing".

As man begins to function as an individual at the psycho-mental level, Mercury operates thenceforth on two planes. Behind the Hand stands the rational mind—until this mind becomes so freed from the bodily organism that it evolves as it were its own Hand. Thus we hear of the power that Yogis or Adepts possess of moulding "astral matter" as if by a mental Hand. The mind, energized by the will, can control other minds, just as men, during the period of muscular power, subjugated others by the might of their hands. The Hand at the end of a wand has always been a symbol of royal power. It is Mercury acting as the visible symbol of Jupiter. Eventually Mercury becomes linked to Pluto. He becomes thus the revolutionary mind of the Civilizer or of the Initiator, glowing with the fire of cosmic visions revealed by Uranus.

Thus Mercury can be seen operating at various levels. The patterns of relationship he weaves at first are framed in by the structure of the loom of the body. The shuttle goes to and fro within the Saturnian boundaries. And lo and behold! a nervous system is born. If only we could read the wondrous hieroglyphs made by the myriads of nerves and nerve currents as they cross each other and tie themselves in knots which become power-stations and centers of awareness and instinctual, then conscious, response! If, above all, we had ways to decipher the magical patterns traced by the life-force within the brain, as the signals from the entire organism intertwist and pursue their wondrous courses hidden to us by the empty word "memory"!

Yet even this amazing tapestry woven by Mercury with the physiological threads of our nerves, is—we are told—only the material representation of an even subtler Work. And if we listen to the teachings of certain types of yoga, especially *Kundalini Yoga*, we begin to see that, behind or within the physical nerves, currents of energies can be perceived to which the Hindu gave the name "*Nadi*". These currents deal with what have been called "etheric" or "astral" energies; and much confusion has arisen in the minds of students of Oriental lore as to the meaning thereof.

It might clarify the matter to say that with these *Nadi* we deal with the essential Mercury realm: that is, the realm of pure organic relationship or "operative Wholeness". These mysterious energies constitute in their totality the *force-aspect* of the human organism; while the physical cells, organs and nerves constitute its *matter-aspect*. Force or energy is the product of relationship. Lack of relation is a symbol of impotency. The absolutely unrelated unit is the symbol of absolute powerlessness. This is the reason why the so-called "Black Magician", he who emphasizes separateness and denies love, is necessarily defeated in the end; because he is essentially powerless. And because he is essentially powerless he must make a desperate show of outer power. The only relationship he can accept is that of hunter to prey. He must be the hunter. He must kill everlastingly, and absorb the vital power of his victims—because he is himself powerless and utterly afraid. He is compelled to kill—or he must give in and be killed.

In this planetary pair, Jupiter and Mercury, great depths

of significance can be fathomed. But in order to do this we must forget the ordinary concept of Jupiter as the Greater Fortune. Jupiter can be also the ruthless autocrat, the high-priest crystallized in dogma, the glutton who lives but to grow fat, the man drunken with pride. And Mercury always becomes polarized by the Jupiter function—which in turn always operates together with Saturn.

Saturn "sets apart" and isolates. Jupiter-Mercury relates. But this relatedness operates naturally *within* the Saturnian boundaries. As it operates fully, man reaches fulfillment and individual perfection. Physiological perfection is the result of a highly evolved nervous system through which all biological functions are perfectly integrated. Spiritual perfection occurs when the spiritual potencies latent in every cell of the organism are gathered together along the spiritual axis of the body —the spine—and through a process of intense and total synthesis are integrated in the brain—or rather in the Solar Center in the Head, the *Sahasrara chakra* of the Hindus.

Astrologically speaking, this process refers mostly to the mysterious cycle, of over eleven years' duration, which links Saturn and the solar photosphere. It is the sun-spot cycle of modern science. In the human organism it refers to the linking of the Saturn-center at the base of the spine to the "thousand-petalled Lotus" on the top of the head, which is the human photosphere and thus has been symbolized in all times as a halo around the heads of saints and buddhas.

But before this ultimate linking up of the lowest and the most high can be accomplished, and before the resulting ecstasy or spiritual bliss can be attained by the individual, it is necessary that the Jupiter-Mercury function should operate most fully. Such an operation is symbolized, in mythology, by the caduceus of Mercury. He who understands thoroughly the various meanings of this important symbol grasps some of the deepest secrets of organic being.

The central rod of the caduceus and the two intertwining serpents refer to the process of synthesis by which the spiritual potencies latent in every cell are gathered around the spinal axis (the central rod) and led up to the head. The entire symbol is one of centralized and rhythmic relationship. It is the hieroglyph of Mercury, the Master-Weaver in action. The weaving Hands go to and fro; and the tapestry of perfected being emerges, from which Man may learn the significance of his own being and of universal life.

Thus Mercury is the giver of understanding and the revealer of significance. Within the realm of Saturn there is nothing that Mercury may not know; for he connects every point of the realm and unifies the whole, so that the Golden Flower of significance may blossom forth, whose roots are in Saturn.

Then the time comes when the realm of Saturn is transcended. Uranus becomes active and a period of transition begins, during which the entire organism is being repolarized at a higher level. This repolarization is harmonious—relatively speaking—if the Saturn period has come harmoniously to maturation and fulfillment. It involves tragedy in proportion as there has been disharmony and lack of fulfillment in the Saturn realm; especially if the Law of Saturn has become a hard shell stifling the life-force. For if this has happened Jupiter has had to turn to the opposite extreme and counteract Saturnian selfishness or formalism with devotionalism and religious fanaticism. The unity of the Whole—be it an individual or a national and cultural whole—has thus been broken. Thus Mercury, symbol of this unity in operation, is cut in twain. The individual is no longer "of one mind". He is rent by mental conflicts.

Then the transcendent inspirations and intuitions of Uranus are compelled to act discordantly. They have to fight against the Saturnian shells. They are moreover twisted and perverted by a discordant Mercury; and as well by a Jupiter who then acts in the capacity of the ruthless *conquistador* and the greedy imperialist or capitalist. Also, as this occurs, the Mars-Venus function becomes uncontrolled and unbalanced. Emotions run riot. Then Neptune must pour his strong acid in order to dissolve the frantic egoic will as well as the feudal fortified castles of the soul. And Pluto becomes the tribunal of implacable judgment, the ruthless cathartic that leaves the organism temporarily cleansed perhaps, yet exhausted and little wiser to face the future.

Mercury is the Hand that weaves the many patterns of the living. It is a servant; at times, a treacherous one. It is a synthesizing agency, which has little to say as to what it synthetizes. It relates everything there is. It co-ordinates. It fashions. It combines the quintessence of all relationships, of all life-functions. It is the Master-Workman, the Master of Works.

Mars:
He-Who-Goes-Forth

MARS IS THE FIRST GESTURE OF BEING; THE FIRST MOVEMENT of organic life away from its own center of bodily equilibrium. It is the blind groping toward an outside something which might enhance and add to this equilibrium. And finally it is the urge to propagate, to reproduce the inherent character of the organic whole.

To move away, to go toward, to reproduce—such are the three great life-operations which Mars symbolizes. Each one is a poem of living which often turns into drama or tragedy. And Mars is the eternal Actor who never tires of going forth —away from the known, toward and into the unknown; the Warrior who ever leads the battle of existence and tends to equalize the inner and the outer pressures of life—until the dissolving power of Neptune does away with the partition separating the outer from the inner, and the difference between I and Not-I temporarily vanishes. Then Mars abdicates and, solemnly or wearily, delivers his sword to Pluto, the Conqueror and the Agent of a Greater Whole.

To move away. Why should organic life tend to move away from its bodily equilibrium? Because to live organically is to generate excess energy; and the loss of energy in passive bodily radiation—such as heat radiation—does not ordinarily suffice to compensate for the increase of potential. The interior pressure of the life-force becomes unbearable, and a definite release is needed. Mars conditions all mechanisms of release of energy from an organic whole that has become surcharged with life-power.

The reason for the increase in organic potential is due essentially to three factors, symbolized by the celestial bodies within the orbit of the Earth. Each of them represents a definite type of relationship—and all power comes from relationship. Every type of energy is born of a corresponding type of relationship established and fulfilled. The greater the fulfillment, the greater the energy generated.

First of all is the Sun and the primordial Will to manifest, which the magic command "Let there be light" sets in operation. This Will is in itself the expression of the awareness of a cosmic need. The One, become aware of the chaotic and scattered Many, wills to be related to them; and this relation is Light—the first type of energy. We now know the source of this Light under the name of "solar photosphere"—the outer Sun. But at the dawn of cosmic manifestation the power that draws this Light out of the "Heart of the Sun", out of the mystic Darkness that antedates all beginnings, is Mars: the great god Eros, *Kama-deva*, the original Rudra—He who tears the Dark and leads forth the Light.

Today Mars is an exile. In Tibetan astrology he is known as *Migmar* and his symbol is the "Eye"—because it is the Eye which calls forth the Light, in a symbology wherein all powers of Nature are created to serve the purpose of Consciousness. Mars is an exile, in the sense that He who was the First-born of all the gods must now fulfill his eternal function of releaser of energy at a more material level. As Consciousness is now centered, for us, on the Earth—then Mars must take his place outside of the Earth's orbit; for he is always the "outside One", He-who-leads-outward, He-who-goes-forth.

After the Sun comes Mercury; after the Will to manifest substantially and so to "redeem" the scattered myriads of particles left over in a state of chaos from a previous cosmic cycle, comes the Will to integrate these particles now gathered within the Saturnian boundaries. Then the Jupiter-Mercury function begins, and Mercury weaves the many threads of relationship between cells and organs within the body—and later the psycho-mental nature. As he does so new internal energies are generated. The cup of organic life overflows. The excess of power produced demands to be used—and for what else could it be used, at first, save to enhance and add to the quality of the organic life? "There must be ways of living more abundantly by venturing forth into the unknown, by using the excess energy to bring more life and to increase the size and stature of my organism"—thus says the blindly groping life within; and communications begin to be established with the unknown world outside—through sensations, through reaching out for food, through commerce, through mental projections and intellectual exchange.

Once more Mars leads the way out. The *Conquistador* and Adventurer traces the pathways along which commerce will flow. Who would there be to blaze the trail save the red Pioneer, He-who-goes-forth, who tears the outer Dark to make way for sensations, for all that the organism may perceive and gather to itself in its will to expansion, its will to grow by assimilating the outer?

And here again Mars is fittingly to be seen as the single "Eye" of the earliest evolutionary days, the Eye which visualizes immediate rapports of being, which instinctively perceives the sense of life-situations and leads the organs of action directly to their goals. Mars is then the one-eyed Cyclops of ancient mythology, the Giant whose prototype is to be seen in the constellation Orion. He is the symbol of Desire. However, no longer the compassionate Desire-to-be which led the One to gather the Many to Itself, but now the Desire-to-maintain-oneself and to grow, which is a correlate of the Jupiter-Mercury function. He will experience a further transformation and become the Desire-to-reproduce-oneself, in association with Venus—his polar opposite and his mate.

This Desire-to-reproduce-oneself is merely an extension, at the level of organic life, of the original and monadic Desire-to-be. In fact this latest manifestation is really the most characteristic, because the original Desire of the Solar One to be related to the myriads of material units scattered through space is after all a desire to project His attributes upon those units. It may be a compassionate desire, yet compassion is desire in its noblest aspect—as is also pure spiritual devotion. The compassion which urges the Great Ones to teach and to love the poor stumbling egos of men is still desire. It is the desire to be the All, to leave nothing separate. It is the will to wholeness, all-inclusive, all-encompassing. To this will the scattered units answer, or may answer, by the pure flame of devotional aspiration—the desire to become one with the One.

These desires are great life-movements which lead the unit of consciousness (or the energy thereof) away from its particular center and into identification with the consciousness or being of other, lesser or greater, units. And Mars is always and at every stage the symbol of such life-movements. But when he operates at the level of human personality, problems arise which disturb the purity of his action.

What is usually meant by human love and its passion of desire is a complex movement of the life-energies—an emotion, a moving-out—which acquires its complexity from the fact that mankind is at present in a transitory stage and is functioning half-way between the physiological and the psycho-mental plane, and actually functioning fully on neither one plane nor the other. Thus the strange emotional confusion which obsesses men, has obsessed them more or less since the time of the Greek civilization, and will obsess them until our so-called morals—the result of a confusion between levels of being and behavior—are repolarized, and human nature is understood in its twofold essence and learns to operate polyphonically.

Originally, the male desire for the female was of the nature of the primordial urge to be and to impress upon chaotic and unorganized substance the integrating will of the One. It was not desire in terms of consciousness, but as a flowing out of will from the symbolical Sun to the symbolical Moon. The solar rhythm was thus impressed upon the lunar inchoate substance; and this rhythm was primordially Light—for Light also is a rhythmic vibration which thrills through passive substance and stirs it into an integrating response. Integration is demonstrated as the child, which is a certain amount of female substance integrated by the rhythm of the male power; nay more —which is (originally and essentially) the living symbol of the integration of the woman as a whole.

Thus it has been said that childbirth is for a woman spiritual "initiation"; and all the ancient and mystic processes of Initiation were patterned after the cycles and occurrences of fecundation, gestation and delivery. This was, of course, at a time when spirituality was in no way separated from the physiological level of being, but rather was seen as the supreme vitalization and integration of body and personality; at a time when the term "spirit" was identical with the term "breath", and "soul" was merely the subtle or essential form of the vital energies. Then woman was substance, and man spirit; and their union had all the characteristics of the relationship between spirit and substance. Woman was "initiated" by man, and integrated through motherhood. Motherhood and the care of the home were the culmination of the woman's nature.

A man's life, on the other hand, was divided potentially into two periods. During the first, he acted as a sun, and established his little solar system—his family—in terms of participation in the life of the greater Whole—the village-community or the state. Then, the children being more or less grown up and provided for, the man could begin to live in terms of a transcendental order, which in most countries meant he could then prepare himself for the great "initiation" that is death. In death was his "initiation".

There were cases however which were super-normal. Some young men were prepared from childhood or adulthood to become "initiated" while alive. They had to pass through a process which *at a psychic level* made of them a woman, being "initiated" by a superior Power that entered into them, spiritually possessed and integrated them. In them the "Christ-child" was born. No woman however could become initiated in these psycho-spiritual Mysteries; for woman was seen operating essentially upon the physiological-racial plane.

But things have changed. With the psycho-mental revolution of the Greek times, with the influence of women like the great Aspasia and later Hypatia, woman began her repolarization at the new level of human consciousness. The result has been a psychic, mental and emotional chaos; a mixing-up of planes, the extreme manifestation of which is now everywhere to be seen as homo-sexuality—the confusion of desires.

Such a confusion in its more normal stages may be due to an over-focalization upon the mental plane combined with a weakening of the physiological organism, intellectual values being substituted—yet not entirely so—for physiological ones; or the mind may become so enmeshed in sensational cravings that all sense of rhythm, seasonal and otherwise, is lost, and desire becomes peripheral and cerebralized. More generally still, the ego of man, now vacillating between the physiological and the psycho-mental levels, deprived of basic earth-power or still in the limbo of the unborn, tries to feed upon the sexual energies of the body. Thus the sexual function—which, when known as an initiatory and cosmic process, is seasonal—becomes over-stimulated by the appetite of the ego.

Mars indeed leads then to the path of self-destruction. He that was "initiator" becomes "god of war". The war of the sexes is the most destructive of all wars. It kills bodies through innumerable diseases. It kills the integrity of minds and psyches. Mars, the Fallen Archangel, becomes now the Destroyer; compassion and devotion are his first victims, lust his progeny. Astrologically, he is seen operating as the ruler of Scorpio—

whereas, as releaser of the encompassing Will of the Sun, his "house" is Aries.

Later on, when the cycle of strictly individual selfhood is ended and man becomes truly a universal being, a microcosm, Mars gives up his rulership of Aries to Pluto, god of rebirth. Pluto acts then as the representative of the Galaxy—the Universal Being. The initiation he bestows is again that of death, but a death which is only the death of limitations and is the birthing of a universal consciousness. Such a consciousness has still an individual center, but it can participate in the consciousness of all things. It has a "home", but this "home" can be taken and established everywhere, for it has the power of universal adaptability.

Mars, unless he has turned destructive, is the captain of the Sun's armies. His essential characteristic is to release energies, to lead any and all outgoings. Therefore he is never a servant of the universal order. His work is always with the particular. He deals always with a "one"—be it a spiritual monad, an intellectual ego, or a body-bound personality. When the stage of Plutonian rebirth is reached, Mars must take a protean character. He must adapt himself to many types of energies. But his place is still at the side of the individual, now become a radiant sun. He is at the fountain-head of all activities. He is the unit of action, the cosmic *quantum*. No atom moves in our universe that Mars did not start upon its circuits.

If we see him close to our Earth, watching outside her gates, it is because our consciousness is now centered upon the Earth. Mars is always the next thing to see outside one's gates. Midway between Mars and Venus, there stands one's consciousness, the individual center of being, the conscious ego; because all forms of personalized life are to be found midway between action and reaction. Mars is centrifugal; Venus centripetal. Mars rules all out-goings; Venus all in-comings. All desires return to their sources, charged with experience. Venus is the path of return and the fruitage of all experience. But within the fruit a new seed will be formed. This seed is the earth-child of the Sun. It too will fall in compassion for the soil, for the chemical elements of the soil which it needs to integrate once more into a plant-organism. Mars will see that the seed falls in its own time.

In this function Mars becomes the captain of all earth-bent desires. Wherever a seed falls in desire, there is to be seen the sword of Mars, cutting loose the seed. All desire is sacrifice— or suicide. Within Venus—the fruition—the seed matures. This seed it is which has grown on earth for ages as the Tree of Wisdom. This is the "Great Sacrifice" of archaic traditions, the Being incomparable, whose seed is seen at the close of every great cycle in the persons of Great Spiritual Teachers, Masters of Wisdom.

But all seeds falling upon the ground do not fall in solar encompassment or sacrifice. Many die of immature desire for the soil. Many experiences do not come to maturity. Many a time Venus longs for Mars, before the time has come for the sword to strike. The seed falls, unripe. It will add its substance to the dark humus of decaying leaves. Such a fall is a suicide indeed. Man cannot hold back long enough the pull of the gravitational forces. There is a haste, a rush of energies. Mars does not properly control the release. It may be that his action is unfocalized by Neptune, or made spasmodic by Saturn. Perhaps Jupiter makes him blind with a glamor of expansion; or Uranus intoxicates him with the scent of the beyond. He may be awed by Pluto, confused by his occult Mysteries. In other cases Mars and Venus may be seen in too close an embrace. Where there is no proper spacing between action and reaction, the seed cannot fall. It remains within the drying-up fruit—either useless or to be garnered and kept in granaries for higher purposes than those of physiological nature.

These are all symbols—and every symbol is a seed. Mars must let it fall within the consciousness, there to germinate in the appointed time and to demonstrate its worth and its significance. One can hardly speak of Mars without mentioning Venus, for how could there be a without and no within, or a within and no without? When Mars is releaser of solar Light, Venus is hidden within the "Heart of the Sun". She is then the Seed of a previous cosmic cycle. And it is this Seed-Host of Beings that falls under the urge of the Desire once more to create order out of chaos. We know that fall as Light —the radiation from the mystic "Heart of the Sun".

Each ray of Light therefore carries something of the "Heart of the Sun"—a quality, a rhythm, a principle of formation. Consider this at the physiological level, and we understand the action of the male seed. All fecundation depends upon the interaction of Mars and Venus in terms of the cycles of the Moon; for it is the Moon which, half of the time inside and half of the time outside of the Earth's orbit, provides the place of meeting for Mars and Venus. The lunar orbit—the sub-lunar realm of the ancients—is the womb, the place of meeting.

But humanity develops its psycho-mental nature, attempts to center its energies therein. The individual as an individual may succeed; but what of the couple constituted by an individual man and an individual woman? Will there be fecundation, or mental-spiritual comradeship? Will the place of meeting be within the womb—or outside of the lunar realm? Will a "higher Moon" offer her hollow chamber, will a Pyramid give hospitality to the King's and the Queen's Chambers?

These are all problems, the sharp and often tragic problems of our new humanity. Mars, Venus, the Moon are the symbols of such vital matters of human relationship and of desire; the keys which may open dark rooms within the subconscious, and set the emotional energies of men and women, at last, free.

Venus:
Queen of the Celestial Bees

The nearest to the earth within the earth's orbit, Venus symbolizes the "inward way", while Mars, guardian of the region which lies immediately beyond our planet's orbit, represents the "outward way". Being so close to us, these two planets stand in sharp relief as polar opposites. In the realm which they symbolize, polarity, the basic phenomenon of organic life, is particularly well defined. It is defined in terms of the behavior of the organism as a whole in relation to any and all types of experience. In any thing that lives there must be a reaching out toward experience and a response or reaction to experience. These two basic phases of all life are symbolized respectively by Mars and Venus, at whatever level the life operates.

The Moon provides the psychic energy required for the operation. Circling back and forth as she does between the realm of Mars and the realm of Venus, she feeds, as it were, the consciousness or ego; now in its Martian venturings, then in its Venusian reactions and evaluations. No planet of itself can be rightly considered as a real source of energy. It however gives direction, form and character to the relatively undifferentiated life-energy which streams directly from the Sun, and reflectively from the Moon. The visible Moon is the essential source of energy for the realm of Mars and Venus. Currents of solar radiations, not perceptible by means of our physical senses, energize the activities of the other planetary pairs. As these activities transcend the normal realm of our actual experiences, the "moons" which energize them are not concrete celestial bodies—at least, to us—but are conceived by us merely as cycles of solar activity.*

Our visible Moon, however, as a true satellite, distributes the vital forces of our body and psyche through the peripheral realm of our being; that realm which, surrounding as it does our concrete vehicle of experience—our body—has been called its "astral" matrix. The tides or pulsations which occur within this matrix control the intensity of our attention and interest in experiences; the intensity of our out-goings and home-returnings. The psychologist usually refers to these processes as our affective or emotional nature; or, if with behavioristic leanings, he analyzes the "stimulus-response arc". The theosophist speaks of the "astral body", the "psychic" nature, etc. All these terms, and many others, are various designations for the most primordial life-processes of action and reaction to the outer world. These processes are the very substance of our world of actual experience.

On the other hand, processes such as relate to the Jupiter-Mercury function, or to still more remote phases of our being, are not concerned with "actual" experience, but with concepts, intuitions—factors which are transcendental, because they are not the immediate results of experience. They are derived from experience through an operation which is truly a kind of *alchemical transmutation.* Venus is the symbol of this process of refinement and abstraction, or extraction of essence. It is therefore the gate to the transcendental mind-realms, the path of the Universals: the Alchemist and the Initiator.

These names however refer to heights of consciousness which can never be fully and vitally understood unless the

* Cf. *The Astrology of Personality.* Rudhyar—pp. 302-309

life-processes which they connote are studied in their more ordinary manifestations, and in terms of everyday experience. Thus we should trace the very first mode of operation of Venus in the most primary form of awareness, i.e., in what we called "sensation". A sensation is to be differentiated from a mere nerve-stimulus. A sound-wave strikes the ears; this produces a nerve-stimulus. Something in the outer world disturbs and stimulates a part of our organism. This disturbance is conveyed to the brain, there to be received by a most complex apparatus of perception. The *sensation* of sound is produced in the brain, not in the ears; and this sensation depends not only upon the condition of the ears but also upon that of certain parts of the brain. It depends to some extent upon previous sensations, upon what we may call organic memory, upon the physiological and psychological state of the whole organism at the moment the nerve-stimulus reaches the brain.

The gist of the matter is that sensation is not a simple fact, but the end-result of a process which, without our knowing, is conditioned by our entire organism. There may even be sensations which originate in the brain—witness such phenomena as those of clairaudience and certain types of clairvoyance; sensations, that is, which may not be caused by any physical stimulus, but instead are due to the direct stirring up—in ways as yet mysterious—of the centers of sensation in the brain. These abnormal or supernormal sensations are also the end-results of a long process of synthesis which takes in the whole of the person's memory, psychological even more than physiological. For this reason the clairvoyant's or clairaudient's "seeing" or "hearing" is conditioned by his past mental experiences. This does not mean that he "sees" or "hears" imagined phantasms of his unconscious, but that whatever strikes his brain is not the only factor to be reckoned with—just as the image made upon the retina is not the only factor in the complex phenomenon of ordinary vision. We do not see with our eyes only, but also with the whole of our past experience. The way in which such past experience has been—or has *not* been

—synthetized influences deeply all our sensations. It is actually a part of the sensations themselves.

What is true of sensations is even more evident in the case of emotions—of what the psychologist usually calls *affects*. To the mere sensation of pain corresponds at a more psychological level the emotion of grief. The ego has gone out, as it were, into the outer world with Martian eagerness, stirred by desire. The world hits back; the desire is unsatisfied. Grief is the result: an affect which manifests in, or is the result of, various organic changes (accelerated pulse, disturbed breathing, upset digestive processes, and glandular changes). Grief, despondency, and bitterness, characterize the end-results of a process which began with the Martian outgoing. They constitute physio-psychological modifications of the vital balance of the organism as a whole. Nay more, they are the quintessence or abstract of these modifications.

This word "quintessence" is worth studying, because more than any other perhaps it describes the life-processes symbolized by Venus, the universal and ubiquitous Alchemist. According to alchemical philosophy—be it Chinese or Chaldean or European—the life of the human organism, and in general of nature, is a combination of four principles, humors, temperaments or essences. To this, the modern theosophist adds that the number 4 is the keynote of the cycle of development of our Earth and of our present humanity. It is the number of the base of the pyramid.

The word "Pyramid" comes etymologically from the root "pyr" which signifies "fire". The pyramid is actually a symbol of the alchemical fire which extracts out of the four-fold base of nature the "quintessence"; that is, the fifth essence, or principle. This operation of extraction, and in another sense of abstraction, is that to which all the true types of alchemy refer. It may be considered at the mundane level, at which gold is sought for, or at any higher level. "Gold"—the quintessence—may mean the elixir of long life; or it may be, on the emotional plane, the purest form of love; or again, in the mental realm, the "pearl of significance". Spiritually speaking, it is the "Diamond Body" of the Chinese esotericists, the purest form of being produced by the mystic "circulation of the Light".

It is also the purest form of sensation: viz., the esthetic sensation, the perception and realization of the Beautiful. It is charm—the quintessence of personality, the "It" of the modern generations—always the result of a process of refining, of extraction of the subtle from the gross, *of the spiritual from the material.* Venus represents this process, in its myriads of aspects and modes of operation, at any and all levels, from the lowest to the most divine. The process itself has been symbolized in countless ways. One of the most common symbols for it has been the pearl—that little sphere of beauty and loveliness born of irritation and pain in an ugly, almost formless mollusc of the sea depths. And, let us not forget, Venus-Aphrodite was seen arising from the foam of the sea, with pearls around her neck.

The sea always signifies the collective and undifferentiated universal life. Out of it is born, through rhythmic motion and cyclic growth (the foam of the waves), the individual. Similarly, out of the ocean of everyday experience meaning is generated. The "pearl of significance" is born out of the sufferings, the conflicts, the arguments and doubts which man experiences. Venus is born of the foam and is carried on a shell lined with mother-of-pearl; for significance presupposes dynamism and the churning of the inert sea-substance of our feelings, and as well, the formative power of the mind represented by the inverted and iridescent shell reflecting the glory of the heavens.

The individual arises from the collective and the racial by the same process following which significance arises from sensations, feelings and thoughts, and the abstract arises from the concrete. It is the same alchemical process of extraction of the quintessence, which has also been symbolized quite universally by the honey-making bees. The flower is already the apex of the plant; the coronation of the vegetable life. And in the flower nectar is distilled. This is the earthly alchemy. Out of the darkness of the humus and the soil, through the hidden, persistent, will-full effort of the dark roots, the flower is born. The more powerful the roots, the more numerous the blossoms. The solar Ray, which materialized itself earthward into or as the root, now ascends skyward to produce the flower. The sap becomes nectar—the *ambrosia* of the Greek gods, the *amrita* of Hindu deities. This is the transmutation of the gross into the subtle.

This subtle attracts winged denizens of the upper regions. The bees draw from the chalice-like flowers the nectar, and another alchemical transformation occurs. The nectar of the earth-grown flowers becomes the honey stored in the bee-hive. It is said in occult books that the bees came to the earth from Venus. And it is said also that Beings, whose names are many —Flames, Sons of Mind, Luciferian Spirits, Prometheus, Kumaras—descended from the radiant planet upon the Earth, at the dawn of *conscious* mankind. Then the Sons of God married the Daughters of Men. And the result was that mysterious "honey" gathered within the stone-hollows of the cities of the Earth—civilization. Every great city is potentially a hive— with its palaces, libraries, museums, institutes, even with its banks and office buildings and vast hotels. Civilization is distilled within all those, as honey is produced within the bee-hive.

Alas, what now is called "civilization" is only the shadowy and perverted—often poisonous—image of what is called at times the "living Civilization". Ancient and occult traditions say that such a "living Civilization" has been pulsating and radiating ever since the days of the earliest *conscious* man from a mysterious sacred City, named *Shamballah*. In this City lives the still more mysterious Personage, whom theosophists call Sanat Kumara, the Eternal Youth, the Great Initiator, the Seed of the mystic Tree, whose branches and leaves have been the great Sages, Prophets, Spiritual Leaders of all ages—and of today. This Being, Father-Mother of all that on earth belongs by spiritual birthright to the regions wherein dwells the

Solar universal Light, may be called symbolically the "Queen of the celestial Bees". He-She is indeed the generator of all "mastery"; for while men, born of the earth, may become "masters", this they can do only inasmuch as they receive within their Soul-depths the "mastery" whose sacred form is "kept in Shamballah"—Venus-on-Earth.

Let everyone beware, however, lest he or she materialize such symbols, vital and actual though they may be. "Shamballah" is no earthly city to be found on the map—even if it has been said loosely to be located in the Gobi Desert. It is the "Hive of Flames" to which none may come save they be carried thither by the "celestial Bees". Ours is the task, humans born of this Earth, to produce as flowers the nectar that shall draw to us the "celestial Bees". This is our transmutation and our alchemy. From the roots of our earthly nature, deep in the pelvic regions, through the stem of our spine, the mystic sap of conscious life must rise, until it becomes within the hollow of the brain—the *Ajna* center of the Hindus—the spiritual nectar of a life well lived in terms of creative significance, of harmony that is love, and of beauty. Then shall come upon us the "winged Glory", and in proportion as we are able to offer to our celestial visitors nectar in the cup of our fulfillment, in such proportion shall we become invested with the "mastery" —the "Robe of Glory" of the Gnostics, the *Sahasrara* of the Hindus . . .

The graphic symbol of Venus is worth considering, inasmuch as it is the glyph of spirit-born man. The Egyptian knew it as the "Ansated Cross ☥, which is a circle or oval surmounting a T; that is, the head of man placed on top of the shoulders and the spinal column. The Venus symbol ♀ is essentially the same, except that it allows for a "neck" between the head and the shoulders; an important point, inasmuch as Venus is said to rule the sign Taurus, and thus, the neck. The importance of the matter increases as one considers that the neck is not only the seat of the vocal organs—the creative potency of the Word—but also contains the thyroid, a vital gland in the body which in fact controls the "alchemical" processes of the organism. It is known that the degree of operation of the thyroid can be measured by the degree of consumption of oxygen. This is the basis for the well-known "metabolism test" of endocrinology.

More generally still, the thyroid controls the speed and intensity of the process whereby the gross elements of the body (including the food taken in) are transmuted into the subtle energies of organic living. This transmutation is accomplished mostly through the use of oxygen, which the lungs send into the blood stream. This is what is called "oxidation". But there is a subtle form of oxidation which transforms physiological into psychological energies, and which is thus the very basis of all psychological processes, especially all thought-processes. For this reason, children born with extreme thyroid deficiency are congenital idiots. In them the Alchemist is missing. They live at the level of the brute. In other cases, the process of transmuting physiological energy into thought is so intense that the body is as it were robbed of its thyroid secretions by the mind, which requisitions all the available supply. Nervous exhaustion follows.

Thought itself comes under the rulership of Mercury; but the process by which the earth-forces are transmuted into solar energies, and body-substance into Soul-consciousness, should be referred to Venus. This process, viewed from a universal standpoint, is what occultists call the Path of Initiation; and the Great Initiator, Sanat Kumara, is therefore said to come from Venus, to give men the Fire of Mind. This is the Promethean gift. This is the Light of Dawn carried by Venus-Lucifer, star of the morning. Prometheus' liver was torn incessantly by a vulture—because the possession of Mind means the crucifixion of the nature of feeling represented by the liver; also because when the thyroid operates too much mindward, the liver suffers from the strain of carrying on the many functions necessary for food-metabolism.

Lucifer was hurled into the bottomless pit—because the possession of creative mind gives a kind of pride which is often man's perdition; not to mention a still deeper meaning, in which the "pit" symbolizes the pit of the stomach, the solar plexus, the gates of unconscious psychic energies. This latter meaning refers to the great test which sooner or later all individuals striving toward spiritual heights must face. It is a test of strength between the conscious ego and the great Unconscious. If the conscious ego is not steady enough in its structural development, it may be overcome or so intoxicated by the inrushing "primordial Images" of the Unconscious, by "gods" of various kinds, that it will lose its form and identity. The rational is then conquered by the irrational; the head-center by the solar plexus. The man becomes a tool of Powers which play irrationally through him.

On the other hand, if the conscious "I am" is able to *assimilate* the energies of the Unconscious, and thus to retain his own structural identity, he becomes a god-like man. Personal pride very often causes the failure. By overvaluing its own importance the ego makes itself unable to resist the shock of the irrational energies. Paranoia may then develop in one form or another; or else some type of mediumship or religious unbalance.

Venus is not necessarily the beneficent influence which astrology ordinarily considers it to be. *Sanat* inverted becomes *Satan*. If the bees are said to come from Venus, so also the ants. The destructive elements parallel the constructive. The bees feed on the nectar of the flower; the ants devour the wood, stem and leaves of the plant. The hives are built in the air; the ant-hills are dug into the earth. Wheat and corn also claim descent, in occult lore, from Venus; but man transforms the brain-building and energy-producing grain into alcohol. To the white Adept corresponds the black magician; to the up-pointing five-pointed star of the Initiator, the down-pointing star of the devil-worshipper—the Disintegrator.

In this star of Initiation, the heavenward point represents the organ of the spiritually creative, within the head. The process of mental creation is based upon the activity of the thyroid—or "throat-center"—and flowers through the higher brain centers. This is Venusian creativeness at its psycho-mental level. But in the earth-conditioned man, the physiologically creative operates through sperm and ovum. At this level the creative energy is marshalled by Mars and becomes procreative energy. The creative principle is still the "Fifth Limb", but it pertains to the process of involution—to the descent of spirit into matter, which calls for the building of "bodies". This too is "alchemy" of a sort, but one which pertains to the realm of the earthly animal kingdom.

Truly *human* alchemy refers to the refining of Earth into Mercury through the power of Venus. And the "marriage" occurring in such alchemical operations is the union of the subtlest essence of the earth with the Venusian winged spirit, or archetype. As a symbol thereof we have the nuptial flight of the future queen bee, mating as high in the air as the bees can reach. The fecundation accomplished, the male falls dead —a sacrifice. Likewise, where Mars fecundates Venus at the high levels of man's consciousness, Mars gives his life joyfully that the Venus-seed may grow into the evergreen Tree of Wisdom, the Tree of Adepts and Christs.

Uranus:
Master of Transformations

SATURN FORMS; URANUS TRANSFORMS. THE EQUATION OF DESTINY set by Saturn is invalidated by the new vistas opened by Uranus. The tribal law, dating from the Golden Age and proclaimed by the race's great Ancestor, breaks down under the restless quest for God and the relentless search for gold, stirred by the divine or devilish discontents that are Uranus' progeny. The traditional and soil-born culture, which is the very emanation of blood and climate, crumbles under the blows inflicted by men of genius, then by virtuosi, finally by phonographs and radios—all servants of the Uranian will that transforms all set things, by pain, by violence, by madness or god-intoxication.

The great key-word of Uranus is: *through*. He it is that pierces through every Saturnian wall; that pierces through the inertia, the peace, the comfort, the rigidity, the austerity, the morality, the practicability and common sense of every manifested and concrete thing there is. He it is that flashes— through every opaque veil, through every protective "complex", through every darkened sanctuary—the light of the realm just beyond. He is the revealer of the next truth to those he has made weary with old unquestioned postulates. He is the rouser of doubt, the breaker of static faith, the iconoclast and challenger. Before every known truth and every accepted fact he stands, menacingly—or in flashing inspiration throwing at the mind and soul of daring men in whom his fire burns, the eternal challenge: *What if . . . ?*

What if there were something beyond? What if men had believed in a gigantic fraud, because of their childish craving for security? What if supposed facts were not facts? What if we were fools and slaves to things taken for granted—slaves or puppets of deified masters? What if gods were man-made? What if our very souls were mere complexes or compensations? What if there were life before birth and life after death? What if there were nothing but ever-fluid, ever-unstable, ever-creative, ever-renewed Life?

Men have turned insane under the weight of such pitiless questions; others became as gods. Uranus forced upon them the confrontations. They either pierced through the ancient shells and emerged conquistadores of the beyond, masters of the threshold, or else they shrank under the light. They saw that their gods were man-made, and became mad as the gods faded into psychological "complexes". They saw through the walls, but returned blind. The Transformer indeed is pitiless toward those who cannot let go of past idols. Once the process of transformation is begun, there is no going back. The form must be renewed—or break. It can never become again what it was before. Uranus does not remember. He has no use for memory. He only moves on from that which is to that *which must be next*. If the "next" is unreachable, then there is nothing but death: death, the transformation of that which cannot be transformed and therefore must be destroyed.

He who conquers death is he who has become transformed. The form is renewed; its wholeness, however, is not sundered. The wholeness—the Self—remains; but with a new delineation, a new formula of operation, an expanded viewpoint, a virgin universe to interpret and to organize. This is metamorphosis. Death is the failure to perform a metamorphosis. It is the failure to recognize Uranus as one's Master, when he knocks at one's door disguised as a beggar or perhaps as a fool. It is withdrawal into the Saturnian limits, withdrawal into the reign of fear. But for Uranus' devotees and friends, there is no death. There is no death for the consciousness that never refuses change, that never shrinks from the most inclusive, the all-challenging transformation. There is no death for him who not only drinks the water within the glass, but the glass itself; not only the contents, but also the container.

It is easy to drink the waters of the glass of self; to change the contents of one's own egoism. This is *modification*—not "transformation". To pass from one mode of action to another mode requires only flexibility of outlook and a good sense of adaptation to circumstances. All planets within the orbit of Saturn are able to modify the character of the Saturnian ego. But the real Uranian "transformation" is a process of actual reconstruction of the form of one's own selfhood. Not only the contents of the form, but the form itself must be "seen through" and "gone through".

In another sense, the process may also be described as "jumping beyond one's shadow"—to use Nietzsche's illustration. It is relatively easy to investigate the contents of one's own nature; but how much more difficult to investigate the investigator! In order to do so it is as if "nothing" were to discuss "something" and pull it to pieces—then rebuild it anew around a new center of light. A fundamentally irrational process leading to a super-rational rebirth of self, from a new "seed" the existence of which could not be realized—because it was hidden by the very shadow of the rational self. Thus the need for jumping beyond the shadow.

Many writers speak of the Uranian process, using the term "regeneration" to define it. Loosely used, this term is adequate; however, Uranus controls only one phase of the total process, of which, in strict accuracy, the word "regeneration" describes only the last phase, symbolized by Pluto. Uranus transforms; Neptune dissolves and at the same time feeds the new prenatal growth; Pluto is the hierophant of the mysteries of actual birth into the "New World". Whoever fails to withstand the transforming power of Uranus must become disintegrated by Neptune. For such a one Pluto is the awesome lord of death. But he who passes the Uranian tests and enters into the Neptunian Sea of Light need not fear Pluto, even through the final ordeal of the Temptation; for Pluto will guide him to the gates of rebirth and of immortality. Immortality: the state of being always different while the same.

Often it is said of Jupiter that he is the polar opposite of Saturn. This however is true only insofar as Jupiter represents a trend of development that leads in the opposite direction from that of the Saturn process. But Jupiter operates *always* in terms of Saturn's prior determination of the form of the being. Saturn contracts, while Jupiter expands. But what Jupiter expands is that to which Saturn gave form. A small sphere may expand into a large sphere; yet it remains always a sphere. A man's ego may expand in Jupiterian optimism, self-confidence and personal authority. Yet what reaches out is still the same ego. The basic form thereof is not changed by the Jupiterian action, even though its outer shape may be distorted or distended as it expands. Jupiter cannot change radically the structure set by Saturn. It can only "modify" its outer appearance and the quality and balance of the organic forces which operate within that structure.

Uranus, on the contrary, deliberately and directly challenges Saturn's power: its exclusivism, its particularity, its rigidity. It "pierces through" Saturn and throws upon the *inside walls* of the conscious ego images of the more universal and freer world which extends outside of these walls. Thus a two-fold operation: the piercing through—then the projection of images. The first phase may manifest in many ways; perhaps through slow stages of progressive thinning out of the Saturnian shells—so that these become finally like translucent window-panes through which the consciousness centered within the shells may behold vistas of the beyond. In other cases, the Uranian action is sharp and explosive. It bores, through the walls of the ego, holes, telescopes, microscopes, channels through which the "flashes of intuition", the "inspiration of genius", may suddenly reveal themselves to the Saturn-bound consciousness. Then there is also the most general process, to which the most vivid and convincing of our dreams bear witness.

In the first case, the Uranian action stimulates and utilizes the power which the mind has to modify, the quality and substance of our individual selfhood. A sort of cooperation is established between Mercury and Uranus which draws upon the Solar Force for the work of transformation. New mental concepts play upon the static traditions which Saturn originated or crystallized. The action of truth after truth, system after system—each a little more inclusive and more dynamic than the preceding one—thins out the Saturnian walls. It is as if layer after layer of opaque substance were removed. Our concepts, our realizations of the nature of "self"—the basic factor of all consciousness—come, at every removal, closer to a state of perfect translucence. The light of the Universals shines with increasing strength and purity through the structure of the particular. Each layer removed makes that light less *colored*— by biases, by particular viewpoints, by earth-conditions—and more *white*.

In other and rarer cases we have men of genius, in whatever field it may be; or real seers; men and women in whom the Uranian power of "image-projection" is very strong, in whom a definite inner linkage between Uranus and the Sun is actually established. A mysteriously creative current plays between the Sun and Uranus, and, whenever other planetary factors permit, a flash of lightning pierces through the Saturnian walls. Then images, symbols, visions, prophetic utterances, messianic impulses are released.

With those, we are entering a realm the nature of which is exceedingly complex and which baffles analysis. This complexity may be better understood if we realize that Uranus can become linked, directly or indirectly, with every planet, and that therefore his action may become adjusted to the tone and characteristic of every one of the basic faculties, the totality of which constitutes organic living. The action of Uranus is therefore protean. It has no definite form, because it adjusts itself to every psychological or social function, to every mode of activity or consciousness.

This ubiquitous and multiformed activity of Uranus is perhaps best evidenced in dreams. Dreams constitute probably the most puzzling phase of man's life, especially because they can be of such varied character, importance and significance. Dreams are inherently connected with the equally mysterious process which we call "sleep". Sleep is a particular aspect of the relation between the Sun-factor and the Saturn-factor in every living organism, the waking state being the opposite aspect of that basic relation conditioning all consciousness, and actually the very foundation of individual existence.

During the waking conscious state Saturn overpowers the Sun; the individual factor of consciousness—the ego—dominates and utilizes for its own end the life-force of which the Sun is the source or symbol. During sleep, the ego withdraws from activity. It is no longer able or willing to control and utilize the life-force for its purposes. It abdicates and retires into a condition of non-manifestation or abstraction. It becomes "pure form" divorced from life-contents and energy; and by so doing it restores itself to its own formal integrity which has been disturbed by earthly activity. As this withdrawal of the ego occurs, the solar forces begin to flow more freely, bringing to every organ and every cell new vitality, clearing away the residua or waste-products of individual and conscious (Saturnian) activity.

Sleep is a time of organic recuperation and organic growth; while the waking state is a time for the individual development and the conscious focalized growth of Personality. Organic recuperation applies to the brain and all its centers of sensation, feeling and ideation, as well as to any other part of the organism. These brain-centers, during the waking hours, are controlled by the Saturn-ego and its *conscious will*. But as this conscious will becomes un-operative in the personality-whole, they are released, as it were, from its grip; and they begin to function in various ways during what then is "sleep".

They can function autonomously. Like children after school, they can romp wildly and exuberantly around, happy to be free from the rigid discipline of the school-master (the conscious ego); or else they may go to absorb physical food—and, if more mature, cultural impressions: reading books, seeing movies, listening to lectures and concerts. They may also, symbolically speaking, make love, enter into new relationships, create.

All such types of activity performed during sleep by our brain-centers—and also by our other centers of sensation, nerve plexus—become the substance of our dreams. Whenever the dreams are the results of the purely automatic activity of brain-centers and nerve-centers, these dreams do not carry any more significance than the play of children stretching their muscles after hours of concentration. Moreover, in most cases these automatic activities are not even recorded as dreams by the consciousness, in the morning. It is only when the conscious activity of the ego has imposed some violent discomfort upon the organic centers of the body—and, we should add, of the psyche—that these centers' expressions of protest are registered by the somewhat aroused consciousness as dreams or nightmares.

How are these expressions of protest registered? As symbolic images. There is no other way. And these images are usually very confused and chaotic, because Saturn's formative power is withdrawn, and only the *organic memory* of conscious formative moulds and of thought-coherency (through the linking of brain-tracts, nerve cells . . .) remains; which is usually not sufficient to make very coherent and sequential series of pictures.

Such dreams are thus to be considered as symbolic images of organic processes, or of organic conditions affecting the brain-centers. They are only "symbolic images". They are not to be considered as *concrete representations* of what is taking place or will take place in the personality-life. Waking consciousness and its objective and coherent (Saturnian) system of perception are needed to produce "concrete representations". Dreams are symbols, which have no value save they be *interpreted* by the ego-consciousness. Then, the physiological or psychological processes and conditions which they symbolize may be of many types. They may be processes tending toward organic disintegration—of either body or psyche—and the dreams may be a desperate warning which the organic centers of body or psyche manage dimly to convey in symbols to the ruthless or careless conscious will of the ego. They may also be processes of growth and of assimilation of collective, racial or universal psychological contents; that is, processes by means of which the lesser whole (man as we know him) expands into a state of direct, conscious participation in the life of the Greater Whole of which he increasingly experiences being a part.

Such processes, whether constructive or destructive, insofar as they deal with "transformations" of the Saturnian structure of body or personality, can be referred to Uranus—and some of them to Neptune. But, more specifically, Uranus is to be connected with the attempts made by Life in general, or various kinds of universal agencies, to bring to the particular personality tidings of a higher and larger state of being. These attempts are the substance of our most significant dreams; dreams which are either symbols of processes of assimilation and integration actually taking place within the psyche, but not noticed by the conscious ego bound by its own intellectual-objective outlook—or else images deliberately aroused in our brain-centers by Spiritual Beings or Intelligences attempting to convey to us vital information or suggestions and to guide and stimulate our growth.

Whether or not our brain is in a condition to receive this information is another matter. It may receive it, yet the very moment the power of the Saturn-ego is reasserted, this power may either obliterate the unwelcome images or distort and confuse them according to its preconceptions and prejudices; according to its "complexes", which are all mechanisms of resistance. Then, even if the consciousness registers the images projected by Uranus as clear and relatively coherent dreams, it may be that the ego will not interpret them rightly, because of subconscious resistances to the information conveyed, or else because of racial biases and intellectual prejudices, or lack of development.

It is the task of the modern type of psychological analysis to enable us to interpret correctly the dreams which reach our conscious state with relatively definite outlines. The psychologist helps us to remove our mechanisms of resistance, just as a surgeon removes a cataract from the blinded eye. He is Mercury, the Healer and Interpreter, working then hand in hand with Uranus, the Transformer and Revealer.

In considering all these manifestations of Uranian activity—whether they be dreams, inspirations of genius, visions, or the like—it is important however to realize that, fundamentally speaking, Uranus, Neptune and Pluto deal with *a process of re-orientation and regeneration of Personality*, rather than with definite factors in Personality itself. Whenever the individual man is the field of astrological interpretation, all trans-Saturnian planets represent essentially the process by means of which this individual personality is being extended, transformed, regenerated. Beyond such a normal human state one may contemplate the possibility of more cosmic developments. These however belong to a larger picture of the universe and of the solar system. When man is seen from a truly heliocentric point of view, that is *as a cell in the Body of that Great Entity which we link symbolically with the entire solar system*, or even with the galaxy, then new valuations arise. Then we are no longer centering our interpretation around man on earth—around the ideal of Personality—but we consider man only as a part of a cosmic Whole; and our perspective necessarily becomes shifted.

However, from the point of view of human Personality,

Uranus, Neptune and Pluto constitute the triune "Path" which links this individual Personality to the vaster cosmic Being whose physical center is the Sun. A *path*, a process. Mankind at large may be said to have entered upon that path since the breakdown of European feudalism in the eighteenth century. But the process of the "Living Civilization" is a long and arduous one, and setbacks are many indeed. And constantly, relentlessly, a struggle must go on between this ideal of a *living* World-Civilization, and its intellectualistic and greed-infested shadow: the pseudo-civilization of our war-torn generations herded in chaotic cities.

These are the two aspects of Uranus: one that is born of the craving for gold—the other that blossoms out of a vital quest for God; that is, for "more wholeness" and "greater horizons". "Civilization" comes etymologically from "city" (*civitas* in Latin); and the word "*civitas*" brings us back to the old roots of *Shiva* and *Siv*. Shiva is in India the Lord of the Burning Ground, Lord of Death and of Transformation. He is the great Ascetic, the Destroyer of earthly things, the Master of all thresholds. "Pass through me into the beyond" is his motto.

But Shiva is also, as Rudra, the Lord of lightning and electric power. He fecundates the soil, releases from the air nitrogen which will serve the purpose of life through the intermediary of nitrogen-fixing bacteria. His progeny is countless. Likewise, immense is the spiritual progeny of the great civilizers who gave men fire, wheels and all the mental tools which have made man both god and devil. But the devil is only a contrast to the god. The Transformer needs also be Destroyer. And there is no death, and there is no hell, save for him who refuses to become transformed. Even he will arise again; for the "cycle of transformations" is ever recurring. At the level of the human individual it is the 84-year cycle of Uranus. At a larger planetary level it is the 10,000-year cycle of the *karma* of civilization—the "cycle of overshadowing of the Buddha" mentioned in occult literature.

Uranus circles on. His is the pattern of the Sky. His is the power of electric Fire. Across all things that bow before the rule of Saturn he flashes his periodical signals to the "Heart of the Sun". Men who interpret them, as they flood their consciousness with symbolic images, become indeed children of Uranus. The burden of civilization becomes theirs. Though they suffer Promethean agonies for the sake of lesser men, they are the Seed of spiritual manhood.

Neptune:
Master of Ecstasy

WHEN MEN HAVE BECOME SHAKEN LOOSE BY URANIAN POWER from the grip of Saturnian egoism and from the inertia of static tradition, they find themselves floating into a new world utterly different from their old habitat. A world fluidic, scintillating with light; a world of strange perceptions—of glamorous mirages for some, of transcendental realizations for others. This is the realm of Neptune, the realm of ecstasy and mystic revelation, the realm of glamor and deceiving phantasms, the realm of hallucination and intoxication, the realm of the "astral sea", perfidious in its shallow waters, sublime where great depths balance the iridescent surface. It is the realm of the collective, where the individual either loses himself in fallacious *nirvanas* or receives the "Robe of Glory", the "Garment of Christ", of which all mystics have spoken: the realm of dissolution and chaos, or the realm of synthesis and transcendent consciousness in which the Face of God is beheld, and the small cell realizes the magnitude and glory of the cosmic organism wherein it moves and has its being.

The entrance to that Neptunian realm is reached through the path cut by the Uranian thirst for the beyond, that quest which makes men leave the known world of their birth, the limitations and traditions of their outer and inner environment, in search for something more extensive, more universal, more stimulating, more permanent and more free. We spoke of this quest as one pursued in two significant directions: the quest for a universal God beyond all tribal gods, and the quest for gold, bestower of a wealth which can be used everywhere and transformed into anything, at any time; a wealth that opens the doors of "society" and courts, that summons at will the glamor of countless pleasures, dreams and intoxications. God and gold are the universal givers of ecstasy. But the ecstasy that is of God is food only for saints and poets, for mystics and musicians; whereas the ecstasies which gold buys may lead all men from glamor to glamor, from dream to fallacy, until they become helpless wrecks lulled to haunted death by physical or psychic drugs.

Seen from the point of view of the individual, Neptune represents the end of the journey. It is the merging of the river into the sea, of the individual into the collective, of the one into the All. It is indeed the passage to nirvana, the final state from which there is no return as an individual personality. Thus the song of Neptune is the song of the sea, and the mauve glamor of sunset. It is the music of "Tristan and Ysolde"—its chromaticism, in which merge and are lost all tonalities, all cultural and traditional forms; its ecstatic surge toward annihilation and love; a love beyond name which is death, because absolute completion—or the illusion of completion.

But Neptune is not only an end. It is not only the acid that dissolves all walls and partitions built by Saturn at the dawn of individualized life, the glamor that covers up all defined and clear-cut outlines with a golden and iridescent mist, the lure of freedom which makes one forget duty and roots, caution and morality for the sake of coruscating mirages. It is not only the death of the individual stream into the collective sea, that disappearance of the earth-cultured and soil-loving peasant into the vast metropolitan mob of office and factory workers.

It is also the prenatal stage of a new life: a life at a new level of consciousness, a life which partakes in a more universal rhythm, which knows itself as participant in an order of being far transcending the earth-horizons of a narrow instinctual selfhood. It means embryonic growth within the Great Mother of universal Compassion, thence to emerge—as Pluto sounds the call—as a "child of God", as a true and responsible "citizen of the world", beyond national barriers, tribal superstitions and passional bondage.

Who is this Great Mother, if not "Mary", mother of Christs; Mäia, mother of Buddhas? She is the one that is many and all, the *Nirmanakaya* of occult lore: She whose vast "being" is for the "Little Ones", the "babes in Christ", the true "Initiates", a home of cosmic love, a home vast as the sea, luminous as the winter skies over snow-covered heights. She is the universal womb of Light: the galaxy or Milky Way. And Neptune is the focal point, the path through which this cosmic love of the celestial Matrix of Souls descends upon those who have refused gold and accepted God as their infinite quest.

Thus Neptune is a symbol of universal compassion and of at-one-ment. For Neptune eradicates all differences, all distinctions, all separateness. Beyond Uranus, symbol of the original genius of the individual Soul, Neptune is the cosmic "melting pot" in which all particular characters and formations vanish and are blended into either a synthesis or an undifferentiated chaos, out of which in due time a new type shall emerge. Thus it is the symbol of the "confusion of castes" which the old Aryans, progeny of the Saturnian Golden Age, thought to be the source of all evil. Today it is the symbol of the proletarian and communistic movement, which is the great leveler of distinctions and the eradicator of privileges and classes; yet which, by the same token, can also be a powerful anti-cultural force, inasmuch as culture is rooted in distinction and particularity of racial-geographical characters. Neptune represents the cosmopolitan ideal, that aspect of civilization which knows no boundary and tends to make all people uniform and monotone in customs, dress, thought and behavior. And yet such a "civilization" is only the shadow of the true and universal Living Civilization, of which Neptune is also the symbol and the promise.

The modern German struggle against civilization and communism, and for culture, race-purity and State-tribalism or paternalism, is the struggle between Saturn and Neptune. The well-known description of Oswald Spengler, in his *Decline of the West*, of the conflict between an extolled cultural ideal and a despised concept of civilization, is this same conflict—in which, however, the purely negative and amorphous aspect of Neptune is the only one Spengler recognizes. In a sense, it is also the struggle between paganism and Christianity, between all tribal forms of worship or ethics and the universal type of religion or spiritual philosophy of which Christianity and the original Buddhism are the outstanding examples.

Unfortunately, very few people today really understand the significance either of world-civilization or of what Buddhism and Christianity brought to mankind. In spite of our international contacts through modern methods of transportation by air, rail and water, in spite of telegraph, telephone, radio and motion pictures, most contemporary human beings are still very much attached to old nationalisms and antiquated cultural biases. The tragedy is that such an attachment no longer means that the human being is vitally and fruitfully rooted in the soil, drawing from it sustenance and stable power or a solidity of response to life. Man today is fundamentally and physically uprooted and rootless. And it is because he senses his helplessness and his lack of vital stability and power that he clings so desperately to *mental* molds and nationalistic fetishes.

This has been made evident by the reaction of our mature generations to the World War. The return to classical forms in the arts, the return to nationalism in politics, the return to such a stable organization as the Catholic Church in the realm of religion—especially of course in Europe—have all been the results of psychological fright at the threshold of the Neptunian realms. The League of Nations is a Neptunian ideal. But nations, afraid of losing their Saturnian "rugged individualism", have fought against it or perverted it.

The conflict between Saturn and Neptune is that between individualism and collectivism, nationalism and internationalism. It is one of the dominant features of this twentieth century. The opposites will have to be reconciled, integrated—just as culture and civilization must become harmonized as vital ideals of harmonic manhood. .

Uranian scientific activities have broken down the partitions between nations and cultural groups, as well as between set castes and classes. The Machine has made the world *physically* one. But it has accomplished this by uprooting men. And men have not had the spiritual courage to face their physical rootlessness and to build a new Neptunian organization established at a higher level, at the level of substantial Spirit, within the unanimous realization of the unity of all men. Men have yet to feel *psychologically* inter-related, united, as a planetary organism.

The Machine cannot do that for them—even though motion pictures and radios are doing their share of the work. Something else is needed: a planetary psychologizing of mankind. Men must lose their fears. Individualism is based on fear. Yet more deeply still perhaps than fear, it is the result of that most basic of all impulses, the impulse to be a "particular" being, to belong to a "particular" group, to have a home in a "particular" place. And unfortunately, the negative aspect of such a desire is the hatred of all that is different; the contempt of the "Elect" for the "barbarians".

Therefore cultural and social exclusivism has been the rule in the past, fortified by religious fanaticism. And we are heirs to such Saturnian shells and venom. The old snakes and creeping things of the slime are still alive in us. We are no longer vitalized by earthly roots, but we are bound by chains of traditional viewpoints which no longer give us power or stability, yet keep us prisoners to old hatreds and old prides. Mental chains are more cruel than physical bondage to the "good earth". They keep our souls narrow while our limbs speed on aimlessly in cars and aeroplanes. They force us to misuse the Uranian Machine, and make us so desperate in our empty lives that we yearn for negative Neptunian intoxications, for physical or spiritual "dope".

Our problem is not to condemn a Spenglerian "civilization" and machines out of our automatons' lives, and to yearn for the stability of the limited and formalistic cultural state. It is to understand *really* what civilization means, and by utilizing fearlessly machines and the new powers freed by science, to transform utterly our social and political structures. We still put electric bulbs on top of make-believe candles, and engines in front of automobiles, because once we had candle-light and horse-drawn carts. And these are but symbols of our general bondage to traditions, of our inept lack of imagination, of our fears in facing the unknown, of our slowness in adjusting our lives and the creations of our minds to new vistas and new ideals.

These new vistas and ideals should repolarize man's consciousness toward the realm of Neptune. They should encompass the whole planet, in terms of social-political organization. They should lead us to a sense of spiritual unity and freedom which would make dreams of "universal brotherhood" realities on earth. We need *universal bodies* in every possible sense of the term; and such bodies are typically Neptunian. Neptune is the builder of organizations which are all-inclusive and which leave no pariah outside of the gates; the builder of "organisms of light"; that is, of organisms whose substance emanates from whatever has reached the stage of wholeness—for every entity that is whole and perfect emanates some degree or kind of "light". This is the positive aspect of Neptune, that it collects the perfume of all flowers, the halos of sanctity of all holy men, the radiant glow of all synthetic understanding, the wisdom of all the wise—and out of it all makes the substance for a new universal manifestation of being, for that "body of light" which is the true "home" of the Soul.

He who has gained that "home", that Sva-rupa—or form of pure Selfhood—need no longer fear the vastness of a world without obvious Saturnian boundaries. He need no longer feel rootless and deprived, because he has reached a realm of universal solidarity in the Light, which is more solid, more steady and more significant than the heavy dirt of this earth and the binding exclusiveness of cultures bounded by climates, by blood and by ancestral gods.

In its negative aspect, Neptune represents all manner of illusion and deceit, and the mental, moral and psychic confusion which takes hold of one who has surrendered his fortress of self to that glamor which, having so many facets and names, is really nameless and formless. With every age this Neptunian glamor takes new aspects. At times men have lost themselves into the glamor of *nirvana*, into the dream of self-annihilation, or rather of a self-centered bliss that meant loss of contact with the many, escape into oneness or holiness. The glamor of sanctity took many Christians to devotional paradises which essentially were but psychological mirages. Even light is a glamor, as it plays upon all things; even its glory is a veil that may lead astray from that central reality, the "Heart of the Sun"—the point of Silence and ineffable Darkness which is the incomprehensible essence of God; "God's utter poverty", as a mystic said. And all great mystics took care lest they be caught into the Neptunian glamor of the Glory of God, and thus forsake the deeper God whose essence hides at the innermost core of the Light—which to us must be considered absolute Darkness.

There is also the glamor of freedom; the illusory sense of escaping destiny and the limits of our particular nature—be those limits considered in terms of parental inheritance and early racial environment, or in terms of Soul-ancestry and karma. The will to freedom is often but a psychological escape into the formless and the un-moral. That freedom which is not found in fulfillment, and only thereafter in transcendence, is usually but the impatience of a youthful soul, as yet unaware of its essential participation in a "greater Whole"— be it society or some more cosmic organism of which each of us is, potentially, a cell.

And there is also the glamor of being a part of some "greater whole", of basking in the sense of being diffused, expanded, released into the substance of that "greater Whole". At the highest level, this is the beatific enjoyment of a so-called "cosmic consciousness", which is but too often a regressive loss of selfhood into archaic images and into maternal security. It is the return to the Mother, the return to the Church, the return to instinctual primitivism, in which men, in the bliss of forfeiting the burden of their individual souls and their too conscious minds, see themselves merged into the vast ocean of the "Great Mother" that welcomes all, yet dissolves all. Subtle indeed is the discrimination one must develop in order not to confuse the *progressive* ecstasy of conscious selfhood, illumined by a greater Consciousness of which one is an organic, individuated part—and the *regressive* glamor found by the weary, disillusioned, perhaps unconsciously defeated soul, when it loses its identity in the mirage of "cosmic consciousness". Heavy indeed is the burden of self. But to drop it and let oneself flow rapturously backward into archaic ecstasies is not the way of the "Sons of God". Selfhood can only be transcended by active fulfillment and participation in some greater and more universal Self.

The same is true at the more normal level of men's relationship to society. The glamor of a social life, the loss of self in an empty round of parties, social functions, amusements, or even cultural devices for spiritual forgetfulness, is a real temptation to those in whose life gold has power. Gambling is another glamor, Neptunian inasmuch as it involves this peculiar mirage of the individual yearning to be lost in a sense of social power.

At the positive pole we find, instead, the joy and ecstasy of conscious and formed organic participation in the rhythm of the national life, the ecstasy of the creator of social and racial values, who knows himself expanded into the communal life in which he struggled and won as an organic part; the realization that every atom of his own individual being has borne to him a progeny in which he will spread himself, and through which he will reach immortality as a social Institution. Thus Edison's individual selfhood burns in every lamp, and his soul sings in every phonograph, which his genius summoned. This is true "cosmic consciousness"; just as the essence of "Christhood" is that in every human heart there is burning the small flame of a potential "Living God" that is the being of Christ universalized, protean, beyond form and particular conditions—yet *only* in the sense that it flows through and permeates all conditions and all particular forms.

This all-pervasiveness, this ubiquitousness, this protean and multitudinous state of being is the reality of true spiritual Ecstacy. It is Neptunian fulfillment. But for one who deliberately, and with burning compassion for the woes of men, strives toward such a fulfillment, how many there are who succumb to the easier lure of multitudinous intoxications! How many there are who drink the cup of dream-laden wine, rather than the Grail of Christ-love! So many indeed, that in all ages a strong symbolic association of ideas has been made between the intoxication bestowed by wine and the ecstasy of the mystic's realization.

In our age of "psychological complexes" and abnormal psychology, men and women come more than ever to alcohol and drugs to release them from the grip of subconscious repressions and inhibitions. The fight between Uranus and Saturn in every "civilized" human being is so bitter and cruel that men are exhausted by the strain. To Neptune they go for relief and peace. Of old, such a relief was found in monasteries and convents; today we find it in drinking, in psychic phenomena, in mediumship of all sorts, in speed driving and flying—

in everything that helps us to forget ourselves and gives us the glamor or ecstasy of freedom and of being "out of gear". Out of the gears of individual selfhood; rolling freely on and on. But what if brakes wear out?

Neptune is also "relief to the unemployed". It is social security dispensed by society to those thrown out of their natural self-expression in work by the machine-age, those who left the earth for the pavements of hard Saturnian cities. Social help, the Whole's care for its parts, is a necessary adjunct to civilization. It is Neptune's answer to problems raised by Uranus, the inventor and builder of our machines and our sciences.

In the realm of religion, this answer takes the form of "divine redemption", salvation by the Grace of God, salvation by the blood of Jesus. At the crucial time of the sixth century B.C., when seeds of the new civilization were first sown, Buddha, symbolically speaking, put upon men's souls the burden of a greater consciousness than they could normally assume. He led them, through rationalizations too sweeping and too daring, to mental and spiritual lives which were too broad and too encompassing for the masses of mankind. Following upon the spiritual vibration that his coming imparted to the whole planet, Pythagoras and the Greek civilization brought to men more mental concentration than they could stand. Buddhism degenerated into spiritual selfishness, Greek thought into sophistry. Thus the religion of compassion of the *Boddhisatva* in India, the religion of compassion of the Christ in the West, were needed to soothe and to save; to take the burden from crushed souls and wearied minds.

This is the answer of the *Nirmanakayas*—universal Beings beyond *manas* or individual selfhood. The universal must rescue the individual. And the universal does so through those Holy Ones who gladly assume the burden and the sins of the world. This assumption, and this sacrifice that is ultimate bliss, are the highest leit-motives of Neptune. This is the melody sung through the great Gongs and Bells which in their mystical shape tell secrets of Neptunian organization, the Bells that blessed from high belfries the cities and fields of intellectual Europe; the Bells also which were "Voices" to a Joan of Arc, and led her to that martyrdom in which a nation found birth.

Pluto:
Sower of Celestial Seed

WHEN, ON THE TWENTY-FIRST OF JANUARY 1930, PLUTO WAS for the first time recognized by human eyes searching for it in an observatory near one of the most sacred mountains of the Indians of Arizona, a new depth of being and of tone was added to human consciousness. A symbol of new perceptions and of a new organization of universal life had been wrenched from the skies, for man to use in his endless quest toward a more cosmic understanding of the meaning of all. Taking its place in the vast orchestra of the solar system, the deepest of all known cosmic gongs was being heard. Men, for the first time, recognized this distant, awe-inspiring, booming voice. The message it is slowly conveying to awakened souls and minds will become the foundation and seed of a new world.

The recognition occurred—by a most symbolical "coincidence"—when Pluto was circling around its North Node, a point traditionally known as that of greatest projective power for any planet. This point was touched first in 1929, just before the Wall Street crash; just before the Depression forced our consciousness into new depths of realization and made us yearn more strongly than before for a new type of social organization. Late in 1912, Pluto had first been in conjunction with the point of the summer solstice, opening as it were the cycle of Mediterranean and Balkan wars which spread two years later to the whole of the globe. More than any other planet perhaps, the slow motion of Pluto symbolizes deep-seated cycles in human history. For, of all planets, Pluto is the one to express those recurrent impulses which, welling as it were from inter-stellar depths, seal the fate of empires and knot the colored threads which will eventually appear on the warp and woof of Time as new patterns of civilization.

It was asked at first whether Pluto was to be considered a real planet, largely because of the unusual eccentricity of its orbit. But we might answer this by another question: Is the seed really a part of the plant? Indeed it grows out of the plant; yet its function is not to be understood in terms of this particular plant which bears it and from which it will fall into the dark humus. It is in the plant, yet not of the plant. It is the messenger of the future vegetation. Its allegiance is to the "new life" that is to come. It belongs not to the particular plant, which, if perennial, begins to die the moment the seed reaches the very first stage of maturity, but to the species of which the particular plant is only one of billions of ephemeral manifestations.

Pluto is only the size of Mars; a small planet compared to Saturn and Jupiter, and far from the root-power of the whole system, the Sun. But likewise the seed is small and ordinarily remote, grown at the farthest point from the life-center of the plant—almost ready to drop away from the plant in its mission of rebirth. For in the seed rests the power of rebirth. In its concentrated, well-protected mass lies hidden the Mystery of mysteries: the mystery of immortality. Because of the seed, death is overcome. The species remains intact, alive, creative —because the seed carries in its shrine the magic Pattern, the potent nucleus, which defies death and again and again brings birth anew.

"Uranus transforms; Neptune dissolves, and at the same time feeds the new prenatal growth; Pluto is the hierophant of the mysteries of actual birth into the New World. Whoever fails to withstand the transforming power of Uranus must become disintegrated by Neptune. For such a one, Pluto is the awesome lord of death. But he who passes the Uranian tests and enters into the Neptunian Sea of Light need not fear Pluto, even through the final ordeal of the Temptation; for Pluto will show him to the gates of rebirth and of immortality. Immortality: the state of being always different while the same."

Thus we wrote while studying the symbolism of Uranus. But now we must go deeper, more concretely, into the significance of the "lord of Hades". We must see him as the symbol of the great seeding process which is the sole guarantee of immortality. Many are the seeds that wither or decay on the ground. But this is because Nature is awesome and reckless in its prodigality and apparent nonchalance. Nature refuses to depend on the individual. It cannot take the chance of the failure of individuals. For each post there must be many individuals ready to assume the function. Immortality, in this sense, is a generic fact. Though the substance of many seeds be lost as seeding substance—it becomes manure to fertilize the soil—yet the seeding process cannot be defeated. It is the process which matters. Substantial immortality is a process and a goal. It is the flag won by heroes, for the Race. Others experience immortality only in a formal and abstract sense; not in the total realization which belongs to the seed that mothers forth the new vegetation.

The seed must needs descend into the depths. Christ descended for three days to hell before rising in his luminous "Christ-body" which is actually to be seen as the spiritual seed of the new manhood. Likewise, Orpheus descended into Hades. It may be that those are all aspects of the universal "solar myth" in which the course of the Sun and its fall in the western skies are pictured. But in ancient symbolism the western lands were the lands of the Mother-principle, and even America is called *Patala* (the antipode, or Hell) in ancient Sanskrit texts—if we accept some modern intrepretations. The

West is the feminine, maternal principle; thus the womb. Into the womb the male seed falls. It is the Hades realm of the seed, whence it arises as a new being after forty weeks (or symbolically forty days) in the darkness of Kali, the Dark Mother.

We should envision Pluto as the solar seed—and in a generalized way as the seeding process, as the Sower of seed. It is the seed of the solar plant. Thus perhaps the great eccentricity of its orbit; thus, moreover, the remarkable fact that its orbit actually intersects for a short distance Neptune's. For approximately eleven years in each of its two hundred and forty-nine year revolutions around the Sun, Pluto finds itself nearer the Sun than Neptune can ever be; even though during the rest of the time it winds its way far beyond the orbit of Neptune.

This is a great symbol. Pluto, during eleven years, forces its way as it were inside of the circle or aura of Neptune. Indeed a cosmic fecundation. During these years the Plutonian seeds are deposited within the orb of Neptune: Neptune being the "Sea of Light", or "astral sea", which is truly a cosmic womb. The two planets represent the two great magnetic polarities of the solar system as a Sun-centered organism; while Uranus is the electrical result of their polarized intercourse. Pluto is the Father; Neptune the Mother; Uranus the Son. Beyond the sphere of Saturn, the sphere of particular and limited beings, they represent the three hypostases (manifestations) of the cosmic Trinity: the three major "Rays" of the occultists; the three primary colors (red, yellow and blue—Pluto, Neptune, Uranus); the tonic, sub-dominant and dominant of European music; and all similar trinities, whose names are countless.

This moment of cosmic fecundation occurred (quoting an official astronomical authority) the last time between September 31, 1736 and July 21, 1747. The significance of this period can readily be seen. It marked the beginning of what we have called elsewhere the great Avataric Period, which encompasses the eighteenth, nineteenth and twentieth centuries. Three centuries; three new planets discovered; three totally different rhythms of human living—the Uranian vibration of the eighteenth century which brought the Revolutionary era, democracy (a new principle of social structure) and electricity—the Neptunian vibration of the nineteenth century which brought communism, Bahaism, spiritualism, humanitarianism, and the total change of the *substance* of human behavior—the Plutonian vibration of the twentieth century which is manifesting through the modern hells of war, but also through the slow birth of a new world-consciousness. The eighteenth century was a period of fecundation; the nineteenth century, of fruition; the twentieth century, of the sowing of seed.

The cycle, in each century, begins most definitely after the twenties, the first twenty-five years of each century being a period of clearing up. The generation of the men who fought the War of Independence, who dominated the French Revolution, was born during or around the years Pluto was impregnating Neptune's orb with its seed. (Thomas Paine was born in 1737; so was John Hancock. Jefferson was born in 1743). Then was sown the seed of the three hundred year Avataric Period, the end of which is not yet in sight. Then began to work great Souls, perhaps unrecorded by names, whose full power is yet to be felt. It was close to the time when the seer Swedenborg "saw" the coming down from Heaven of the New Jerusalem: not a period of results, but one during which causes were formed and seeds sown. While Pluto was then passing through the zodiacal sign Scorpio (which it rules, according to some), Neptune was in the early degrees of Cancer—the degrees of the summer solstice, which symbolizes the "Marriage of Heaven and Earth"—thus the beginning of the seed-process. As Pluto reached that point in 1912–1914, the cycle of the Great War opened.

Of previous Plutonian fecundations we need only mention that of the late fifteenth century which sounded the real keynote of the Renaissance; that of the late tenth century which marked the early beginning of the Gothic period. Interestingly enough, musical activity of great significance seems to impress its stamp upon such periods; witness the apex of classicism in

Bach, the climax of medieval music, and the consummation of monodic plain-chant during the three periods above mentioned. These periods are fulfillments which are also beginnings. They are *karmic* periods, in a planetary sense much more than in an outer human sense.

If the first phase of the present Avataric Period began with a Uranian keynote, it is because, from the point of view of human evolution and growth in consciousness, Uranus represents the first step. Says the Christ: "He that hath seen me, hath seen the Father." Behind Uranus stands Pluto. But it is only after the subtle, dissolving and compassionate action of Neptune has operated that the path which Uranus opened can lead to the Glory of the Father. Rebirth must first be dreamt of, envisioned by seers and poets, before it can be actualized and experienced in substance; and Neptunian love needs to water the soil before the Plutonian seeds may take root.

Seed, Soil and Sun: this trinity of elements constitutes life in all realms. Ancient Scriptures often mentioned it, under many names. To us now it takes a new meaning, because of new symbols to which it may be correlated. Pluto is the seed, the Earth is our "soil" and the Sun is the great vivifier, the Source of Life and Light: God-in-the-Highest. But to this God-in-the-Highest, that is the Sun, answers the God-in-the-lowest, that is the seed.

The seed must descend into the depth and the darkness of the soil, there to give witness unto the power of the Sun, unto Life. And this is the great challenge of our Plutonian century: the challenge of the seed, the challenge for men to become as seeds, to demonstrate God in the lowest depths of the Earth-womb, to be shrines of the Living God where the darkness is the deepest, in the eternal Western lands where the Sun sets. Farthest away from the sunrise, farthest away from the triumphant God of the skies, seed-men are needed to incarnate the Plutonian urge, to consummate the cyclic sacrifice of all seed, to sink themselves into the matrix of futurity; thence to emerge some day as the new Life into which they died. For the seed must die, that the new plant may live.

God-in-the-lowest is not the celestial Being of splendor and omnipotence worshipped by the devotee. He is the God-seed that sleeps in the center of the head of men; the solar disc that is there hidden by veils of *karma* and of material thoughts; the divine Eucharist which is the true presence of God within man. This presence of the God-seed within man's skull (Golgotha in Hebrew means "skull") constitutes the great mystery of the divine Incarnation. God, the Universal, assumes the limitations and racial *karma* of man, the particular—that man may manifest divinity in his consciousness. Thus also the universal Center demonstrates itself to and fulfills every point of the circumference. Each man is a point on the circumference of God's being—just as each cell is a unit of the organic whole that we call the human body. This body is never perfect until man—the consciousness of the whole—experiences himself in every one of his cells, in every part of this whole. To experience oneself is to sow oneself: it is to project one's "Son" into the farthest removes of one's "earth".

This penetration of one's depths, and this revelation of oneself to oneself in every remotest part of one's being, is Pluto's Great Work. Psycho-analysis is the product of such an urge, especially as it is able to face and interpret the "collective unconscious". The Ancients spoke of it when they told the tale of the fisherman plunging into the deep to tear from it the "Pearl of Significance"—the pearl that is grown out of suffering; the iridescent sphere hidden in visceras, imprisoned in heavy shell.

Pluto is the mark and seal of the new messianic Revelation of God within the depth. Messiahs of old were reflections from the heavenly spheres. It is only since Gautama the Buddha and Jesus the Christ that men of this earth have borne the full burden of the God-seed; have borne it as Sons of the Earth as well as Sons of God. In this century, the great universal Revelation which has already spread through two centuries, is reaching bottom—is reaching the heaviest layer of the soil, whence only it can germinate, upward again, toward the Sun.

The message of Pluto is that of divine substantiality. The Soul can be made substantial. It can be made concrete. It need no longer be but a breath of heaven, but an astral vapor, but a thought soaring toward universal heights. The substance of the Earth *can* be regenerated. The substance of human souls *can* be redeemed. The race-*karma* of mankind *can* be burned. The thick pall of darkness surrounding our globe can be lifted. Men *will* be free to demonstrate in radiant bodies, in prosperous lives filled with abundance and health, the gods they are. This is the "abundant life", the life full of seed; man, the eternally filled granary—man, the Ark everlasting, bearing the seed of all that lives—man, the perfected microcosm which is today PERSONALITY.

This is the great message of Pluto, whose presence became revealed even in the midst of a bitter Depression; for men can only learn the lesson of abundance in poverty, the lesson of health in disease, the lesson of operative wholeness in injury and deprivation. It is the message of the Far-West, the great Womb—the message of America, the vast granary. And Pluto's message is also that of democracy; for the God-seed is hidden in every man, irrespective of birth-condition and of environment. There can be no king where every man is king by divine right. There can be but one rule: that of law. "In America the law is king", said Thomas Paine, father of democracy.

Because of this, America has been a welter of lawlessness. No kingship of the law can be established in the heart, mind, and soul of men, save after the experience of lawlessness. Pluto may "rule" gangdom; but it symbolizes also the Parliament of Man, the New Jerusalem, the "White Lodge of Masters" who are indeed the perfected Seed of mankind, who together constitute the "Seed-Manu" of theosophical lore.

Sun, Soul and Seed. Within the earthly bodies of men God

has been sown. This is *Kali Yuga*, the age of the Mother, the gestation of a new humanity and a new earth. The age is dark and wet with blood. But after forty weeks, forty cycles of ten thousand years—but accelerated years no doubt—the new birth is to occur. This is the age of great arousal. The germ is stirring within the seed. The radiance of the living God is come. Many are the heralds. The Source of Power is one. Far in the West Pluto was discovered. Far in the West the new City may rise, the prototype of a liberated manhood; God-the-Host within the depths of men that are whole, men that sing Life; whose songs bless the earth with fulfillment.

Asteroids and Comets:
Servants and Messengers of Universal Harmony

Gong-music, music of bells, music of the orient mysterious in its fullness as well as in its transcendence, music of ancient troubadours whose *viola d'amore* vibrated to the quivering of sympathetic strings, music of some modern orchestrations which blend in mysterious resonances intricacies of overtones—in all such music we hear, if we listen deeply enough to the message of that which lies beyond the obvious, the throb of countless tonal multitudes. What we hear thus is not to be found on the printed page. It is not to be given names familiar to old conservatories bred in the intellectual desiccation of the classical seventeenth and eighteenth centuries. It escapes scales and tonalities, rigid patterns and conventional relations which link stately, cut-and-dried notes. It is a mystery of imperceptibles of tone, a breeze of sound that caresses the ears as floating perfume the nostrils.

We may speak of "resonance", of "overtones", of "sympathetic vibrations". Names matter little. What is heard is that which moves and has its being between the classified notes; that which links tone to tone in a quivering continuity of vibration; that which escapes analysis, yet which is the very soul of synthesis. It is the vibrant aura of music, where music is really alive in substance and in tone—and not merely a matter of intellectual craftsmanship or abstract patterning. Such a living music is not all contained in a few obvious notes or scales. These constitute only the structure, the skeleton. Likewise the solar system, and beyond it the ever-widening spaces of galaxies, are not a mere sum of planets or suns with easily recognizable masses. Space is not an emptiness in which these suns and planets alone move with rigid *tempo*. Space is a fullness of being. Its denizens are multitudes. Between the known and set entities sharply etched upon the background of our consciousness are vagrant hosts, unrecognizable and elusive. These hosts are the throbbing substance of Universal Harmony. They link the proud suns and weave garlands across planetary fields, in order to blend, to unify, to sustain, to remember.

Today we know that a number of small planets or asteroids revolve around the Sun, within that wide band which fills in the space between the orbits of Mars and Jupiter. We know that they occupy roughly the place which, according to the Bode law, a planet should fill. We know some of their mythological names: Ceres, Pallas, Juno, Vesta, Eros. We know that the dimensions of the vast majority of these asteroids are very small, the largest one, Ceres, being not even 500 miles in diameter, while the last to be duly catalogued is only half a mile in diameter, and thousands of others may be still smaller. We have heard it said that perhaps as many as 50,000 such small celestial objects are found spread all along the zodiacal belt. Yet do we fully realize what their presence signifies?

We come closer to such a realization if we consider that these asteroids are not the only objects, besides the well known planets, to overrun the fields of space which are polarized to the central power of the Sun. There are also countless comets moving through such fields; comets whose orbits lie in all directions, whose paths, regular or irregular, may lead them even farther than the boundaries of Sun-centered space.

Then there is cosmic dust, blown perhaps by winds unrecognizable by mortal minds. And who knows how many particles of substance, some of which might be discoverable only by eyes tuned to rays of light beyond our normal spectrum, may move around and between the more distant planets of the solar system, to be condensed perhaps, some day, into rings similar to the rings of Saturn?

We do not know; yet we may grasp something of the significance, in terms of life-symbolism, of such multitudes of celestial objects circulating through the interstices of the planetary structure of our solar system. And our previous musical analogy may be the key to such an understanding. We need this understanding in music, in art, in psychology and in this system of celestial symbolism which we name astrology. We need to recognize that analytical and analyzable structural elements are not all there is. We need to realize that the intellect and its categories, the conscious and its clear-cut projections, do not tell the whole story. We have to account for the intellectually un-accountable; for prae-sentience, presentiments, forebodings, as well as for memory. Precise events are not the only one reality. The conscious present is not all there is. Somehow, somewhere, there are *reflectors* which mirror the past back to us (memory), but also which mirror the future ahead of us (presentiments). There are mysterious presences in between all set things—not only presences that may belong to other realms, but even such as are unnoticed because of their apparent inconsequence, yet whose reflective and condensing power forces upon us the unexpected, be it out of the forgotten past or of the future as yet unlived.

These little factors of life! How profoundly they affect our destinies, although we seem unable ever to trace their comings or goings! Small may be the seed which some day will grow into the giant redwood tree. But smaller still these bacteria, enzymes, hormones, viruses upon which our most dynamic urges depend, or whose orbits mark paths upon which death silently rides. All these imponderable, all-powerful factors—may we not see them translated to the skies in the form of asteroids, comets and meteors?

Dangerous presences these are for those minds who cling

too closely to the structural patterns of the "Harmony of the Spheres"! But the moving, unfathomable tides of Bergson's élan vital, of this vital surge of a life that refuses to be trammeled by intellect-born clocks and yardsticks, and Jung's mysterious Unconscious whose irrationality compensates for our "cramps of the conscious" show us that our destinies are not only ruled by rationally moving planets, but are also the products of incalculable factors which escape analysis. This conclusion is also suggested by the puzzling fact found in all astronomical calculations that all cycles are measured by irrational numbers and never by exact integers.

There is order in the universe; but that order is not the whole of the living. There are Archetypes and rational Forms, whence all things that have names originate. They are the masculine seeds of the visible universe. But the nameless also is; and there are women! Wherefore the wise intuition of astronomers led them to give to the asteroids the names of goddesses, and to one of them of changing luminosity the name of the most irrational of all gods—Eros, god of love. Truly, love is a ceaseless alternation of shadow and brilliancy! And the mysterious wanderers, the comets, have long hair of light; their faces always turn to the Sun. And their paths are elongated ellipses, far from the "perfect form" of the circumference; ellipses whose two foci are far apart, because in the irrational realms, the polarities of being are necessarily also remote from each other.

Sometimes these comets travel in series along the same path —like mysterious, haunting thoughts that rise from the Unconscious. Sometimes they seem to experience strange transformations as they near the Sun, whose vivid light perhaps overcomes their phantasmal nature. At other times they must have broken into swarms of meteors, whose cyclic appearances may have more significance than most astrologers would admit. Witness perhaps the *Leonids*, or November meteors, whose orbit seems to link directly those of Uranus and the Earth; and the *Perseids*, whose presence is a regular feature of August skies.

These spectacular visitations do not find room in the rational systems of astrology; but if astrology is a symbolic system of interpretation of celestial events, how could we ignore them? We can not give them assuredly a *structural and rational significance,* because of their vagaries and their anomalistic behavior by reference to the paragon of all geocentric celestial motion, the Sun. But the domain of the irrational is open to them; and we can no longer ignore it, after having escaped from classical mechanism or formalism and from Victorian moral hypocrisy.

The Heavens contain more than the rational and the archetypally ordered. They reveal and symbolize the whole of the living. Comets and meteors are visible and spectacular, and they have been related to ominous messages of destiny. But they should not be considered evil. The irrational is not the evil. It may disturb our intellectual and traditional self-complacency; but we should welcome its visitations, for it brings, at least to the strong, a breath of the beyond. And we need the beyond, that we may learn to laugh at our littleness and our pompously ordered interpretations.

Pluto was believed at first by some people to be more like a comet than like a planet, because of the eccentricity of its orbit. Pluto contains indeed something of the irrational. All seeds do—because they are too much alive. Their cycles move too widely from an extreme of self-sufficiency and self-containment (when they bear within their rigid envelopes the future of the Species they serve) to an extreme of self-sacrifice and self-immolation (when they give their all so that the plant may be). *That* is irrational. It presupposes two very different types of polar attraction; two foci far apart, and thus an elongated orbit.

With the majority of the Asteroids, however, we are not dealing as much with the irrational as with those subtle and almost imperceptible factors of being which sustain the continuity of all living processes—and particularly of consciousness. They constitute essentially a *chain of reflectors* all along the path of the Sun and of the planets. They sustain the effects of those mighty Entities, after they have passed on; they foretell their coming. They link all forces released within the zodiacal belt—as experienced from the Earth. They may be "fixative" also of celestial influences that come from the vast womb of the Galaxy.

These processes will be better understood by considering again the illustration of "sympathetic strings". These strings are found in most Oriental stringed instruments roughly resembling a violin or a cello. They are found in the *viola d'amore* of the Renaissance. While the modern violin has only outside strings on which the violinist actually plays, these other instruments have, besides the outer strings, a great number of finer invisible strings stretched inside the instrument's body and vibrating in sympathy to the outer ones when the latter are played upon by bow or plucked by the hand. Thus tone is produced, as it were, at two levels, or is of two kinds: active, positive tones, and passive ones throbbing softly in constant blending, emphasizing the active tones, but also sursounding them by an aura or halo of sound.

These sympathetic resonances bring to musical tone a continuity through which all separate notes are blended and partake of each other. A note struck continues to vibrate after a new one is played, because the hidden strings sympathetic to the former keep vibrating until their period is completed; and perhaps it is not completed before this same note, or one very closely related harmonically, will start them vibrating again. So that vibrations will go on and on, unceasing, subtle and eerie. The modern grand piano with its highly tense strings and resonant sounding board produces somewhat the same effect, if the pianist keeps his foot steadily on the pedal; yet the principle is a little different.

The few active strings played upon deliberately by the musician represent the planets whose vibrations constitute the rational and structural "Harmony of the Spheres". The many sympathetic strings, resonating softly yet unceasingly, symbolize the asteroids. We do not see these asteroids; save perhaps Ceres, on exceedingly clear desert nights. But neither do we see Neptune and Pluto, who are symbols of such powerful significance. Their size is small, but size is no indicator of planetary importance in astrology. The most recently found asteroid is the celestial body closest to the Earth outside of the Moon. Who knows that its high pitched vibration is not of the greatest significance as the overtone of some more ponderous planetary lord?

The asteroids bring us to the threshold of consciousness, to a vibrant penumbra of being which has little room for classification. They prolong the conscious moment into a memory of that which has been and is not yet quite gone. They make us dimly aware of the coming of future events, just as, denizens of the plains, facing the high mountains, we can feel the approach of the rising Sun when we see the towering peaks aflame with a reddish glow.

These asteroids practically fill the entire zodiacal belt, spread at varying intervals through it. They constitute indeed—if seen in their entirety—a ring around the smaller planets of the solar system, a ring dividing the solar system into two strikingly different zones: the zone of those planets which might be called the satellites of the Sun, and that of the larger planets which perhaps are truly suns in the making. Thus the ring of asteroids may be said to be to the Sun almost what the well-known ring of Saturn is to that planet.

However, from the point of view of our earth, the significance of these asteroids lies in the fact that they are links, messengers between the Sun and the planets which move through the zodiacal belt. They are the hosts of servants who press around the great planetary personages in the pageant of the year. They are the many resonators whose hum fills the high regions with overtones of the planetary gongs. This hum never dies. There is never any stretch in the path of the Sun which is without one of these servants of the universal Harmony.

There is no emptiness, no break in the cyclic vibration of solar life.

We call them "servants of the universal Harmony" because they reflect, each and all; because they are too imprecise to be given specific and rigid characters. Their significance is in their ubiquity, in their being here, there, everywhere. They vibrate to so many things that they belong to the All. They are glittering threads of gold woven everywhere through the tapestry of solar, lunar and planetary being. They reflect light and make the many objects blend in an undulating tide of light. Some of them, whose orbits cross the set planetary circuits, may partake of the nature of comets. But in general their nature is presumably very different. For comets, and all celestial visitors which glow through our skies, should not symbolize the servants of our conscious faculties, but instead the fiery sparks welling from the depths of unconscious being and setting the consciousness aflame, for brief moments, with inspiration.

These represent truly the irrational; and if their purpose is to be set down, it must be indeed that of being messengers of the supra-rational—messengers of the stars. Many of these comets come presumably from outer reaches of space beyond the orbit of Pluto. At any rate, they serve to integrate the realms of the distant "planets of the Unconscious"—Uranus, Neptune, Pluto—and those bounded by Saturn's orbit. They bring the cosmic and the universal into the particular. They force paths of fire across Saturn's realm, paths which give entrance to those regenerative factors which help to make man more than mere man—paths through which great stars may send their power and their love.

In the individual, Uranus, Neptune and Pluto may operate directly as the process of regeneration of the earth-born entity, because man contains in his nature the totality of cosmic factors—in potentiality, if not in actuality—and therefore regeneration is merely the summoning of as yet unrevealed factors into the light of clear consciousness. But where collective and planetary values are considered, there the need will be seen for concrete and objective messengers and pathmakers, if the universal realm of the stars is to be linked with that of the Earth. These are the comets. They are the vital symbols of that constant interchange which goes on between all realms of being, that interchange which is the highest essence of life itself.

Life is the very power and the very act of universal relationship. Life laughs at all water-tight and mind-tight compartments. It ever has ways of piercing through all walls. Uranus is the symbol of this process of "piercing through", when expressed in terms of, or related to a special faculty of the human soul. But comets are the concrete symbols of such a drama of universal relationship, potent agents who carry out the integrative and harmonizing purpose of the cosmic Whole: the Galaxy. They are sparks of the electric fire that is God's Will.

Little wonder, therefore, that men of old bowed in awe before their unheralded appearances. They were signs of divine judgment. And this judgment is awesome to forms that have crystallized and refused to open to the power of Uranus. It means fire and destruction. And yet Fire in its sublimest meaning is the very essence of the Deity. All the living is born of Fire and progresses onward through the ministration of Fire. The entire universe is a constant paean to Fire; and Fire only reveals its true intensity to those who can experience beyond, yet within, mental structures the swarming multitudes of lives that, circulating between all set and rigid things, weave tapestries of flame on the transcendent fields of galactic space.

The Constellations and the Milky Way

A T A TIME WHEN MEN, BEHOLDING IN AWE THE MAGNIFICENCE of the starry night, imaged forth astrological cosmogonies to correlate the glory of the heavens with the vast process of genesis of the Earth and of man, it was thought that spheres after spheres surrounded the Earth. Each of these spheres was seen to be the abode of a planetary Spirit, and as these spheres revolved in harmonious and cyclic motion cosmic powers appeared to be released and brought to a focus in the Earth and in man, its creature. The farthest of these planetary spheres was that of Saturn. There the planetary Rulers who held under their sway all earthly and earth-conditioned natures found the limits of their kingdom. And the sphere that extended beyond this Saturnian realm belonged to another order of values. It was the sphere of the Fixed Stars—farther than which was conceived only the abode of the primordial, eternal and unperceivable Mystery, whose name was cryptically expressed as the *Primum Mobile*—the Source of Motion and the Beginning of all there was, is and ever shall be.

The Fixed Stars have been grouped for ages so as to form constellations, prominent among which were those that lay on the yearly path of the Sun: the constellations of the zodiac. Because they were "fixed" and not "wanderers" ("planet", etymologically, means a wanderer), it seemed evident to men, awed and bewildered by a world of constant change and uncertain happenings, that they must belong to a much higher level of being than the planets, whose behavior seemed often so puzzling in their forward and backward movements. The very fixity of the Stars' formal groupings vouched for their divinity; for only gods could remain eternally what they were, beyond all change, constant in their operations, neither waning nor waxing, established in their own universal potency.

Thus we know that the constellations became the symbols and the very centers of operation of these great Creative Hierarchies which, in all ancient cosmogonies, were considered the formative agencies of the higher universe. Essentially, the Creative Hierarchies were twelve, and they were a background of power to the Sun. It was the Sun which released their formative energies as, each month, his course made of him in turn the focal point for the operation of one of the Hierarchies. Yet behind and beyond that part of the Constellations' power which was brought out into physical and earthly operation by the Sun, the Constellations, as universal and transcendent wholes, remained.

While it was only indirectly and through the Sun that certain of their vitalizing energies could operate on Earth, nevertheless man, because in him burnt a fire that made him more than a creature of the earth, could become correlated with the Constellations *directly*. In his lower nature man was under the sway of the planetary Rulers who had dominion over all earthly elements, and thus over the physiological essences of his body and psyche. This was the "astral" realm. But above it the "celestial" realm extended; the realm of pure form, of Archetypes and Ideas; the realm of the Constellations.

In that realm man, the Individual, could transcend earth-conditions. In that realm he could find the "fixity" of his being: his immortal Source, or Monad, or Star. He could find his true and eternal "place" in relation to his Companions, together with whom he constituted indeed a constellation of "solar beings", a slowly forming Host. And in time this Host was to become heir to the work of the earlier celestial Hierarchies, who would then move on "beyond manifestation" to ever more transcendent realms of universal being, once they had formed and trained their successor, MAN.

The astrology of the Fixed Stars in this ancient cosmosymbology was indeed a magnificent poetry of spiritual unfoldment through realms which modern theosophy but too often materializes. Perhaps a little more light may soon be thrown upon a process which today we somewhat divine under the scheme of progressive "Initiations". We may realize that Man-the-whole, rather than being related to or designated as one of the celestial Hierarchies, should be considered a whole new "sphere of the Fixed Stars" in the making. The totality of the Fixed Stars is the symbol of Man-the-whole slowly forming itself, through countless races and civilizations—slowly discovering its total world-wide pattern, its synthetic fulfillment in the state symbolically called the "Seed Manu". Every human Soul *is* a Fixed Star; and when every human Soul will have learnt to find its place in the total chord of Man-the-whole, and to function in creative freedom and co-operative intelligence illumined by the presence of Wholeness which men call "love" —then "New Heavens" will have been constituted. The Father-Hierarchies will have passed beyond to greater depths of light, and Man-the-whole, their "Son", will assume their creative, formative function in terms of some "new Earth".

In the realm of the Fixed Stars, however, a strange sight had been noticed by the Ancients. We know it today by a name widely accepted through the world: the Milky Way. The name itself is a symbol, and this symbol, whatever may have been the many mythological or literal interpretations, refers always to the principle of Motherhood. The Constellations and the Milky Way: the celestial Fathers and the great Womb of souls —for as Plato wrote, repeating the age-old tradition, Souls are born in the Milky Way.

The most recent world-picture made possible by our telescopes and spectroscopes confirms the wisdom of the ancient symbolism. For the first time in several centuries the astronomer is beginning to deal with the universe as a Whole, with vast organizations of stars as wholes. He fashions through daring hypotheses a new universe of galaxies—millions of them, each an "island universe" whirling at terrific speed in spaces so inconceivably vast that the light takes several millions of years to link them. Each of them is a vast organization—may we not say organism?—of stars, star-clusters, bright and dark diffuse nebulae and, perhaps, planets.

Our Sun is but a medium-sized star in what appears to be one of the largest regular-shaped galaxies of the vast universe. And if we study all celestial objects which shine in our earthly skies we come to the conclusion that we must differentiate between the stars which we are able to see individually as *stars* and the diffuse streamers of starry light which we call the Milky Way, and which are constituted of prodigiously numerous stars so distant that we can see them only as a crowd.

The Constellations were conceived as groupings of individually perceptible stars; and so they remain to this day, to the naked eye. All these stars are relatively near us. Together with them we may be said to constitute a "local system of stars" which has presumably an independent existence, as independent perhaps as that of countless other "star clusters" which border the galactic whole. But what we see as the Milky Way is the zone of greatest condensation—from our point of vantage quite off center—of those myriads of stars which are parts of our galaxy, yet not perceptible as individual points of light. They are, symbolically and in relation to us, *non-individualized* star-light.

Because they are especially condensed, we see them with the naked eye; but today the telescope pierces through what before was sky-darkness. It brings to our vision everywhere a "Milky Way". Thus the galaxy surrounds us completely. We are swimming in its tremendous ocean. We see a fragment of it as the Milky Way; but the Milky Way is all around us, far beyond those Constellations of individually perceptible stars which may be said to constitute in their totality our own system of stars; those to which we are *individually* related.

The Milky Way, our galaxy, is indeed the appropriate symbol of the Great Mother, who is—to us—the undifferentiated sea of universal Wholeness. She is the great cosmic Womb, whence all stars come and to which all shall return. She is, figuratively at least, the womb of all souls in that symbolism which sees in every individually perceptible star a Soul—an immortal Identity of consciousness, a Monad, a "Fiery Spark of the Universal Wheel"—as the ancient occult books say with "prophetic" literalness indeed! Prophetic, because the entire galaxy is now seen to be exactly that: a whirling Wheel of Fire with a bulging hub. Another simile would be about as exact: a disc-like gong with a large knob at the center—as is the case with most Javanese gongs. Wombs of Souls; womb of stars; womb of cosmic tones—for men who are suns and can hear the throb of the Great Mother's heart.

Constellations and Milky Way: an eternal dualism of the higher realms of thought and being. We might use other words which would have the same meaning: the *group* and *society*—while the entire solar system would refer to the *individual personality* in its final or perfected state of development. And by "groups" here must be understood any and all types of human associations of a relatively permanent character through which, and through which alone, the human person is being moulded. It may be the tribal group, or it may be the spiritual brotherhood. It may be a formative group on the physical, on the cultural, on the mental or on the spiritual planes. But *formative group* there must be; establishing a certain rhythm of being, a pattern of behavior, a structural order or framework of consciousness within the individual.

The Creative Hierarchies, in the ancient cosmogonies, constituted the universally formative group of Man-the-whole. Through the Sun and the Moon, as they passed from one sign of the zodiac to another, the Hierarchies poured those energies which were necessary to build the physical organism, born of the earthly father and mother. But their work was not limited to this. They were seen operating also on inner psychological planes. They moulded the cultures of men, laid down the pattern-ideas of civilizations, through geniuses, seers and adepts; we might say through Uranus, Neptune and Pluto. Farther still they remained, waiting for the daring Soul who had passed the awesome portals of the three trans-Saturnian planets, to accept him into the Company of the Immortals, into the Celestial Chord of Man-in-the-making, into the seed-tone that is also the Word, or Logos.

But even such a cosmic Group is only a point in the total magnitude of the galaxy. Through the father, through the teachers and through the companions, the individual personality is moulded into the pattern of his own solar being. But all the while another Presence, more diffuse, more encompassing, yet less individualized, hovers around. At the purely psychological level, it is the Moon, the physical mother. But beyond the obvious plane of physical motherhood can be seen the nearly invisible motherhood of the Race. It is a subtle Presence which has no name, yet which gives foundation and solidity to the teachings of all the wise men, to the dreams and inspirations of seers and geniuses, to the realizations and powers of all adepts.

This Presence has been given many names, though it is essentially beyond all names and definitions. The Eastern occultist will understand what is meant by the mystic name, the Nirmanakaya. It is the "Sea of Bliss" and the "Ocean of Wholeness". It is the never ceasing resonance of the sounding board of the universe, from which all tones surge and into which they are reabsorbed. It is *Tao* as a cosmic reality, as infinite power in stillness and in light—before which all thinkers and teachers, all seers and adepts bow.

The beauty of the symbolism lies in this, that though the galaxy as a totality is indeed a thing of incredible magnitude, though the universal Wheel of Fire holds power beyond all imaginings, yet all that we, mortals of this Earth, can see of it is a scarf-like streamer of pearl-white light in the clear skies! It is so remote, so mysterious, so evanescent. Yet it is the one and only Reality of this our "island universe". It is only through the use of our finest instruments—symbols of our deepest mental powers of concentration—that we may realize its ubiquitousness, its all-pervasiveness, its all-encompassing presence. And it is only then that we learn to know that that soft and flowing opalescence is a congeries of much more than a hundred billions of stars. The number of stars in our visible constellations pales to insignificance compared to such an inconceivable multitude.

Yet can we not imagine something close at hand of the same magnitude? Consider mankind today, and its approximate two billions of living men, women and children. But this is only the number of the living. Auguste Comte once said that "Mankind is composed of more dead than of living". Perhaps we believe in personal immortality for every living soul. If so what would be the number of discarnate souls, after a few millennia? The figures would be staggering; and even if we believe in some form of reincarnation and a limited number of human souls, there might still be many times more souls in mankind than stars in our galaxy.

Who knows? Perhaps the number is the same; and perhaps this same number would reveal how many atoms a human body contains—or is it rather that there are as many atoms in the human body as there are stars in all the galaxies of the total universal Whole? Such a number would be in the category of 10 followed by twenty-seven zeros, according to a modern physicist.

Oceans of souls! The skies show us galaxies at all stages of development, from that of a round ball of fire to that of a much flattened disc whirling at terrific speed. Through this development we may trace symbolically the process of growth of human souls, out of the undifferentiated condition of the primordial Group-soul to that of bright suns joining with others to form Constellations and pleromas of Constellations —the star-clusters of modern science. We may point out critical phases of Soul-evolution, danger-spaces like the dark nebula called the "Coal Sack" in the Milky Way, the yawning Pit or the dark "Horse's Head" in Orion (the Dragon of Intellect); and we may show the "Mystic Gates of Heaven" in the Northern Skies, whence souls may pass beyond the "Ring of Manifestation"—a fascinating symbolism which has never been written down consecutively.

Suffice it to say that in such a system we see, pictured in hieroglyphs of light, the super-rational or super-conscious realm of Intelligence and Being. Here it is no longer a question of linking together the paths of the planets, of filling in the interplanetary spaces with myriads of tiny reflectors, such as the Asteroids, or with cometary messengers shooting lines of fire across the set motions of the steady planets. These refer to the imperceptibly small. But the Galaxy tells tales of the unperceivably great. Man, the living and thinking person, stands between the two infinites—between the cells, of which his body contains billions, and the stars and galaxies, which also number billions in the Universal Whole.

The great mystery is that the imperceptibly small mirrors the unperceivably great; that even modern science finds keys to the secret doors of the atom while contemplating the fantastic recession of nebulae across the extra-galactic spaces through which light-rays flash yet seem to make no speed. Wholeness is active within any whole; and just as we see Saturn surrounded by rings of infinitesimal particles of substance which seem continuous, so the Milky Way, this multitude of stars, appears to us continuous. *Such continuity is the omnipresent symbol of Wholeness.*

Our faculty of perceiving continuous substance enables us to see our body as a solid whole, to feel a chair as solid substance—even though science today tells us that the apparently solid substance is an illusion, merely the effect of the whirling of widely separated atoms. Solidity is a symbol of solidarity and unanimity. Our body appears solid because of the relative solidarity of its constituent cells in terms of our total consciousness. Saturn's rings appear continuous, as a symbol of the self-containment of that principle of structural permanence which we call the ego, the "I am". The Milky Way appears as a continuous stream of light, because to us it stands as the limit of our *unaided* natural and earth-born perceptions of spiritual Being—as *Nirvana*.

On the other hand, Constellations of Fixed Stars represent groupings of divine Individuals who act, co-operatively and in groups, yet still in terms of individual attainment and brilliancy. They are the Creative gods. But beyond them is Light, apparently continuous, utterly homogeneous and solid, it seems, in its unanimity of being.

And yet, to the transcendent mind, the continuous must ever break into Hosts. The body is seen as a whirling of wheels within wheels, as a complex circulation of myriads of lives. The Saturnian ego breaks into "complexes", and the galaxy into multitudes of remote stars. Wholeness therefore must always admit parts. Unity—even homogeneity or unanimity—is a dream of consciousness yearning for the absolutely "totalitarian" state, never to be reached—even in that greatest of all dreams, *nirvana*.

From the mountain top all the sounds rising from fields, seas and cities merge into the vast throbbing resonance which has been called the tone of Nature; the middle F of our keyboard, the great tone *Kong*, around which the harmony of Chinese civilization was seen to revolve. The many sound as one.

Similarly, we may attune our hearing to the "Harmony of the Spheres"; we may listen to the great gong-tones of the planetary orbs as they fulfill their destinies in the service of the Sun. If our ears are keen, we may sense, between the booming voices of the planetary choir, the mysterious elusive hum of those myriads of lesser lives which are catalytics to the larger operations of cosmic being such as planets represent. And if our vision soars to the greater heavens, where stars of great glory, bound in comradely love, masterfully control the threads of destiny which are the very warp and woof of evolving souls, we may readily wonder where their magic powers, co-operative yet individual, shade into unanimous being—the mysterious borderland between stars and Milky Way, *between Masters and Mastery.*

Still beyond all these, there remains the yet greater abyss which hides the essence of Motion—the sphere of the *Primum Mobile.* Beyond all tones, be they separate or blended into galactic resonance, there is Sound. Beyond—yet at the very core of everything; for there is no stone and there is no cell that is not throbbing with Sound. And perhaps, in the last analysis, the most profound reality of astrology lies in this omnipresence and omnipotence of Sound. The whole universe is a Chord whose harmonies vibrate through realm within realm, through whole within whole. And destinies are built and destinies are shattered through the universal magic of Sound, the tone within our heart answering to the Tone within that star which is our glorious "place" within the Body of the universal God.

Meditations at the Gates of Light

1.

At the Southern Gate

The sun lies low in the southern skies—a face that has seen death and now glows with the confidence and the ecstasy of rebirth. The light glides softly over the whitened earth, caressing trees that stand bare, abstracts of the life that was. This is Christmas. The shortened days vibrate the mystic tone of solstitial life. I stand facing the gates of light which rise toward the south.

... The song of the light! I would capture its elusive melody as it curves throughout the year, as it waxes and wanes with the pilgrim's errand of the sun through the skies; for the year is but a cycle of light, a poem of solar pulsations, now low, then high, carrying with their rhythm the message and meaning of that supreme Being, whose presence is light and whose name men stammer in many tongues.

Throughout the ages the mystery of time has baffled human minds. Poets and philosophers and scientists alike have brought their vacillating answers to the altar of human consciousness, overshadowed by this mystery. What is time, I ask, save the awareness in men of light and darkness, of changes in light and life, save the awareness of days and of years?

Because men are subject to the fatality of sleep, because

therefore the cycle of day and night forces upon them and includes for them all the periodic states of being which range from full sense-awareness to the utter unconsciousness of dreamless sleep, this day-cycle must ever be understood as that of individual selfhood. Between the most lucid consciousness and the most profound unconsciousness the individual self balances its activity and its realization of itself as well as of all that is not itself. This is the cycle of the mansions of the self, the cycle of the days and the nights of consciousness, of the above and the below, of light and darkness.

But light itself must change. Life is not only an alternation of states of consciousness and unconsciousness. It includes many qualities of consciousness, many degrees of response to the supreme Source of Life. Because every living thing sees all there is from its own center of vision, it must needs interpret its varying response to this divine Source of Life as changes in the intensity or the quality of that which emanates therefrom. Thus men of old spoke of the waning and the waxing of the sunlight; unaware that it was only their position on the globe of the Earth which produced these apparent yearly changes in the sun's radiations.

Nevertheless, these men were profoundly right. For while we may know today, with intellectual knowing, that the cosmic sun does not move northward and southward, we have forgotten that this outer sun is only the symbol of that Source of Life which dwells within our innermost being as surely and potently as it shines in the distant spaces of the world. And when our illusioned eyes witness the slow swinging of the sun in celestial declination, our unerring intuition should know—and eternally knows beyond deceiving words—that this very same motion is occurring in our most intimate depths; that the inner Source of our Life actually swings in correlation to that outer rhythm.

It is this motion of the inner sun within man that the ancient hierophants and mystics described in glorious and revealing myths. The northward and southward pilgrimage of the sun from solstice to solstice brought to men meanings and realizations that brain-intoxicated man today has forgotten. Bound to sensorial data, and to the intellectual interpretation thereof born of rationalistic logic, man is hypnotized by the fact that the sun can be studied by instruments and formulas, its distance measured and its substance analyzed. And what if it can? Does it make the sun within less subjectively real? If there were no sun within man, who would there ever be to measure the outer sun? If the individual did not rise in consciousness and power out of the sea of mass-instincts, who would there ever be to produce a cultured society, and to create a civilization, objectively exteriorized for all?

Nevertheless every phase of thought through which mankind rises has meaning, correlating as it does to vast, cyclic modifications of universal Life. Intellectual and scientific materialism is a great conquest, in spite of the beauty it has torn to shreds in its naïve contempt for all subjective values. And even today science is being repolarized toward a new kind of subjectivism. It is therefore for us to salvage from the memory of the past seeds that have lain dormant for centuries, and to warm them with the power of a more lucid and inclusive understanding, that they may give birth to a new vegetation of symbols potent with a new life, sources of a new vision for a new race of men.

The new subjectivism—or shall I call it mysticism?—of science is founded upon three great mystery-ideas: space, time and light. The entire cosmology of the modern physicist rests upon an attempt to re-interpret, correlate and integrate these three concepts—or shall I say symbols? It is not without significance that a modern English philosopher, Alexander, gave a book the title *Space, Time and Deity*. He might as well have named it *Space, Time and Light*; for light is our only adequate symbol for Deity in operation. God is That which radiates light—all conceivable modes and qualities of light. And this is why science is at present entering the fields of a new mysticism; because it has destroyed all illusory objects; because it has left behind the realm of opaque and material things. It has entered boldly the realm of light.

The scientist's universe—ever since the dawn of the twentieth century and the discovery of radioactivity and the quantum theory—is a universe of light. It is measured by the velocity of light. Its atoms as well as its remotest galaxies are known to us solely by the radiations of light they emanate. All we know of the world is reflected or radiated light. Ours is no longer a world of objects, brilliant or dark. It is a world composed of radiated and of reflected light. We may infer and induce from our observations of light the existence of Sources of light. But we have no possible way of really and actually penetrating beyond the emanated or reflected light to the source of that light. We are lost in light. We know nothing but light; endless variations, combinations, blendings, conflicts, modifications of light.

Is this not indeed cosmic consciousness? Are we not reaching a direct or indirect awareness of the Glory of God, which is precisely "light"? Space-time is seen by modern thinkers as a mere structure. What fills this structure or framework is light: nothing but light. Indeed we have entered a realm of intellectual mysticism, a mysticism built painstakingly through rationalistic formulas which are nothing but gates leading to the incomprehensible and the unformulatable. There, reason admits of that which is beyond reason. The formulas of non-Euclidian geometries, of Einstein's cosmology, of intra-atomic physics, are but symbols of a mystical reality which will ever elude our sense-bound intellect. They are strained attempts by the intellect of light-reflecting entities—men—to grasp the mysterious behavior of light as it streams out of still more mysterious centers so utterly minute or so utterly remote that one may only postulate their existence from the observation of the escaping light—precisely as men of old postulated the existence of God from their observation of the magnificent order of universal Nature.

It is well therefore that we should re-polarize our interpretation of ancient world-symbols in terms of light, rather than force upon an unbelieving generation the concepts of unknowable entities that are the postulated Sources of this light. Let it be the seer's privilege to pierce through the light, through the Glory of God, and to stand in the presence of that emptiness and that silence which the greatest of mystics have realized as being the very essence of God, "God's utter poverty". Let the most occult of scientists stand in uncommunicable understanding at the very core of the atom, before the innermost "Heart of the Sun".

As for us, as we try to reformulate the cosmic symbols of old in a modern tongue, let our vision be that of ever-changing, ever-fluctuating light. Let us understand the waxing and waning of that glory whose rhythm marks the yearly tides of our human time; nay, is the very essence and significance of time. Let us stand at the four great gates of light, at the four signposts of the year, solstices and equinoxes—that we may sense and perceive the qualities of the light which floods our seasons, which gives keynotes to vegetation and to human souls alike, which men once symbolized as the fourfold Zodiac and its twelve sub-divisions, the signs.

Such a Zodiac is a poem in four great cantos and twelve stanzas: a poem of light. It will not be our purpose to detail the words which flow through the stanzas—for our understanding of light and of its subtle modifications is very imprecise and we can only sense the significance of the greater moments of the poem. But standing at the four great gates of light we may watch with understanding the larger sweep of the cycle and commune in spirit with the essential qualities of the light at the crucial points of the year.

We begin at the southern gate, crowned with the majesty of Christmas. There the Sun enters upon its northward journey— a journey which has been described by seers and poets in beautiful symbolism, for it brings to men, and to all that lives, the great hope of rebirth and self-renewal, the glad tidings of Christ-birth. The sun lies low in the southern skies; but the miracle of winter light as it caresses the hills white with silence and with peace is hardly to be described. Only those who have lived where pale skies pour molten white gold over horizons glistening white under the robe of the snow can know the magic of a light reflected by an earth so pure that it actually seems the source of light drenching a darker sky.

It is that light which hides in truth the face of the cosmic Christ: a light which heralds a new day, as Christ announced a new humanity. The magic of the winter light is veiled deeply in the myth of the Virgin Youths, ascetic and pure as the snow, who came to the Earth from another cosmic realm to bring to man the tidings of the mystic rebirth. Though their names be many, they are mostly known as *Kumaras*, as pure Archangels who, in their love for struggling life on earth, bent low toward the human hills to touch them with the winged glory of their translucent light. They are the mystery hidden beyond the zodiacal sign Capricorn.

Some reflections of their light may be seen here and there in the purest of Capricorn types, in light, clear eyes which seem transparent and open as winter skies. Such eyes reveal the mystic type of the new Aquarian Age; they glow with a light that transcends the Aquarian sympathy and self-projection, a light that has known the snow and is rooted in the vast purity of white spaces. It is the light which will flow from the mighty urn carried by the Aquarian man. The Christ-light has yet to be shed upon the souls and minds of men. Its release so far has been mostly symbolic, irradiating only those who could respond to the mystic song of the winter's light, whose souls were neither bent earthward, charmed by the tunes of the pipes of Pan, nor hiding, frightened, in frozen repressions. We do not yet know the Christ-light. We have only heard the name of Christ; we have worshipped blindly at the shrine of a word. We have proclaimed loudly the incarnation of this "Word", yet have groped in the ugly darkness of wars and passions, confused by the noise of our proclamations of sanctity.

Man must ever climb slowly toward the light that flows earthward. His steps are symbolically revealed by the backward motion of the equinoxes. Man—earth-man—is the equinox, a point in the structure of his own world and his own need for above and below, rising and setting. Man-the-equinox moves toward the light which pours from the one Source; one Source which becomes four streams in order to fit into man's framework of consciousness. As man moves through Pisces toward the Christ-light, it seems to go forward to him, matching his every step. Where they meet, such a place has yet no name. It is the place of downpour of the Christ-light. It is the *Avatar*, the consummation of power for the winter. It is early February, the mid-point of Aquarius, the spirit of the waterfall— which today we harness as electric power to illumine the darkness of our cities. A day will come when that mystic "Waterfall" will bring illumination to myriads of human souls, when the Virgin Youths will become visible to all men, who then will no longer need to kneel before a crucifix, but will know in fact and with evident knowledge that quality of the light which men worship as the Christ.

It would have been so easy for men to have made Christ, the incarnate Son of God, take birth at the spring equinox, when all nature heaves with the yearning for birth and life takes visible form once more under the rosy-green light of adolescent dawns. But the birth of Christ is a birth of whiteness, in the cold of night, a birth in lowliness where there is no hope, and great darkness indeed. And no one may know it save those who are very pure or very wise, the most robust and the most frail.

The birth of the green earth is a miracle wrought by another stream of the light, whose culmination is reached at the height of the prolific power of Taurus, the ancient "Great Mother"— bestialized into the acme of procreative power since the advent of cultures based on male power. Here, may we ask of the reader that he forget the symbols of the realm of bodies and emerge with us into the new symbolism of the light—which is a symbolism of power. This world of power will reveal itself through an eightfold rhythm of alternated positives and negatives. Eight is the ancient number of the Sun; the number of the "Diamond Soul" and of its eightfold Path. It is the number of the Christ—the number of the light as man becomes aware of it in his world of number and form. The galaxy is a vast diamond-cell cut in an eightfold pattern, because it is for us the symbol of the universe of radiant light; whereas all bodily substance, which is but reflected light, presents itself in mystic symbolism under a twelvefold form encompassed by the sphere of divine love—as Pythagoras taught in the days of Greece.

The four gates of light are the points of positive release, the fountainheads of power. But midway between these gates there are four centers or culminations of power which are the cosmic places where the "marriage of Heaven and Earth" occurs. Through this union of light and form is born consciousness and might. As light becomes consciousness through form, so power becomes likewise might; that is, power that can demonstrate itself through effective and directed action—as consciousness is light made to act in terms of meaning. These four "places" are the four Avatars of Light, symbolized in the realm of earth bodies as Bull, Lion, Eagle and Angel; in the world of light bearing new names significant in terms of the "circulation of the light"—within the mystic's body as well as through the pageant of seasonal skies.

The light indeed is universal, but also individual. Its circuits are known to beholders of earth and sky, but no more than to those silent ones who have made of their own organisms a universe of light. These, by so doing, generate powers of an avataric or god-like nature; for in these men also the four gates of light and the four avatars are to be found along the serpentine path which simulates the number 8 at the very core of their bodily organisms. Light is everywhere. There is no place devoid of it utterly. Within our densest organs, there too is light. And this light may be made to respond to the rhythm of the seasons; and as it flows throughout the whole of man's being there is gladness in his heart and reality to his soul. He knows himself whole: a cycle, an eon, a fullness of light and life, whence consciousness and might arise. Wherefore this zodiac of light is a song of consciousness and might—for whomsoever is able to pierce through the symbols and to catch the eyes of significance laughing bright under the mask of rhythmical words.

. . . Christ and the "Waterfall": source and consummation of that Power which is generated by the flow of pure, crystal-clear Being from the heights of Spirit-realization to the depths of Earth-foundation—from Neptune to Saturn. It is this flow from the higher potential of cosmic wholeness to the lower potential of earth-solidity which generates Power, that very Power which enables the solid Saturn-bound earth to glow into the likeness of the universe of light, which transfigures the dark carbon of our earth-nature into the resplendent diamond of our cosmic identity. Such a flow, under whatever name and condition, is the mystic "Waterfall". It is the descent of Uranian waters in Aquarius. This downpour occurs throughout the winter cycle. It occurs beyond time.

Would we truly understand these meditations, we must transcend our normal awareness of time as a succession of events. We are not dealing with three separate zodiacal signs following each other through one season, but rather with three essences or qualities which are synthetized in the reality of the light itself. The year of which we speak is a poem of light in four episodes, and each episode, as a season, is a whole, triple yet one; and the beginning and the end of each of these four chants of light are to be seen merged in a synthesis of opposites. Jesus said: I am the *alpha* and the *omega*. In this he spoke both as Jesus and as Christ. For Christ and Jesus are one, as Neptune and Saturn are one. They interpenetrate and flow into each other. Jesus is born of the Jews, the tribe of those whom Saturn-Jehovah chose as the incarnators of the solidity of the earthly ego, the tribe of men of carbon who through the purifying fire of world-wide suffering may glow into the diamond of planetary consciousness. Jesus is born under Saturn in Capricorn; but Neptune is the Presence of Christ. Yet the birth of Jesus is the "signature" of the Christ-light. The beginning and the end of the winter are one, as god and man are one. Where they meet, there is the place of down-pour of the Waters of the Spirit, the Presence of the Holy Ghost, the mystic "Waterfall". Capricorn and Pisces are synthetized in Aquarius.

Through the Piscean age men worshipped an event. They made of the first flow of this Christ-light in a planetary sense a unique happening, an "only begotten Son". They lived on the memory of that event, which they placed in the past. They did not understand that Christ-birth is eternal, that it pervades the whole cycle. The Southern Gate of the light is never closed. Christmas is never in the past and the "Waterfall" never does dry up nor leave the earth barren. This is why the *Kumaras* of ancient Aryan lore are shown as Eternal Youths— foremost among these Holy Seven being Him Whose name has been given as *Sanat*, the Youth of Sixteen, the pure Diamond—for sixteen is the square of four; that is the earthly cube or stone in a condition of higher power.

From this condition of higher power the crystal-light of wholeness constantly flows upon the dark earth; Christ is born as Jesus, and Humanity in Pisces finds itself focalized as a whole in the few mystics in whom Capricorn is raised to the higher power, the Youth of Sixteen. But now the earth itself is fecundated and in travail of Christ. The sweep of the cycle is moving toward the moment of fulfillment, when the planet as a whole will become transfigured by the "Waterfall", by the Aquarian Avatar.

Today we foreshadow this transfiguration by releasing electric power and all types of Uranian energy. We harness the physical waterfalls and light cities and plains with the glow their power summons into magical existence. Deliberately we utilize all differences in physical level or potential to release the power produced by the flow from higher to lower. We are perhaps at the threshold of an era in which this same release will be sought in the realm of the psyche, when differences of spiritual level will be seen to make possible the generation of Power, just as differences of earth-level can be made to generate electric power.

Then we shall be indeed at the threshold of a conscious civilization of the Spirit, energized by the ever-flowing "Waterfall" of Christ-like sacrifice. Mankind will be understood as operating at two levels—symbolized by the Pentagram and the Square, the Five-pointed Star and the Cube; and men will know that civilization itself and all spiritual outpouring, be it through its Saviors, its Seers or its Geniuses, is a process of downflow from the higher to the lower of these levels. It is the ancient and eternal process of Sacrifice. And Light is the sacrificial bestowal—the crystal-light of the Southern Gate, light which white snow alone is pure enough to receive and to reflect in adoration back to its solar Source, the innermost reality of the Christ.

This sacrificial essence of light has been known in all antiquity. Hindu cosmogony spoke of *Viswakarman*, the First of all Sacrifices, the pouring of light out of the very Heart of the Sun through that God who was conceived as the Source of all light and life. This process of sacrificial outpouring—*Yajna*—was seen as the substance of all life-processes; and the *Bhagavat Gita*, the great Hindu scripture, speaks in vibrant terms of this wondrous and constant gift, not only of light, but also of rain, of soul, of intelligence, through which evolution is made possible. Blavatsky's *Secret Doctrine* tells in beautiful words of the great One whose name has already been mentioned, the highest of the *Kumaras*, the one Initiator, the Great Sacrifice. Every fragment of spiritual thought known to the world joins in the reverent and grateful homage which the pure among men—the virgin snow—pay to that mighty Source of crystal-light, reflecting back to His sky-realm the wonder of His rays.

Today the thoughts of most men are very distant from such a contemplation; yet in a curiously intimate way we are playing every moment with that electric power which ceaselessly flows from higher to lower potential—a symbol, nay the very reality of a cosmic power the nature of which we are too immature even to consider. If these powers have come to men it is because the magic of their presence has been revealed by the sacrificial gifts of Great Souls. Our cities are vibrant with Aquarian energies, with streamlets of that mighty "Waterfall" which in due time will reveal its awsome power and shatter to the last the Bastilles built by our Saturnian egos.

The time is not yet. We can see it, alas! too well, by looking at the usual Capricornian types; by scanning the records of men who played politics instead of releasing the mighty power of collective sacrifice, who segregated nations in a world electricity has made one, who preached national aloofness, partisan politics and class privilege when masses have gone hungry and spiritually desolate. The only privilege of the higher is to flow into the lower. The privilege of all true aristocracy is to give of itself unstintingly, that civilization may be born through inexhaustible giving. If there need be a high level, it is only because the difference of level is an absolute requirement of the generation of that Power which is the very fountainhead of life and evolution. The true Capricornian is aristocratic only that he may sacrifice himself to the masses as civilizer and beacon of guidance. His politics is pure initiatic leadership. And the darkness of our world of men is well shown in the character of many of its Capricornians.

In Aquarius we find power in operation. Who has not witnessed the iridescent splendor of rainbows playing upon waterfalls? But who has not known also the senseless glitter of many an Aquarian ego? Here again we witness among present-day men the shadow of the light. And when, turning to history, we read of the crimes condoned or accomplished by Piscean churches which should have reflected in adoration the pure

Christ-light as snow reflects the wintry splendor of the south-bent sun, our hearts are heavy with the despondency of a seeming failure.

Yet this failure is only that of youth and immaturity. When man left the realm of green and earthly things to move back to his Source, he ventured forth into a realm of Power which brought him face to face with abysses so deep that he recoiled in awe or sank to levels hardly recorded. What more pitiful sight than city streets filled with melting blackened snow! Yet what could be more glorious than fields of pure whiteness iridescent with the setting sun, or even meadows dripping with melting snows through which crocuses and yellow shoots of imprisoned sunlight dart with all the ecstasy of spring?

We are in an age of readjustment and repolarization. Men, for untold eons, have lived on the fruits of the great Sacrifice of ages ancient beyond reckoning. Now the time is come when Man himself must be the sacrifice. Wherefore he is advancing as a host toward the Aquarian place of sacrifice. Man himself must be the mystic "Waterfall". He is the Waters as well as the Water-bearer. In humanity, total and integrated, Christ meets forever Jesus, as the winter light meets the snow.

In this meeting is hidden the mystery of winter. Through the Southern Gates the crystal light flows. Oh, blessed is he who opens his heart to the inflow of that light, for in him shall be born even the Christ-child; and great will be his burden, but great also his overcoming. And his light will be poured upon all men that are barren and desolate; a promise of Spring, a song of "glad tidings", heralding the increase of life and the splendor of noons ever more vibrant with fertility.

2.

At the Eastern Gate

FROM THE ETERNAL AND SYMBOLICAL EAST THE SUN EVER RISES to bring to man the promise of fulfillment through embodied existence. This is the gift of the Constellations to man: that Man-the-Spirit may prove and fulfill himself in man-the-personality. It is the gift of birth on the green earth, birth within the rhythmic tides of the red blood: birth as a body, birth as an ego. And to this most wondrous and most total of all gifts every star in the heavens contributes. In this chorus of celebration every Constellation sings its part; for man-the-whole, man as the potential Living Person into whom Mastery eventually descends at some future Christmas and in whom the "Diamond Soul" radiates the fulfillment of the Christ-light—man thus realized is the living embodiment of the entire cosmos. Toward him all the powers of Space flow; toward him all galaxies radiate their cosmic light. He is the Son of the All . . . yet he knows it not.

To know it, to feel it, to act it—this is man's eternal task. Man is born of the All. Man must prove himself consciously the Whole. This is the great human ritual of development; the Path of Woe, which is ultimately known as the Path of Wholeness—when the goal is reached, at least in consciousness if not in deed. This Path leads from the pipes of Pan to the

"Diamond Soul", from the toneful vibrancy of Nature to the crystalline ecstasy of the Christ-light.

Ancient symbolism began the cycle of the year with the birth of man in the kingdom of mighty Nature; because it was yet filled with the echoes of the song of Pan which flows westward from the realm of the rising sun. It followed human growth, thus, from vernal birth through estival fruition and autumnal transcendence or death, to the state beyond the human symbolized by winter and its Christ-light—or by the pure *nirvana* of a snow-white dream state in the Spirit. But this sequence refers to the realm of bodies born of the earth. It is indeed the cycle of nature and of earth-vegetation: the true cycle for men who begin their calendar year with the Spring equinox. It is no longer significant for men who celebrate beginnings under the ecstasy of the Christmas light, close to that other day recognized by occultists all over this globe as that consecrated to the Virgin Youth of Sixteen, Sanat Kumara.

We do not realize how significant such a change of calendar is. We do not realize what occurred about the time of the life of Jesus the Christ, and why since this approximate period most nations of the earth celebrate the birth of the year close to the winter solstice. Yet so much can be gathered from such an event! A new era has begun. Mankind is slowly rising from the realm of natural bodies to that of the light. Our vision soars toward the galaxy, while our bodies have grown wings and lost their former roots in the provincialism of soil and blood. Truly there is a grave danger in this state of rootlessness. Uprooted mankind is feverish with a sensing of spaces its mind can hardly grasp and its feelings are too weak to experience. And everywhere there is a clamor for solidity and a new anchorage. Everywhere men are eager to worship as an embodied god some leader or master. Blinded by galactic immensities and frightened by unthinkable atomic smallness, modern minds cling to the sense of body and personality, worshipful of Pan under many comforting forms.

Nevertheless the call of the light is strong, and none but

those that belong to the common realms of the human masses can deny this summons. New symbols are arising. A new zodiac of light is being born in the consciousness of the few whose souls are light. Such a zodiac is not to begin with the actual birth of Pan in nature, but with the symbolical birth of Christ as Jesus: with the remembrance of a still more ancient event, far back in the dawn of time, when Mind descended upon man and the Promethean Spirit gave man the Fire from which civilization was engendered in its ceaseless ascent toward the light.

This gift of Mind can be seen symbolically as a lightning which as it struck the earth produced the first fire. Civilization was born with it, and from fire to light mankind is wending its arduous way, through cyclic ebbs and flows. At the Spring equinox civilization takes substantial embodiment and the dawn of culture manifests through races who worship the "Great Mother" and sit under "Bodhi trees", as Gautama the Buddha did, conquering at last all nature-born illusions. At the Summer solstice, men look with increasing awareness to the freedom of the light. They arise from earth-motherhood to the fatherhood of the individual Spirit—the Living God in every human soul. They sign the mystical Declaration of Independence, on the symbolical Fourth of July, which is the evolutionary counterpart of that day, early in January, consecrated to the descent of the Flame which brought to men Mind. The green earth is left behind. Man faces the "Desert" and the Sun —the Avatar in Leo.

Lastly, at the Fall equinox mankind, having passed through the "Desert" and communed through nights of glory with the stars, having grasped the secrets of the Sphynx and built its own inner Pyramids, reaches the "Sacred City" and beholds the "Golden Flower" within. Man the individual becomes Man the unanimous Host. The golden synthesis is reached. As it pales toward whiteness it arouses an answer from the center of the galaxy in Sagittarius; and as question and answer become one, the "Diamond Soul" is revealed. This revelation is Christmas—the birth of the new cycle of light.

In Easter skies the sun rises with the fervor and flush of early adolescence. A rosy fire spreads, visibly or invisibly, throughout heaven and earth. It is that fire which, concentrated and focalized, will give color and warmth to the blood of the higher animals and of man. In answer to this rosy light the earth pushes upward millions of tender green sprouts. And with the deepening of the light, the pale green of the myriads of buds darkens into jade; until the emerald of Nature in Taurus fully answers to the ruby of late Aries light. Because our senses are attuned to the vibrations of the earth we do not catch easily the color of the hidden and inner light. Yet it flows in our innermost self; it conditions the tides of our blood—and astrological symbols are but gates to an understanding of realties so intimate that we fail to acknowledge their existence or significance.

With the realm of manifestation dualism arises. The unified crystal light of winter, one in essence yet multi-colored in its iridescent reflections, changes as Spring begins, flushed with the pale rosiness of earthly dawns. Its redness will turn to purple and blue as summer advances; reaching later to the wondrous quality of the mauve light as Fall begins to dream of the crystalline purity of winter skies. And while the light passes thus through its cycle of transubstantiation the things of the earth, following after the pageant of the light, reflect the polar opposites of its successive colorations. Green earth in Taurus becomes yellowing earth in Leo, and turns to gold and browns as the Fall equinox sounds the call for transcendence or eventual death in Scorpio.

. . . The ritual of Crucifixion, to which the Christian world has given such a haunting prominence, is the ageless symbol of the downpour of ruby light during the Aries period of the year. The pouring of the redeeming blood of Jesus is but another phase in the process which begins with the shedding of the blood of the "little children" by Herod as he heard it told that a newborn child of the Jews would rule over Palestine. This blood of the "little children" symbolizes the first rosy light of the Spring equinox, the Easter light, while the "blood of Jesus" which saves all mankind is the ruby light which, once incorporated by mankind, makes of every man an individualized soul, a self-reliant ego. This, because the seat of the ego is in the heart, and the emotional power of the ego flows according to the tides of individualized blood.

It is said also that, in ancient secret terminology, the Initiates were called "little children"—because man had to regain the purity and simplicity of a little child before he could be allowed in the presence of his own divinity. Thus the "massacre of the Innocents", among whom Herod hoped to have the newborn Jesus destroyed, is really to be interpreted as the cyclic destruction of those Initiates who pave the way for the Great One, and whose sacrificial deaths leaven the soil in whom His mission is to become rooted. These Initiates represent the John-the-Baptist phase of the avataric descent. They are heralds as well as martyrs. They close a cycle, and make the opening of another possible.

We find the same series of happenings in the Bahai traditions. The Bab and the thousands of his followers who underwent martyrdom leavened the soil trod by Baha'u'llah, the "Glory of God". And we may see the same process at work in other manifestations of the avataric descent, which is glorifying this and the two previous centuries beyond all recorded events of such a spiritual nature. The rose-colored blood of "innocent children" must be shed that the gates of Easter light may be opened wide for the coming of the cosmic Ruby of Splendor, He-who-leads-forth, the divine Ares or *Arhat*, the incarnate *Manu*, the cyclic Progenitor of all manifested beings throughout the cycle his coming opens. The symbol of such a coming is the letter R—from which, according to the system of language and the perception of this or that race, come all divine names beginning with either AR or RA.

A Manu, in Aryan spiritual philosophy, is the Progenitor of a race, or more generally, of a cycle. He is essentially the Seed-Idea of that race or cycle: God's Idea of what race and cycle are destined to represent. He is thus symbolically the "birth-chart" of that cycle, the Archetype or Pattern of Wholeness thereof. Yet he is not only archetype, but also prototype. He takes birth, that thereby he may be seen as the divine Exemplar of all that man should develop during the cycle, as the Image or Ideal set in concrete form in the memory (conscious, then unconscious) of the race. He becomes thus the great Father as well as the great Hero whose life will be recorded by bards and depicted by sculptors and painters, whose deeds will inspire countless generations.

This process of incarnation of the divine Seed-Idea through which a type is set for an entire cycle of human development takes place at various levels. As a result at least three basic interpretations of the yearly cycle are possible. Here, however, the plane of physical Nature is the only one considered. On this plane, which is that at which mankind as a whole still operates, the projection of the divine Seed-Idea occurs at the Spring equinox under the zodiacal sign Aries. On other planes, which transcend the normal possibility of human experience as we know man today, this projection occurs under the two other "fire signs" of the Zodiac; in which case physical Nature, being altogether transcended, can no longer give us symbols to record the events, and the light which is then to be described is no longer light in the ordinary sense of the term.

In Aries, therefore, the "blood of the lamb" having been shed for the redemption of the "sins" of the past cycle, and for the fecundation of the germinating substance of the new, the ruby light of the great Progenitor and Leader floods the virescent earth. This light is a song of fervor and of exuberance. It breaks through all inert things, stirring in them new life and new blood. It challenges the dark earth. It tears from trees and humus green sprouts as mates for its adolescent loving. It forces buds to swell and to throb with yearnings for seeds. It calls forth rose-white blossoms to transfigure orchards. It flushes virgin cheeks with the rapture of dreams. Everywhere it longs to become blood and sap. It summons future seed through the lure of flowers. It chants itself to the earth, the Great Mother of the yet unborn.

The descent of the Avatar occurs symbolically at the midpoint of Taurus: its symbol is the "Hymen". This symbol has literal as well as general and social meanings. The month of May has most often been associated with the idea of courtship and marriage. The sign Taurus is said to be ruled by Venus, goddess of love; and its symbolic stone is the green emerald— while that of Aries is the ruby. In the organic sense of the term, the "hymen" suggests by its shape the Moon, who is "exalted" in the sign Taurus. The "place of power" at the physiological level is the hymen—the point where the fecundative impact of spirit meets the resistant inertia of matter, yearning however to be fecundated.

In Taurus, therefore, the might of the active power of life, which *is* on every plane the positive aspect of the "Avatar", manifests as a fecundative energy overcoming the resistance of the earth's past. This past is symbolically the Moon, occultly considered to be the mother, and thus the ancestral-karmic inheritance of earth-born mankind. The type of avataric power which we find active through springtime is indeed different from that which was symbolized, in Aquarius, by the "Waterfall". It is no longer power flowing in pure self-sacrifice from a higher to a lower level or potential; but power released under the stress of desire, of the eternal urge for more life and for personal immortality—be it physiological or spiritual.

This great Taurean urge begins in Aries with the process through which the divine Seed-Idea or Archetype becomes incarnated in the person of the *Manu* or Leader. Under the magical power of the cosmic impulse toward manifestation in a body of earth, the divine Idea takes form within the Chosen One, the *Manu*—and within those who follow after him, the first Pioneers of the new cycle. At first this impulse is still closely connected with the realm of the Spirit. The light is rosy. The blood shed is that of the "sacrificial lamb". Soon however the rosy light grows brighter, stronger. And in Taurus ruby and emerald face each other with earth-passion. Theirs it is to redeem the earth's past by giving one more chance to the spirit of man to overcome in his body Earth and Moon, to overcome duality and the need for more birthing; for the body is the only path for overcoming. It is the alchemical vessel in which only man may transmute the earth substances into the gold of spiritual understanding. Thus overcoming, man becomes a buddha . . .

It is said of Gautama the Buddha that he was born, reached liberation and died at the full Moon of May. While this may be at least an approximate historical truth, the significance of the tradition lies in its profound symbolism. It is said also that the Buddha's mother was named Maia, which means the great Illusion, the eternal womb of Nature, ever-changing, ever-renewed, ever-deceiving with its hollow promises of happiness in fleeting bodies corrupted by the imminence of death.

Under these allegorical names and facts one may easily discern the ageless teaching which has been particularly close to the inspired minds of hot, passionate, teeming India. A teaching of overcoming; overcoming by understanding and by directed will; overcoming by the power of objective contemplation and of courageous confrontation. The full Moon symbolizes such a power. While it brings to some a peculiar madness well known in tropical Asia, it also leads the strong and integrated soul to self-conquest. At the full Moon the Sun and the Moon are located on either side of the Earth. Man-the-earth stands thus between their opposite pulls. He may be torn, disintegrated. He may face his objectivized past—the full Moon—with the power of the Sun hidden within, and having faced it without terror and without regret, he becomes free. Such a freedom is that of a buddha, who having accepted all there was on this earth—from the most beautiful to the most abject—transcends it all and is at peace, eternally.

But in order to reach this state of objectivity man must arise from the deepest experiences which the sign Gemini can give. He must have known all the recesses of mind, all the labyrinths of the intellect. In him the end of this Spring season—Gemini—must have met and been re-energized by its beginning—Aries—in the magic synthesis which alone may ever lead to full liberation. The mercurial nature of the Twins is of itself helpless to reach such a high goal. Only through that mysterious alchemy of end and beginning can the middle point of the cycle bear its most wondrous flower: the flower of buddhahood. The pure will of Aries, blending with the dualistic intelligence of Gemini, may overcome the earthly fatality of Taurus. Man, in the process, is brought to the gates of renunciation and of compassion in the mystic place in mid-Taurus where the Avataric Descent occurs, where the cosmic Wholeness blesses the all-encompassing One.

Under the Bodhi-Tree, which is the Tree of ever changing life and of fecundity, the tree of the "body", the Buddha sits and overcomes all passion and all pride. He conquers the resistance of the earth. He pierces through many a mental membrane. He pierces through the occult "Ring-Pass-Not"—the boundaries of Saturn—and emerges into the cosmic Womb of Light—the Galaxy.

Indeed the Buddha is a conqueror. In him the power of the *Manu* becomes spiritual might gained through that understanding which can only come through the full use of the discriminative faculties of the mind. The name of Mercury in India is *Budha*. Through Mercury, Venus is controlled and overcome—but only if Mars gives to Mercury the fire of the divine Will, the sacred Sword which cuts a path through the luxuriant growths of earth-nature, through the prolific jungle and the deep woods of human desire.

If the symbolism can be translated in so much that deals with sex, it is because Spring indeed is the domain of the mating instincts. But these instincts can be raised to a higher potency. The Bull can be dominated by Orion, the mighty

Hunter. Betelgeuze points out the way of overcoming—and Sirius is nearby, shining as the goal and also as the Silent Watcher of the conflict. Today Betelgeuze, the great orange star of Buddha-light, is very close to the summer solstice—and Sirius, the blue-white diamond, has just passed beyond the position of the Sun on the symbolical Day of Independence. When Betelgeuze actually reaches the solstitial point—next century—a world may overcome and Man may become fecundated by the wisdom and the strength of the buddhas . . .

Intoxicating is the light of the Eastern gate. It is a potent drink that sets blood and ego aflame with a surge of passionate desire. It calls with compelling fervor for more and more bodies to be born, for more and more future to redeem the heavy past. Spurred by the inner sense of unexhausted *karma*, it goads men and trees, plants and insects, to prolific hymen. Yet men should never forget that the source of this light is a pure rose fire that wells up from the cyclic holocaust of the "little children", from the crucifixion of the Lamb of God. They should remember that the bearing forth of life is on high a sacrament performed in compassion for the *karma*-laden sons of the earth; that the first love is the love of love—and the last love is the love of the whole.

Easter light is the light of love. But of love there are many degrees. And that which forces its passionate way as the mighty Bull is also that which transcends all fire and becomes one, as Buddha, with the universal light. The rose light of love is a song of chastity and renunciation. The Vestal in the temple balances the great Mother bent over the sod to tear fruits from the arid earth, and to the marriage that binds helpless children of the soil in threads of blood-fulfillment answers the mystic hymen of the Enlightened One and the Light.

3.
At the Northern Gate

The vehemence of natural earthly love is limited by its very fruitfulness. The desire which sweeps through the bodies of earth is fulfilled in progeny, exhausted in satiation, or overcome in the renunciation of the Buddha—as the case may be. The song of the solstitial light of summer, the song of St. John's light, is a song of fulfillment and integration for those who live purely and fully according to the rhythm of physical Nature; but it is always a song of climax. Satiation also is a climax for those who crave for impossible self-aggrandizement through the body—a climax of futility. And renunciation, fire of the daring mind, as it burns high and clear through the perils of the Gemini nature, leads the overcomer to a climax of freedom at the symbolical Fourth of July, when he is born of his noble Purpose as a citizen of the spiritual New World.

As June ends in a blaze of purple light, the sun stands high on the throne of the sky. His royal will bears no contradiction. He possesses the earth. He establishes his dominion through the Cancerian home which is being built as an altar to his power as well as a cradle for his progeny. The fulfilled earth is great with child. He is established in her progeny. He is secure in her mother-love to be. The realm of objectivity is conquered, because solar man has been able to demonstrate his might, to prove himself in his fatherhood, to objectify himself in the child that now is conceived. He is secure indeed, rooted in the fertile earth. His security is a paean of regal light.

To the purple-blue light of the skies answers the yellow song of the soil pregnant with maturing crops. The royal will of the Spirit consecrated as lord of manifestation finds its answer in the mature intelligence of the human soul, in the yellow of objective intellectuality. A culture is born, weaving its antiphonal patterns under the sustained vibration of that solar impulse which once was known as the great sacrifice of the Manu and now is solidified into a code of laws, a "rule" of behavior, a discipline of individual and social formation. To the changeful moods of vernal light succeeds the steady glare of summer skies. Light has made of the earth its home and is known in the realm of physiological endeavor by its growing fruitions.

But this physiological realm is not essentially the realm of the light; nor is it the true domain of man. If for a brief time man finds himself glorified in this earthly realm, it is merely in order to root himself in preparation for further endeavors. Man, having experienced through the rapture of love the fulness of the May-day, having known the body and drunk deep of its potent liquor, having danced the ritual of fecundation, arrayed in the glowing beauty which Nature painted upon his emotional soul as a witness to the glory of the mysterious alchemy which Spirit performs through the body—Man, having passed through all this earthly coronation, is now ready to face a nobility more royal, a glory more transcendent. He is ready to enter the "desert", to merge utterly in the ocean of light, and to become an atom of divinity.

No one has ever known the light who has not experienced the desert. It is only when the heavy moisture of the fertile plains is left behind, when the watery power of the emotional life has been dried up, and space is no longer cluttered with chaotic masses of trees, jungles and virgin forests pushing intemperate and superfluous growths to moist skies, that man can experience the purity, the glory of light—the magnificence of stars. Humid fertility belongs to the lunar realm of Cancer. That intense profligate greenness which spreads over the earth with overbearing femininity; that dominant motherhood of love too human, love of bodies and of physical progeny—a motherhood which stifles as well as nurtures; that material pomp of earthly dominion and earth-bent intellectual culture, belongs to the watery symbol of Cancer: the animal that claws and never lets go.

The truly spirit-born man, having fulfilled the needs of nature and rendered to the earth what belongs to the earth, moves on, away from the steaming plains, to the plateaux where the air is clear, translucent and dry. He enters once more the realm of fire. Born of the fire in Aries, he faces rebirth in the light of Leo. He crosses the mountain passes which guard the dazzling vastness of the desert. He becomes one with the light.

The desert's light is a steady light of intense lapislazuli dotted with gold. Its intensity, its fervor, its vibrancy pierce through and through the wanderer who offers himself to the nuptials of light—nuptials not to be celebrated in this body of flesh, but in the very vibration of that light which not only possesses the desert, but *is* the desert. Man enters the desert. Man becomes the desert. Then man merges into the light. And in the terrific intensity of this embrace, which is a holocaust, deep sources of life are tapped. Earthly depths are reached, beyond ordinary knowing. In him who did not fear the possession of the desert's light a miracle of life occurs. An "oasis" is born. Palm-trees surge skyward from the fecundated sand, blessed by water. They pray to the sun. They rise, sheltering their trunks in their own dried leaves. They rise, magnificent images of glorified man; and golden, luscious dates hang from the high foliage, filled with sweetness, potent with strength, poems of spiritual fecundity.

All symbols—desert symbols, difficult perhaps to fathom for those who have not known the magic of oases, the majesty of date-palms, their roots heavily watered by springs which stream up from great depths, their glory-crowns of stately leaves radiating darts of green flame to the sun which plays through them, weaving arabesques upon the torrid sands. Yet magnificent symbols of a realm of life, which is that of flaming spirit —spirit in its intensity, in its superhuman might, in its disregard of the merely human—spirit, tragic to the weak, devouring fire for the watery soul, song of exultation and drunkenness of space to him who is noble and strong, whose power reaches upward like palm-trees, and, because it is watered from the deepest depths, can bear forth the clustered wonder of amber dates to feed the multitudes.

Desert light—desert storms. The sands swirl madly, whipped to frenzy by howling storms. Palm-trees sway in the wind, singing strange dry songs with their sharp leaves. Tremendous extremes meet in violent embraces. Desert-man must face them, unconquered, unbent, singing always his power-chants, his nostalgic songs. This is the life of the man who has faced the spirit and entered the gates that leave behind the soft greenery of the earth: the life of the man who has made an oasis his home—who has faced, therefore, the need to be alone and to make that solitude rich and fruitful.

Solitude is an oasis. Every man reborn of the spirit is alone —alone in the desert of men who are spiritually unborn or dead—alone without rain to soothe his parched mind, his starved longings for cultural ease and softness—alone with the one spring, water surging from his own depth—alone with the stars through intoxicating night, stars shining so large, so close, so vibrant that they are near-presences, loved ones, divine songs that tell strange, ineffable secrets of cosmic wastes, tremendous spaces, in which they too are alone, shining, radiating, giving of themselves . . . but alone.

Solitude in the desert. Man in communion with stars. Myriads of them, unknown to steam-laden plains teeming with clinging humanities. Great pageants of glittering light uttering messages which each man of the desert must decipher for himself, must listen to with his own soul reaching upward, straight, strong, like palm-trees. Like palm-trees, men of the desert must be erect spines, columns of life crowned with a sphere of radiating leaves. How symbolic these long palm-leaves, like hardened feathers, so geometric in the patterns they weave on skies and sands, so beautifully grouped round the stem! Symbols of the brain and its myriads of fan-shaped nerves; symbols of those still more mysterious whirls of energies, chakras, of which the head is but the material structure. All the power of the earth concentrated in the head; water of the deepest depths surged skyward; a pulsating, living fountain of life become, as it falls back to the earth, golden clusters of dates. The Date-palm and the oasis—symbols of the avatar, in Leo.

The waterfall in Aquarius represents the descent of spiritual energy to the earth-realm. In Taurus, through the act of fecundation, we see power becoming embodied, energy made into living substance. In Leo, we find man freeing himself from the green earth, communing with the light within, becoming a majestic witness to the spiritual reality that is God—indeed, an atom of divinity. In Scorpio we will find spiritual power stabilized, made collective and forming itself as a Host, in preparation for a new descent. Four aspects of Power based upon four modes of manifestation of the one light.

The Northern Gate of light is a high gate through which light streams forth in a commanding and climactic manner. The summer solstice is a moment of consecration. But what is being consecrated is that which descended into manifestation at the Southern Gate, took embodiment at the Eastern Gate and will reach perfection at the Western Gate. Sacrifice, embodiment, consecration, perfection. Summer light is the light of consecration. It consecrates the home, in Cancer. It consecrates man, the Soul, as an atom of divinity, in Leo. But man can never arise as a solar being unless he has found within his mind that discontent with earthly things, that craving for self-perfection and self-purification which is of Virgo. The Wife and the Virgin meet in his soul; the former to bring him security, the latter divine discontent. The Mother gives him a sense of power; the Vestal, a sense of dedication to a greater selfhood. If he follows the woman in the home he remains bound to the green earth and its yellowing crops; bound to the harvest, as the king is bound to his subjects. Leo, at the physiological level, is king over subjects at the bidding of her who yearned to be queen. The consecration of the home in Cancer forces him into being a leader of men; and he who leads others is bound to others—and bound to his necessary pomp and his necessary showmanship; for these are required of rulers.

The man who feels the mysterious inward pull of the Vestal within, and in whom the song of the Flame resounds—such a one will arise from his earthly home and take himself to the roads that lead to the desert. And if he has been strong and daring enough; if he has tapped the wells of his deepest depths, and if these depths have watered his own oasis and summoned the great palm-trees that sing in the winds the magic chant of the desert—then, one day, as he ventures beyond the oasis and toward the vaster spaces, he will encounter the great symbol that stands before the Western Gates: *the Sphinx*. And in the Sphinx his Virgin-Self will confront him and ask him to pay the "price" to the Guardian of the Gates; the price of Initiation—his spiritual pride.

The Sphinx: a lion's body with the head of a virgin. Thus has been symbolized the cusp between Leo and Virgo, the solemn moment of choice between the "oasis" and the "sacred city", the path to which lies through the "pyramid". The avatar in Leo is a fiery expression of divine power. It is neither universal, as Aquarian power, nor earthly, as Taurean power. It is *individualized* power, divine power meeting the established personality (or "home"), formed in Cancer. The negative aspect of the Aquarian avatar is diffusion; of the Taurean avatar, materialism or over-concretization. The negative aspect of the avatar in Leo is individual pride. Here man glories in his wonderful home, his wife, his progeny, his intellect and culture; or else in his superb renunciation, his heroic solitude in the desert, his spiritual experiences, his divine guidance. Here man gets drunk with leadership or with stars and with space. Here man loses all sense of perspective, and makes of his home or his oasis the center of the world, the unique in a world of commonplace.

Spiritual discrimination is needed. Virgo provides it to those who understand the lesson of the Sphinx. For to the self-intoxicated Leo is shown that the lion-part of the mystic symbol is only the lower, sustaining part. Dominating it is the Virgin's head. Just as Pisces needs to bring a sense of summation and synthesis to the diffuse Aquarian power, just as Gemini is needed to intellectualize and make conscious the fecundative energy of Taurus, so the discriminative, self-purifying and self-perfecting activity of Virgo alone may show the Leo power how to reflect upon itself and its past, how to study the records of all those other individuals who also were noble and heroic, and thus to gain mental objectivity and a correct sense of spiritual perspective.

Such a type of activity is symbolized by the head of a sacred Virgin, because objectivity and perspective are only characteristics of a mind unbound to a particular manifestation of divine (male) power. The "married" woman represents the earth impregnated by a particular impulse of spirit, and as such limited in perspective by the boundaries of the home of her progeny, which are those of the sphere of power or wealth of the father. But the "Vestal" is consecrated only to the Fire, which burns all particular forms and emphases, which is free from name and from self.

The sacred Virgin belongs to the All and to no man. She is therefore the smile of universal light, the radiance of the unattached and the free. She is inscrutable as light itself. She answers to all, yet gives herself to none. She tames the lion of pride and directs it. The Sphinx is the Guardian of the Gates of Initiation. It makes of the proud king a servant of the All. It humbles the wise. It leads the individual to the great Host of Those who, as servants of the Fire, are the hierophants of the Pyramid's Mysteries. And within the Pyramid the heroic personality who sang his desert song to the stars will receive, after great ordeals, the directed blessing of that Star which is his true Higher Self.

Behind our Sun stand mighty Stars who guide the destinies of its system. Behind our individualized personality is that other Star which gave it birth, the Monad whose "Ray" it is. No one may reach this Star in consciousness and in actuality who has not passed through the desert, who has not stood as a palm-tree bearing its golden dates under the fierce light of the sun—even though some may feel the Star's guidance in unconsciousness and inspiration. No one may experience its reality who has not been initiated in the Pyramid—the altar to the universal Fire. For the pyramid stands facing the Western Gate of light, and none may enter the "Sacred City" who has not passed through the Fire as a Sphinx, guided by the "Virgin of Light" within his Soul.

The "Virgin of Light": such a name recurs many times in all occult and mystical books. It symbolizes the universal "Sea of Light" as its tides operate rhythmically within the illumined Souls of those who have left behind the green earth and its heavy fluids, circulating slowly within rigid Saturnian structures, allaying the thirst of earth-bent bodies. The mature Woman stands for the fruition of this body-realm, her generous breasts cupped in the image of the Moon, ruler of Cancer: redeemer of the past. She is life particularized, embodied, attached to a "one". But the "Virgin of Light" is life as pure energy flowing through the All at the level of universals; life ever-present, ever rich with unconditioned potentiality, ever radiant, ever potent with the Mystery of the veiled presence of Isis.

The Disciple on his way to Initiation into the Mysteries of Light must have overcome not only the pull of earthly fecundity and of self-establishment in a home, but the pride of his individual realizations as a Soul. Only then can he commune with the Virgin within in the pure ecstasy of translucent September skies. Only then can he know the universal "Beloved" and drink of the "Wine" of mystical life. To him who is bound to his own pride the "Virgin of Light" can be but a mirage of the desert, a projection of his own thirst and his own longing. He has left the Woman behind, and her fruitful love; but now he yearns for an escape from his solitary and heroic selfhood. He yearns for a dream really, for a phantasm compensating psychologically for what he has given up.

Only as he gives up also, irretrievably, the pride of having given up does he cease to dream, to long for the unattached effervescence of un-married youth, for the lithe suppleness of virginal forms and emotions that float like clouds in adolescent skies. This desire of mature man for the earthly virgin is but the yearning of his pride for absolution or dissolution. He longs to forget himself and to escape from his spiritual or social responsibilities as an individual. He desires to drink of the sparkling wine of a love evanescent and unburdened with memories; a love which he dreams will have the power to revivify his being, burdened by a home or burnt by the desert's intensity and loneliness—a love which he dreams to be mystical, yet alas! which is but a mirage of his own individual thirst.

This is the negative lure of the Virgin. Where it prevails, there we find symbolically the virgins "thrown to the lions" in the Roman arena, to satisfy the mentalized lust of men and to make settled women sadistically rejoice in the security of their own homes: Christian virgins, virgins who were dedicated to the universal God, who were poems of spiritual light . . . But in the Sphinx, it is the Virgin who dominates and guides. The "lion" becomes a vehicle of power for the consciousness of the Virgin; because, in the purified Disciple and Candidate to Initiation, it is that virginal and consecrated consciousness of universal life which uses the power of the individual Soul in order to become utterance and revelation.

The "Virgin of Light" is unfocalized cosmic energy. It is radiant space before Milky Ways are born as homes to countless suns. It is a sensitized plate upon which the infinite modulations of Light register as voiceless potentialities. It is the unbreathed breath of Wholeness. But the lungs through which this vitalizing breath will pass, releasing its spiritual ozone into the blood of a "Master of the Light", must be purged of selfishness and pride. The alchemical "red-lion" and its hot desires must have been tamed by the Virgin, who will have become in fact the very head or directing force of the lion.

Thus the Sphinx. Every candidate to the Initiation of Fire, which is celebrated in the omnipresent and eternal Pyramid within every man, must become a Sphinx as he approaches the sacred entrance. His consciousness must be transfigured into the mystic countenance of the Virgin. He must have become a Universal, borne by the tamed energies of the individual Soul to the Place of Rebirth, where the Virgin's consciousness will become fecundated by the Star of Initiation, and the lion's body will take wings to soar toward the "New Jerusalem" descending from the skies: the Seed of spiritual mankind.

This spiritual fecundation of the "Virgin of Light" by the Star was often materialized in ancient temples by sacred rituals of fecundation in which consecrated virgins and the High Priest participated. But such ceremonies belong to the realm of Taurus, or else they were perversions of a fact of purely spiritual Nature, the "Immaculate Conception" or Virgin-birth of the Initiate in the sacred chamber of the Pyramid. However, with the Pyramid we enter actually the realm of autumnal light. What has been born of sacrifice at the Spring equinox is reborn of understanding at the Fall equinox. The mysterious nature of this understanding, which is creative and regenerative, is veiled in the enigmatic figure of the Sphinx. Who dares to lift the veil of Isis with a pure heart shall experience the reality of the Sphinx.

This Sphinx is the child of the desert. He is born in those who have fulfilled the desert in their lives, who have not let the roaring lions enter their oases, who have grown a rich harvest of golden dates, whose Soul has communed with the constellations, opening itself to the desert song and the harmony of multitudinous stars. To such a one the Pyramid will have no terror, and the Western Gates of the light no pitfall. He will assume that peace that passeth understanding, that poise of the Middle Path which is wisdom and bliss. And as his feet climb the steep inclines that lead to the snow-white splendor of the Sacred Mountain, he will behold skies of translucent purity and mauve ecstasy. And around his haloed head there will be seen, shining with ineffable radiance, the glory of the Golden Flower, Chrysanthemum of the skies.

4
At the Western Gate

IN THE ETERNAL AND SYMBOLICAL WEST THE SUN EVER SETS, TO bring to man the promise of transcendent life and of rebirth into the vastness of an always greater Whole. As the light of the flamboyant ego of the skies pales into the translucent ecstasy of autumnal dusk, out of the darkness, one by one, stars emerge. Through the gates of night is seen the pageant of the constellations. The one and only sun is forgotten in the wonder of the communion with myriads of stars. The one has died into the many—but such a death is a revelation. Wonders beyond imagining are open to the vision of the man who, having died in the death of the sun, rapturously arises with the stars. Unmeasurable vistas meet his eyes soothed by dusk, cured from the blindness of sun-seeing. Where before he felt oppressed by the intensity of the one implacable God, he now expands into an ineffable communion with the brotherhoods of Celestials. Where before he felt himself a slave tyrannized by the relentless power of the one light, he now senses his comradeship with the stars, and in his mind exultantly grows the certainty of his being one among the multitudes of radiant centers of light, the intuition of his place in the constellations welcoming gently his quest for the ultimate Whole.

This mysterious change from day to night, from the burden

of solar light to the sense of companionship with the stars, is a symbol of that greater change which is experienced in what men have hidden under the name of "Initiation". Initiation is a word of so many meanings! Here, however, we are expressing through it first of all that tremendous step, taking which, men emerge from the realm of the solar Autocrat and into the company of the universal Brothers and Companions—revered under many names, yet distinguishable always by the freedom and the comradeship they proffer to those whose eyes have been cured of the emotional blindness of fervent devotion to the one Sun, the personal God.

God, the one Person—God, the Host of the "Companions of Space". God, the Autocrat—God, the Mystery. Two poles of the ultimate reality; as day and night, as the Individual and the Companions. Perhaps the greater cycle of consciousness makes their alternate emphases necessary, as the rotation of the earth forces upon men who live on its surface the alternation of day and night, of culture and civilization, of peasant and citizen, of farmhouse and skyscraper, of devotee and responsible thinker. True and cosmic Initiation is a passing away from dependence upon the sun, and the emergence into a state of interdependence with the stars. Between the two states the soul must endure, through seemingly endless moments of twilight, when light seems gone for ever, the chill of dusk settles, and no stars are yet to be seen.

In an earlier type of symbology such a transition period corresponded to the trials experienced by the neophyte while progressing through the dark passage-ways within the Pyramid, until the night of a mystically induced sleep opened to him the magical realm of archetypes and of stars in which he learned to recognize his own place and function within the cosmic whole, the City of Light, the mystic *Shamballah*—in truth the living wholeness of that Constellation which is the company of the Perfect, the Chord of harmonized "masteries". From this Chord issue forth the vibrant Tones which we call "Masters", and in it they that go forth find their strength, their relatedness and their place of power, where only they abide actually as Masters. For a Master is only a Master when unified with the "mastery" that is his Source and his Star.

This vision of the City of Light and of his own place therein indelibly impressed upon his soul, the Initiate of old awakened to earth-consciousness. The first thing he saw was the Star of Initiation shining before him through the long and narrow opening so accurately directed that that star—whatever it was—would at that precise moment of awakening be visible to him while yet lying in the sarcophagus. This was a symbol that now he had found his own star and could henceforth function as one in the midst of his own Constellation, as a sun among suns.

In the allegory of the year's cycle, this moment of Initiation is the Autumn equinox, the first point of that season during which all things fall to the ground: the leaves, to decay and become manure for future cycles of growth; the seed, to remain as receptacles of unconquerable life, as mothers of a new vegetation. All things fall to the ground, because the power of the sun has faded away, which held the products of the earth as mirrors and devotees of that central celestial will. The leaves will decay because they did not go beyond this magnetic binding power. The seeds, because they conquered the sun while fulfilling the purpose of the Life beyond the sun, will remain and will know that willing death of consecrated giving which is a warrant of immortality.

The magnetic power of the sun is that of emotional radiating light which is needed in order to gather together and integrate the remains of the past cycle. It is the power of Eros, which raises crops from the soil, and causes martyrs joyously to die for the embodied god they worship. It is the power of the great Artist of the heavens who radiates his magnetic personality to stir people into being more than they are, into transcending their little selves and surrendering them in utter love for him, the *avatar*, the divine mover of Souls. It is the power of heavenly emotion, which binds while it liberates.

He who overcomes that power and that divine glamor does not die the death of Eros and of ephemerals, because he has become free from the great White Serpent of the cycle. Having fulfilled the cycle, he has become free from it. He is now a seed; and the Fall, which comes amidst the reddening glory of those who are to die, which smiles upon the golden magic of chrysanthemums, and makes twilights sparkle with mauve ecstasies, is the herald of his entrance into a greater realm of wholeness. As he enters the gates of Initiation he must, however, pay the price to the keeper of the gates. And the price is the sacrifice of the seed. The personality is indeed to fall like a seed into the soil of the surging era. This fall is the ransom of Soul-immortality: a conscious, clear, unemotional centering of the total power of personality into a "work of destiny", after which the personality become seed will die that the new plant ultimately may be. But the immortal Individual, fulfilled thus in sacrifice, will have passed the gates of the City of Light, thence to shine as a star among his welcoming Brothers.

The realm of the sun is the realm of Eros and of emotional radiance. When a sun is considered as the one and only giver of light to planets entranced by the glamor of his all-powerful and all-dominating vibrations—rooted as they may be in compassionate love for the many craving to be redeemed and integrated; when a sun is not seen in a relation of inherent equality with his companion suns, thus as a star—then we are dealing with the realm of emotion. The realm of stars is that of the mind and of archetypal form. It is known through the night because it is only while the solar glamor is sunk below the threshold of consciousness that stars may be seen. And it is only when divine Personages are *not* walking among men that men may know that they themselves are gods.

Wherefore the great Powers of Mind, the mighty *Asuras* and Lucifers, the Flames and *Kumaras*, are shown in ancient mythologies to be Powers of the mystic and incomprehensible Darkness. And through that Darkness only can the Unknown

God, the MYSTERY, be revealed. It may only be fully revealed through Initiation.

Following the ritual of the year, we find ourselves thus facing in Libra a great change. In the "night house" of Venus we may enter the communion of the Elect, and become ready for All-Saints Day—a festival which hints at the great reality of the spiritual Constellation of those who are stars in the skies of eternal humanity. And in Scorpio the mystic power may be given to us on the summit of the "Sacred Mountain" where earth meets heaven in the pure splendor of the snow.

The Sacred Mountain: a potent symbol of attainment and consecration. And in every land we find alive the tradition of the existence of one or more Sacred Mountains, the abode of the gods—from the Himavat of the Hindus, the Olympus of the Greeks, to the Fuji-Yama of Japan, still reverenced by an entire nation. There may be variations due to geographical factors, yet certain characteristics are almost inevitably associated with such sacred mountains. These are particularly well exemplified in Fuji-Yama, which stands as the almost perfect archetype of such mountains.

The sacred mountain should be, and most always is found to be, an extinct volcano, and its mass should rise in as perfect as possible a cone formation, from the surroundings. Moreover, eternal snow should be found on its summit, if the symbolism be perfect. The most significant point is the fact that it is an extinct volcano—which links it in a meaningful way with the zodiacal sign Scorpio. This, because it must be realized that without fire at the base of the crucible no alchemical operation is ever possible. Fire is the foundation. Earth-fire overcome, passion become wisdom, telluric strength kept within bounds and consecrated by pure snow—such are the requisites. The power that did not consume and tear through all restraint in the earlier stages of being is hardly power fit to enkindle the sacrificial offering of those who climb the slopes of the Sacred Mountain. But for power to flame forth is not enough. It should do so within perfection of form. Thus the archetypal cone of those volcanoes which kept within the law of their being and built their own perfectly geometrical slopes out of the very fury of their eruptions. Another great lesson for the fiery soul who would spout its enthusiasm in irregular and formless ways!

Then the long period of quiescence. Wisdom sought and purity found. The consecration of the virgin snow that falls from heaven, blessing the brow that pierces through clouds and communes with eagles and with stars. Thus heaven meets earth, and angels abide. Great "breaths of life", shining Ones, *devas*, planetary Spirits, dwell upon the summits. Men who have overcome ascend the steep walls. Hermits and seers meditate, links between the brotherhoods of stars and the chaotic society groping through the plains.

The Sacred Mountain symbolizes the avatar, in Scorpio. Traditional symbolism tells in parables of the scorpion which becomes eagle. But this metamorphosis is implied also in the transformation which makes of the passionate volcano the snow-covered, perfectly shaped Sacred Mountain. It is a drama of the fire within, which ends in an apotheosis of light. Beyond this change however is the fact of the permanence of the Mountain, the stability of this magnified pyramid of earth which stands against time and change, a cosmic symbol to all that lives within sight of its splendor. Men become initiated in pyramids made by human hands. But a step further is reached when the cosmic forces of the earth itself raise a symbolic monument of universal natural mastery. Here is overcoming and perfection shown on a scale which involves the cosmos. Planetary mastery is implied.

The message that Scorpio delivers to man's consciousness has ordinarily been misunderstood. The obvious linking of this sign of the zodiac with sex has led many astray in the consideration of its essential nature. The urge which burns through Scorpio is fundamentally the urge to transcend the limits of individual selfhood. It is a power generated by the organism in order that the boundaries of this organism may be transcended, and its generation is therefore caused by something beyond the purely physiological level at which this organism normally operates. Scorpio is procreative power only insofar as through procreation the human being acts in terms of the vaster racial whole and thus, becoming an agent of the race, expands into the purpose of a greater life—transcending its petty limitations as a self.

In Taurus the avatar-force is sheer creative power; the urge of the self to project itself and to impregnate materials of the earth. It is an elemental urge to fecundate, almost indiscriminately, and for the mere purpose of stamping oneself upon substance and to see oneself mirrored and multiplied in a progeny. Taurus is the symbol of pure and spontaneous fruitfulness; of the inherent, natural, *karmic*, unavoidable projection of abstract consciousness into the concrete reality of the earth. There is no intelligence, no self, in the projection. It simply *is*: a force of nature, a compulsion of being. It is seasonal and animal sex-power, undifferentiated and undisturbed by thought.

Scorpio power is of an entirely different nature. It is power born of the personal self yearning to transcend or to transfigure itself. It is the result of a dissatisfaction with the narrow boundaries of self-centered personality; a search, often frantic, for means to forget self in some ecstasy, to forget one's burdens and one's complexes by participating in some transcendent vital activity. And because this search is often frantic and desperate, everything which hinders the apparent success thereof arouses the most violent feelings of frustration: thus jealousy, revenge and all the exacerbated passions into which Scorpio power transforms itself when repressed.

In its positive sense, this autumnal power is a fervent reaching out into a larger whole. At first, a family and a long line of progeny in which the individual expands his sense of personality and attains a kind of physiological immortality; then, a national whole, a planetary whole, an entire cycle or eon. In Scorpio life, become personality, reaches out for conscious immortality. The Scorpio avatar is therefore that power which makes of an individual man an immortal Self. It establishes the Initiate, who has seen in Libra—the Pyramid—the vision of the celestial Host to which he belongs by spiritual birthright, as an immortal participant in the life of that Host. It gathers around the "I am" axis of his being (the spine, at the physiological level; the "rod of power" of the *Kumara* at the psycho-mental level) all the peripheral energies of his being and concentrates them in the Sacred Mountain within the head, on the apex of which man, the individual, receives the consecration of celestial light and becomes established as a "star".

The token of this consecration is depicted symbolically as the golden halo surrounding the heads of saints and adepts. In other forms of symbolism it is known as the "Golden Flower", the glowing chrysanthemum, the thousand-petalled effulgence which shines under autumnal skies—for such a glory can be seen on earth only after the hot intensity of the sun has waned. Then the light of summer becomes a mauve golden radiance, whose intoxicating tints may be perceived after the fall of the sun beyond the horizon. Even the leaves of trees sing with golden tones an epithalamium with the beyond, and life moves inwardly toward the iridescent whiteness of the snow through dusks scented with autumnal magic.

Such is the highest significance of Scorpio, a power of vital synthesis gathering in all energies of the individual being and transmuting them into a flame leaping upward to the summit of the Sacred Mountain where transfigured earth meets the sky, where man made immortal is welcomed in the celestial Brotherhood of his peers in spirit. Such also is the highest meaning of *kundalini*, the serpentine Force, through which every energy of the physiological and psycho-mental nature is drawn and integrated into the "pillar of fire" of the "I am", to serve as the root of the immortal being of man-the-star.

The negative aspect of Scorpio is a desire for escape from the intolerable burden of individual selfhood, a yearning to elude the responsibility of one's own destiny by surrendering oneself to some larger being in which to relax in emotional ecstasy. This escape is sought first of all in sex; for in sex we may temporarily forget our personal selfhood and transcend its heaviness in the relative bliss of a surge of emotions or of power giving us the precious illusion that we are losing ourselves. *Through another,* who becomes merely an instrumentality for psychological escape, we may be able to find a way to the sea of undifferentiated and self-free life-forces. Some may call this great illusion of freedom "cosmic consciousness"—yet it remains an escape and a glamorous dream.

The more men become "individualized", in periods of intensified intellectual civilization and strong ego-centric individualism, the heavier their sense of self and the more tragic their craving for escape. Therefore the stronger the emphasis being laid upon sex without responsibility, unprocreative sex, sex as a means to reach an emotional *nirvana*. The only other way is to repress sex utterly, as the Puritans theoretically did, thus developing a masochistic emotional self-exaltation—the equally illusory ecstasy of the martyr.

Sex is a desire for progeny *only* in the sense that through having children—in old natural cultures—man reaches, in his progeny, the only possible merging into a Greater Whole: viz., the tribe. He thus transcends himself. Today, the tribal order of society having been largely forgotten, men do not feel so deeply this self-expansion in a progeny, so they care less for the body-generating result of sex, and yearn for that emotional release and escape from self found in ever-repeated and ever-deceiving unprocreative sex, sex bent toward emotional *nirvana*.

Likewise, in many present day women mother-love is perhaps more than ever an escape. What the woman cannot bear of and in herself she yearns to release into her child—"my own flesh and blood!" Thus natural, healthy motherhood becomes in so many cases a psychological complex. Just as the jealous passion of the male for his woman, the possessive love of the mother is a psychologically twisted yearning, no more noble than the yearning of the drug-addict for the chemicals which lead him to his particular *nirvana* or artificial paradise.

In order to free themselves from these negative aspects of the Scorpio power, men who have been drawn into the vortex of the artificial "city", its escapes and its lusts, may call upon the realizations which are symbolized under the zodiacal sign Sagittarius. Through the power of Sagittarius and its flaming arrows man may overcome "Sodom and Gomorrah"—the *Satanic city*—and wind his way toward *Shamballah*, the City of Light, in which is enthroned *Sanat Kumara*, the blazing five-pointed Star, the Spiritual Identity of our planet, that glorious center of cosmic being which links the Earth as a whole to the realm of stars.

In Libra the individual self becomes, at the lower level, a "social" being taken up by the company of his fellow-men; at the higher, a companion among those who represent the spiritual collectivity of Man, the Lodge of Free Men. This leads him in the first case to the town and metropolis, in the latter to the mystic City of Light. In Scorpio the power released by such associations is demonstrated: on one hand, sex as a social factor conditioned by the man-made artificialities of city-life, a pastime, a search for emotional escapes or for acute sensations; on the other, the great magical power of life-synthesis, the *kundalini shakti* of Hindu occultism, born of the fulfillment and abstraction of intra-organic relationship, at the psychological as well as the physiological level.

Sagittarius balances Libra and helps man to conquer the pull of the negative Scorpio power. It is the faculty of generalization and abstraction, of synthesis and understanding. Through the use of it man surveys the new world opened to him in Libra, and gives value and significance to the multiplicity of impressions which assail him after he has passed through the gates of the city—be it that of matter or that of spirit. In order to produce intelligent valuations, man must learn to generalize, to deduce laws from multiple phenomena, to recognize simple types among the many individuals he meets, to understand human nature, or that higher nature of the realm of spirit.

It is only by the use of understanding, by ardently searching for the source of the many human phenomena encountered and the goal to which men aspire, that the individual may keep his balance when the power of the Scorpio avatar stirs his organism deprived of the elemental earth-stability of the tribal self-centered state. Understanding is mind brought to bear upon life-relationships, which encompass many factors and situations in which the self is only a part of a larger organic whole, social or spiritual. To understanding is added the ethical sense, a sense of the fitness of parts within the structural pattern of the whole. And it is this sense of structural or moral fitness alone which can overcome the tendency toward fallacious *nirvanas* and glamorous escapes from reality.

As December comes near and the sun is falling lower and lower toward the south, the glorious flaming quality of the autumnal light begins to vanish. Golds and scarlets turn to deep browns. Life seems to shrink inward, letting go of all things, to concentrate fully within the seed. Christmas is not far away, and a mysterious stirring is felt within the seed as every thread of life is drawn towards the center in preparation for the new birth.

The City of Light is soon to elect its new messenger, whom it shall send forth among men as a new sun, once more to gather and integrate the failures of the past, the ruins of the city of matter. Even now the cyclic Barbarians are invading its precincts, just as the fallen leaves turn into dark and pungent humus under the autumnal rain, soon to become snow. This messenger shall be endowed with the combined power of the Brotherhood. Upon him shall descend the "mantle of power", the "Robe of Light", which is the foundation of spiritual mastery.

Indeed, at yuletide the whole species is concentrating its life upon the seed. The synthesis of the end of the cycle becomes drawn to a single point, which is source and beginning: the new Logos, the Christ-to-be, the Word that is becoming flesh as the sun falls lower toward the south, toward that death in matter which is birth. A glorious birth, though hard be the path that leads away from the cradle toward an eventual Golgotha. For in that birth the power of the Constellation and the purpose of the Brotherhood are brought to a focus in that tiny seed within the head of the Christ-child.

This is the God-seed which is latent in every man of this earth since the ancient days of the Great Sacrifice, when He that is the planetary "I am", the Initiator, took His abode upon our shores. And in this seed is contained in potency the total glory of the Brotherhood; in this seed all the stars of the Constellation that is Man celestial and triumphant, weave patterns of light. It is indeed, this seed, a miniature of the City of Light. Every man, whether he is to grow heroic or dwell in the marshes of sin, contains his own *Shamballah; Shamballah* as he shall experience *its* glory on the day when, freed at last from the heavy burden of mankind's failures, risen out of the darkness of his own fears and frustrations, he shall look through the Western Gates and, his eyes aglow with the vision, shall tread the sacred grounds of his own immortality.

5.
The City of Light

"... And he carried me away in the spirit to a great and high mountain, and shewed me that great city, the holy Jerusalem, descending out of heaven from God, having the glory of God: ... And I saw no temple therein: for the Lord God Almighty and the Lamb are the temple of it. And the city had no need of the sun, neither of the moon, to shine in it: for the glory of God did lighten it, and the Lamb is the light thereof..." (*Revelation* 21)

The "holy city, the new Jerusalem, prepared as a bride adorned for her husband ... the Lamb's wife" is the Biblical symbol for the City of Light of which we spoke. The Light that shines in it, however, is neither sun nor moon light. It is the effulgent Glory of God. It is the Light of the Host, of the divine *Pleroma*—a Light which transcends the obvious, emotional, overwhelming light of the sun. It is the emanation of the Logos, not the radiation of the divine Eros. Not even exactly an emanation, but as is said in *Revelation*, the "wife" of the Logos. It is the mastery of the Master, the "Robe of Glory" in Gnosticism, the *Nirmanakaya* Vesture in Eastern esotericism, of the man who has passed through the four gates of the light and reached the fifth—which is not a gate but the actual welcome of the City of Light, whose "key" is placed into the keeping of him who thereby becomes a Master.

We can trace this symbolism in the Buddhistic or theosophical teachings concerning the four great Initiations, the four Paths, and the step beyond which is the winning of the mastery. We can trace it, though less clearly, in the Gnostic systems of our first centuries, or rather in the few remains thereof which have resisted the spiritual vandalism of the Fathers of the Church. In our previous "Meditations" we reserved the term of "Initiation" for the fourth "Gate", symbolized by Libra and the Autumn equinox. There is justification in this procedure, for it is only at the fourth gate, the Western gate, that man, as a spiritual Individual, takes the great step from which there is no return; a step which involves a complete repolarization of spiritual being and the rebirth of consciousness at a truly universal level.

At the three preceding gates the Individual was growing ever more perfect—if one considers the cycle of transformations at the purely spiritual level. And perfection was gained through hard struggles and by overcoming many crucial tests in the true spirit of sacrifice. But until the fourth step is taken the Individual may yet fall. From this point of view each of the "avatars" represents a test of power. In Aquarius, the Individual's willingness to dedicate his power and consciousness to those of a lower level is tested. In Taurus, the purity of his motives and the strength of his focalization in Self—so that he be not drawn into the whirlpool of the earth's elemental energies—are the issues at stake. In Leo, the solar man is tested for his pride.

These tests constitute indeed initiations, if successfully passed. Yet the true "entrance into the Kingdom of God" is not made certain until the power of the Scorpio avatar burns through the Individual; who, thereafter, rises as a phoenix out of his ashes. This supreme experience regenerates the Individual utterly and beyond recall. The Individual thereby becomes a focalization of the celestial Whole. He dies as a solar Individual and is reborn as a Ray from the Universal, a star within the Constellation. This death is described in occultism as the destruction of the causal or solar body—the final Crucifixion. After this, the Initiate of the Western Gate, or Arhat, is formally received in the City of Light and invested with the mastery of his Ray; that is, the power of all those who belong to this Ray or Constellation becomes his to use, within the limits of his individual ability to use it efficiently for the Whole.

It is this unanimous power of the Host which constitutes the "Bride" of every perfected Adept. A truly significant designation; because the wife of a man—in all pure and natural earth-born societies—represents actually the total power of the tribe for the man to use, in order to bear forth a progeny and thus to serve the purpose of the perpetuation of the tribal whole. The pure bride is concentrated virgin potency, to be fecundated and made operative by the man's action. She is the "Virgin of Light" who meets the would-be Master on the inner side of the City's walls. She is the mastery to be assumed by the Initiate. Through this assumption of power and responsibility, he becomes actually a Master, the bearer of a progeny of universal deeds through which he truly proves himself a "Star", a participant in the Life of the Universe of Light which is the Body of the Deity.

In ancient Hermetic books it is said that there are twelve "Virgins of Light", who thus correspond in *Revelation* to the "twelve apostles of the Lamb" whose names are inscribed in the "twelve foundations" of the wall of the new Jerusalem (21-14), or to the "twelve angels" guarding the gates on which are written the "names of the twelve tribes of the children of Israel" (21-12). The *names* of apostles or tribes are written on the walls or gates of the City; a name representing the form or individual structure of being. But the "Virgins of Light" themselves are the *substance* of the City, differentiated according to the twelve Constellations or Rays to which the Initiates respectively belong by spiritual birth-right.

In Hindu occultism and in *The Secret Doctrine* we hear of the six *shaktis* or universal life-potencies synthetized in a seventh which is called *Daiviprakriti*, the "Virgin of Light", and which represents the fifth cosmic plane. It is so, because it is only after the four steps, stages or planes are left behind that man reaches in the fifth the actual power of mastery—the possession of the *shakti* or Virgin of Light. The fifth refers to the apex of the Pyramid, to *Sanat Kumara*, to the realm of stars, to the Creative; whereas the realm of suns—considered as suns because of their relation to a system of planets which as Individuals they energize—is that of the four.

The City of Light "lieth foursquare, and the length is as large as the breadth . . . twelve thousand furlongs . . . and . . . the wall thereof, an hundred and forty and four cubits, according to the measure of a man, that is, of the angel." (Revelation 21—16, 17.) All these numbers are based on 4 and 12 (4 under a threefold differentiation); but they all refer to the *outer* shape of the City, to the foundation, the walls and the gates. This is so because the fifth is to be conceived as existing either within or above the four. The *foundation* of mastery is the regenerative event of the fourth stage on the Path. In Rosicrucian symbolism, the Rose blossoms out of the heart of the Cross; and the Rose is again the "Virgin of Light", the "Bride" of the reborn. The fifth is contained within the fourth; the City within its walls. And the substance of this City, which is Light itself, is an emanation from the "Glory of God".

If it is written that the new Jerusalem "comes down from God out of heaven", this means that, even in the crucial happening of the fourth stage—the true Initiation—the man who dies and is reborn is actually reborn "from God" and "out of heaven". This is the mystery of the "Marriage of Heaven and Earth". The new Jerusalem is the *sacred Cube* "clear as crystal" which descends upon and fills the *vacuum* left by the "death" of the Initiate. The substantial man has vanished, burned in the fire of the sacrifice, but his form—the exact space he occupied—is there, a vacuum to be filled with God-emanated substance.

The "measure of a man" remains; but when it is filled with Light "out of heaven from God" one may no longer speak of a man, but of an "angel". The vacuum that was man is occupied by the City of Light, and the Master is born. Only the *substance* dies the death of all things of earth, however pure and radiant; but the *form* or "name" remains. A Master is the exact form of what had been a perfected man, filled with the mastery which is the "Glory of God".

Obviously such symbols can but awkwardly describe the reality of a process which transcends our earth-conditioned imagination. Thus the fact that the images overlap and are not always absolutely consistent. Various angles of vision are needed even to suggest what is occurring, and only the intuitive understanding may lead one to sense the continuity, coherence and rationality of a process which essentially is beyond rational moulds of thought. Rationality provides only the form of the process. It can never lead us to the perception and realization of the Light. It can never draw to us the "Virgin of Light"—any more than reason can ever give birth to vibrant and life-giving love. And in an emphasis upon the form of the process it is easy indeed to find oneself without a real awareness of substance; a beautiful structure with no indwelling life; a perfect lamp without fuel; a would-be master without mastery.

At less exalted levels, the same process can be said to operate. Here mind may be found unmarried to soul, intellect bereft of feelings. The City of Light can be seen reflected in pools of materiality and selfishness, as the "*Ville Lumière*", Paris—a symbol of European creativeness turned sterile and perverted; as the metropoles and Broadways of the old and the new world. To the Living Civilization is opposed the purposeless and spiritless cosmopolitanism of modern capitals, the congested emptiness of our Fifth Avenues and Main

Streets. And motion picture stars dispense emotional thrills to a mob of office workers who have no roots anywhere, no spiritual or earthly stability in lives barren of happiness and of love.

Yet through means dark and chaotic mankind is stumbling upon the way to a progressive mentalization and objectivation of consciousness. It may not seem that it is so in a period when emotionalism, be it religious or political, is sweeping most nations, and intellectual sanity is rarely to be found. But men are almost unavoidably led to emotional fanaticisms and irrational enthusiasms or fears when they face conditions which they cannot understand. The machine has so transformed our living conditions that we face helplessly vistas of power and problems of organization with which we cannot cope on the basis of precedents. And, their habits disrupted and their frameworks of thought and feeling shattered, the masses, and even the *élite*, break down in worship, in fear or in hatred.

Dictators arise. Suns autocratically rouse and vitalize helpless planets and the lives thereon. Streams of emotional power sway the confused, the weary and the oppressed. A new age may rise. A new dawn may be hidden beyond towering skyscrapers and mountains of greed. The awesome complexity of economic and social relationships need not bewilder us any longer. Men learn quickly the techniques of new machines and new industries. Will they not be as quick to learn the technique of living in a world of cities when benevolence takes the place of selfishness, and cooperation supersedes fierce competitive struggles?

Yet before such a change can occur men's earthly personalities must become light, emerging from the realm of dark, from light-reflecting planets to effulgent, light-radiating stars. Only to learn the use of intellectual powers will not give mastery to the individual. Machinery and the knowledge of intra-atomic forces will not lead mankind to the perfect Synanthropy, the organic wholeness of all men.

Therefore the ancient Books made it clear that the practice

of the "great virtues" was necessary, if the first Initiations were actually to lead the individual to citizenship in the City of Light; if the tests of the avatars in Aquarius, Taurus and Leo were to be met successfully according to the "Law of Light", which is that of conscious sacrifice and of intelligent love. Therefore *Shamballah*, the City of Light of the Buddhist esoterists, is located in the fastness of the Gobi Desert—symbolically if not literally—beyond the Himalayas standing as a barrier which only the purest in heart and the most daring may cross. The symbolical pilgrimage of Hindu civilization led from Southern India to the Himalayas, then to the beyond. It was exemplified in the life and deeds of Shri Sankaracharya, the great Southern Indian Initiate, from whose famous commentaries of the *Bhagavat Gita* sprang eventually the devotional movements of early medieval India. Upward rose the devotional tide, unfurling over the foothills of the Himalayas. But how many succeeded in crossing the forbidding ranges and reaching the City of Light, the abode of *Sanat Kumara*, the central point of the total spiritual consciousness of Man, whose Presence dwells within the "sacred cube of Light"?

These may be symbols; but they may be realities. And perhaps symbols are the only true and permanent realities, because they are not of the earth alone, but "out of heaven from God". Every symbol which has lived in the hearts and minds of generations has proven itself to be, in ever so little a way, a City of Light. The light that dwelt in that "City" is the light of Meaning that ever radiates from the altar whereon burns the fire of pure and living Intelligence. Emotions sway human souls hither and thither. The passionate tides of the sun vitalize alike the things that creep in the mire and the things that soar toward the resplendent summit of the Sacred Mountain. From the humus of the past all seeds rise under the compulsion of the loss of equilibrium which is *karma*, born of action; all things bear progeny under the heat of desire, be it the purest or the most elemental. But secure beyond the snowy ranges of every soul's Himalayas, *Shamballah*, source and symbol of all true Intelligence, remains, unaffected and serene—a Constellation of cool and radiant stars.

This Intelligence that resides at the core of all that is truly human—fire that burns phantasms of passionate suns and of troubled moons, fire which surges clear from the altar of wholeness and equanimity standing at the last milestone of the Middle Path trodden by the Wise and the Free—may it illumine our humble quest for that Jewel of Significance mounted upon the Rod of the One Initiator! Behind the altar stands the wondrous Countenance, lifting His wand of power and of peace. In Him all the light of Meaning seems to concentrate, so dazzling is He who gave to mankind the fire of Intelligence. Indeed He is Himself the altar, the fire and the light. And in that threefold essence He lives and radiates within all *Shamballahs*.

For in every man there is a potential *Shamballah*, and in every man may burn the fire of Intelligence upon the altar of wholeness and equanimity, at the center of the City of Light. In this City is revealed the mystery of Form which is also Radiance, Mind which is also Love, Beauty which is also Compassion. In this City there is perfect Order, but also intense livingness and free spontaneity; and the core of all is Meaning.

Every initiation is an entrance into a new realm of Meaning. Through it, symbols that were only passing realities acquire that supreme seal of significance which makes them immortal sparks of the fire of Intelligence. It is that very fire which burns throughout the worlds. From it, galaxies receive their multitudinous light; and men who are true to the divine pattern are set aglow with its flaming power through long vigils of search and solitude. A flaming power which orders all things, yet is as nothing. A fire whose intensity burns through the most inert crystallizations of substance, yet which is cool and pure, unswayed by emotional storms of suns and planets alike.

How can one speak of that Intelligence in whose simplicity is hidden the greatest mystery, in whose exaltedness all spiritual quests find peace and fulfillment? It is in every one; yet only one here and there is alive with its fire. It lights all things; yet men prefer to struggle through the heat of earthly or solar emotions. Every moment reveals it operating; every day is singing with its melody—yet eyes do not see and ears fail to hear the revelations of the Presence that quickens all things that have form and name.

Sanat Kumara! Eternal symbol of that all-vivifying Intelligence, living Fire that burns in the souls that are creative and free, great Purifier and Giver of light—we accept the challenge of thy Sacrifice, and ground our search in thy significance. Divine Youth, who came to this heavy earth from the Morning Star, bringing to us the Promethean gift, we accept thy name as our standard. We go forth in the light of Intelligence, bearing thy gift to those who yet shun its costly splendor and fear its responsibility. And may it be this, our nobility, that we shall grow in understanding and wisdom, in the power to bring to the confused and the weary new names and new symbols in which thou shalt truly abide, O Master of Names, Source of all Meaning. For each name and symbol is a potential *Shamballah*. And while the City of Light abides beyond time and change, yet, because men weary of the old and become confused by the accretions which cling to once pure Images, as barnacles to a ship, it is needful indeed that new names be revealed—new streams gushing forth from the immortal Rock of Significance, a new feast of symbols for hungry souls, new mansions for new men.